D0893499

THE *FUTURE* OF THE INTER-AMERICAN SYSTEM

Published under the auspices of The American Society of International Law

THE FUTURE OF THE INTER-AMERICAN SYSTEM

edited by

TOM J. FARER

PRAEGER PUBLISHERS
Praeger Special Studies

New York • London • Sydney • Toronto

Library of Congress Cataloging in Publication Data

Main entry under title:

The Future of the inter-American system.

Bibliography: p.
1. Latin America--Relations (general) with the United States. 2. United States--Relations (general) with Latin America. I. Farer, Tom J.
F1418.F99 301.29'73'08 78-31153

ISBN 0-03-047391-8

The views in Chapter 1 are the author's personal views and should not be construed as representing those of the U.S. Government.

PRAEGER PUBLISHERS,
PRAEGER SPECIAL STUDIES
383 Madison Avenue, New York, N.Y., 10017, U.S.A.

Published in the United States of America in 1979
by Praeger Publishers,
A Division of Holt, Rinehart and Winston, CBS Inc.

9 038 987654321

Printed in the United States of America

To the memory of Orlando Letelier, martyred in the perpetual struggle for justice

FOREWORD

John Lawrence Hargrove

The relationship between the United States and its hemispheric neighbors to the south has long been viewed as "special"—whether in the context of the Monroe doctrine, or from the standpoint of former colonies of other metropoles trying to assert the perquisites of sovereignty in the face of the dominance of the "colossus to the North," or as an aspect of what has come to be called the North-South dialogue. It may well be that history has overtaken the "special relationship" and the network of traditions and institutions, including the Organization of American States, that has evolved in response to it. One may well ask what that system has become, and some have asked whether, indeed, it has a future.

In an effort to explore that question, the Society, with the support of the Rockefeller Foundation, assembled a panel of experts in late 1975 following a technique which its research and study program has used and refined over a number of years. It brought together economists, political scientists, international lawyers, government and international organization officials and others, some of whom prepared draft papers on various aspects of the problem in accordance with an overall scheme of analysis. Most of these were critically examined in working meetings of the group, which was chaired by the editor and co-author of this volume, Professor Tom J. Farer. Papers commissioned during the later stages of the project were jointly considered at a conference in May 1978 by the Society and the Latin American Program of the Woodrow Wilson International Center for Scholars. Portions of Professor Farer's contribution to this book have appeared previously in the essay, *The United States and the Inter-American System: Are There Functions for the Forms?* which was published in 1978 as No. 17 in the Society's series of occasional papers, *Studies in Transnational Legal Policy.*

Special thanks are due to the Rockefeller Foundation for its support of the project, as well as the Woodrow Wilson International Center for Scholars, and in particular Dr. Abraham F. Lowenthal, director of its Latin American Program.

The views expressed in the book are not necessarily those of the institutions with which the authors or other participants may be associated, the Rockefeller Foundation, the Woodrow Wilson International Center for Scholars, or of the American Society of International Law (which as an organization characteristically does not take positions on matters of public concern).

CONTENTS

Section B: Human Rights

Section C: Security, Peacekeeping, and Arms Control

LIST OF TABLES AND FIGURE

INTRODUCTION

THE CHANGING CONTEXT OF INTER-AMERICAN RELATIONS

Tom J. Farer

The Inter-American System is an idea corresponding never very precisely to a set of formal institutions and legal norms. It is also an association for mutual defense, political accommodation, economic development, and cultural exchange. But above all it is the still evolving, tangled, and problematical relationship between the United States and its southern neighbors.

Some 27 independent states, they differ dramatically in size, density, history, race, culture, wealth, development, and just about any other facet of national existence that the mind can conjure with the partial exception of language. Yet it has long been assumed that history imposes on them a collective relationship to the United States that frames and colors their diverse bilateral ties with the northern behemoth, and often with each other as well. This is the so-called "special relationship"—variously defined, sometimes lamented, occasionally questioned, and perpetually present.

Although the great weight of the immediate U.S. economic and strategic concerns lies in other parts of the world, although American planners do not see the Western Hemisphere as the primary arena for confronting any of the great issues of contemporary international life—from pollution to nuclear proliferation to the allocation of wealth and the terms of resource transfers between developed and developing states—no president and no secretary of state has been prepared to renounce a special U.S. interest in and, as a corollary, preferred status for Latin America. President Jimmy Carter reiterated the traditional position in remarks before the Latin American foreign ministers and diplomats attending the session of the UN General Assembly:

> As far as my stay in New York is concerned, I have saved the best for the last, because I feel closer to you than to any other region of the world.

The Inter-American System is, as already suggested, far more than the cluster of formal agreements and official institutions that are its most concrete expression. They are only the moving parts of a pluralistic system that comprises the much larger network of relationships between and among public and private entities—intelligence agencies, churches, trade unions, universities, armies, foundations, corporations. And then there is the idea itself, this way of thinking about the hemisphere that inevitably influences public policy. The formally bilateral question of the

Panama Canal Treaty would not, for instance, have been so charged with political significance had it not been implicated in the larger bilateral relationship felt to exist between the United States and its collective southern neighbors.

Although their virtues have been absorbed into the conventional wisdom of the United States, becoming a point of intellectual departure for editorialists, politicians, and the portion of the public that imagines itself literate about foreign affairs, neither the idea nor the formal institutions that give it flesh are any longer sacrosanct. Heterodox opinion within the foreign policy community has on occasion gone beyond calling for reform to proposing institutional demolition. Before becoming assistant secretary of state for inter-American affairs, William Rogers wondered publicly if it were not time for the United States to withdraw from the Organization of American States (OAS). Although withdrawal was too sharp a démarche for the State Department professionals, a policy of malign neglect has found supporters who imagine a time when the institutions are so clearly moribund that they could be interred, without commotion, virtually by unanimous consent.

Are the heterodox right? Have the norms, customs, and official institutions of the system lost their capacity to promote the interests of the United States or most of the other participants? Are they relics of another age, obstacles to the conduct of an enlightened diplomacy? Should they be reformed or should they rather be dismantled on the grounds that they help to perpetuate an outmoded conception of national rights and obligations in the Western Hemisphere? These are the questions addressed by the essay in this book.

THE SYSTEM'S PROGRESS: THE PROBLEMATICS OF SUCCESS

The character of the system's formal institutions—principally the OAS and the Rio Treaty—is premeditated. If, as citics maintain, the institutions need to be changed, it follows that the underlying reality of inter-American interests, relations, and beliefs that animated their architects already has changed. How has that reality altered in the course of the nearly three decades which have elapsed since the adoption of the Rio Treaty and the OAS Charter?

The Aims of the Founding Fathers

One begins, necessarily, with the original premises. Latin as well as American statesmen were concerned in the aftermath of World War II with external threats to the hemisphere. It was, after all, the Latins who, during the drafting of the UN Charter, tenaciously insisted on a quasi-autonomous security and peacekeeping role for regional institutions. In other words, it was not simply the United States that wished to "multilateralize the Monroe Doctrine."

However differently they may have appraised the prospect, U.S. and Latin American political leaders assumed that the United States would play the central role on the Latin American stage. It was without rival as a source of investment capital and imports and as a market for southern exports. Its nationals had more investments in Latin America than in any other part of the world. And although the United States had not intervened militarily since the inception of the Good Neighbor Policy, World War II had plainly strengthened its capacity to employ force throughout the hemisphere. Thus the United States represented at least a potential constraint on the autonomy of every Latin state.

Leftwing critics of U.S. policy in Latin America tend to see the institutions that grew from this premise as an elaborate sham designed to conceal the imperious thrust of American power. From time to time they have served that end, most notoriously in the cases of Guatemala and Cuba, rather more equivocally in the Dominican intervention of 1965. But these instances of collaboration with imperial intervention hardly suffice to support the claim.

A striking feature of the seminal negotiations that finally produced the Rio Treaty of Reciprocal Assistance and the OAS Charter was the evident enthusiasm of the Latin participants. Why would political leaders in countries so sensitive to the risk of American intervention have promoted institutions that, according to the critics, would serve merely to cloak or even thinly to legitimate American threats to their political independence? The simple answer, of course, is that they would not and did not. They devised the institutions of the Inter-American System not to legitimate but rather to contain American power. Containment was their dominating purpose. And the charter and the treaty were its imperfect expressions.

Unlike the UN Charter—which, by centralizing coercive authority in the Security Council and conceding vetoes to the Great Powers of 1945, frankly recognized the material inequality of states—the OAS Charter and the Rio Treaty collectively signify the triumph of formal equality: one state, one vote. There is, to be sure, a kind of veto power since decisions compelling enforcement action by the member states require a two-thirds majority. But this was no concession. Rather, it was a counterweight to U.S. influence, a hedge against the anticipated capacity of the United States to marshal a friendly majority.

The intent of the Latin founding fathers to circumscribe U.S. power—a power they could not in any event exorcise—also is apparent in the charter's categorical and multiple prohibitions of intervention except in the case of "measures adopted for the maintenance of peace and security in accordance with existing treaties," that is, measures adopted by a two-thirds vote. Article 15 states:

> No State or group of States has the right to intervene, directly or indirectly, for any reason whatever, in the internal or external affairs of any other State. The foregoing principle prohibits not only armed force but also any other form of interference or attempted threat against the personality of the State or against its political, economic and cultural elements.

The prohibition is echoed in Article 16's stricture that "No State may use or encourage the use of coercive measures of an economic or political character in order to force the sovereign will of another State and obtain advantages of any kind." And it is reechoed in Article 17, which precludes recognition of "special advantages obtained either by force or by other means of coercion."

The inhibition of U.S. power being its regnant aim, why was the charter acceptable to the United States? In part, no doubt, because the financial, moral, and political costs of a legally naked hegemony must have seemed even more onerous in 1947 than in 1933, when the United States renounced any unilateral right to impose its notions of propriety on the hemisphere. In part, as well, because U.S. statesmen saw no fundamental antagonism between the national interests of the United States and those of the dominant classes in Latin America. Fascism, which during the 1930s had flourished in some Latin states, had lost its allure—if not for its delinquencies then certainly for its defeats. Communism was no more popular in Latin capitals than in Washington.

Economic interests also seemed essentially compatible. The Latins needed U.S. markets for their commodities and U.S. capital in lieu of the internal savings that most states still were unable to marshal, even where there was much of a surplus to save. The Europeans, for many decades vigorous participants in the economic life of Latin America, had neither capital nor markets and products for export.

But there were potential difficulties. Nationalism had lost none of its emotive force in Latin America. Although unalloyed with communist or explicitly fascist ideology, it could again threaten U.S. investments; Mexican oil nationalization remained a rankling memory for the U.S. business community. Moreover, as in the past, some of the smaller states particularly might prove feckless about repaying public debts to U.S. creditors. But with the cold war already coming to dominate the views of the U.S. elite, these concerns must have seemed secondary at best. What really mattered was collective security against the emerging Soviet challenge. However it may have been perceived by U.S. statesmen, the challenge was defined in ideological terms: liberal capitalist democracy versus totalitarian, aggressive communism. A security system democratic in its form, resting on notions of equality, nonintervention, and mutuality of interest, nicely underlined the declared stakes of the competition.

Apart from the cold war, the democratic forms of the OAS system appealed both to the self-consciously idealistic strain in U.S. foreign policy and to the natural inclination of a status quo power—necessarily delighted with the postwar dispensation—to consolidate and legitimate its position in terms of prevailing values. And the values that prevailed, in the aftermath of a war against their antithesis, were respect for the independence of small states and rejection of force as a tool of diplomacy.

Success and Its Discontents

The promise of converging political interests was essentially fulfilled. Whenever East-West issues surfaced at the United Nations or in other global forums, the bulk of the Latin states generally followed the U.S. lead. When Cuba broke ranks, a clear majority of the OAS supported U.S. efforts to isolate the apostate. Within the OAS, few governments questioned the compatibility of the Bay of Pigs incident with the nonintervention norms of the charter. And as the issue of guerrilla-led revolution in the Third World became salient in U.S. strategic calculations, most Latin governments proved enthusiastic collaborators in Washington's effort to coordinate a global program of counterinsurgency. By formal resolution, the OAS anathematized Marxists and implicitly authorized relaxation of nonintervention norms as a means of cauterizing the revolutionary threat.

Developments in the economic sphere coincided logically with the common struggle against the guerrillas. In most of Latin America, increasingly professional military establishments and a growing class of civilian technocrats opted decisively for the capitalist road to high technology development. Among its other consequences, this choice entailed a relatively receptive attitude to foreign investors, heavy reliance on hard currency financial markets, a drive for new or enlarged export outlets in the industrial West, tolerance of high levels of unemployment, and accelerating inequality between the upper one or two quintiles of the national population and those at the bottom.

Now, in ironically dialectical fashion, that profound convergence of interests has succeeded in generating prickly differences between the United States and a large number of Latin governments. In the 1960s, development aid and the struggle against the left were the preeminent themes of hemispheric discourse. Now they have been displaced. In the political realm, debate over issues of human rights agitates the hemisphere; in the economic realm, discourse is infused with the whole complex of north-south issues, though with particular emphasis on trade, the transfer of technology, and the regulation of multinational corporations.

Human Rights

The increasingly acerbic dialogue over human rights relates in at least two ways to the earlier successful effort to destroy the revolutionary left. On the U.S. side there is a sense of having strayed from the path of traditional American idealism and a kind of penitential desire to find the way back. Catalyzed in some quarters by remorse for the devastation inflicted on Indochina, the mood is regularly reinforced by reports of government-sponsored brutality in countries that the United States encouraged and assisted throughout the 1960s under the banner of counterinsurgency. The U.S. public no longer is comfortable with the worldly cynicism epitomized by a possibly apocryphal comment on Trujillo frequently attributed to FDR: "He may be an s.o.b., but he's our s.o.b."

Latin governments, for their part, sensitive under the best of circumstances to "Yankee intervention" in what they might choose to regard as their internal affairs, have greeted the freshet of American criticism with anger as well, of course, as deep concern, heightened by a sense of betrayal. As one young Uruguayan officer is said to have told a visiting American,

> We are doing precisely what you encouraged and equipped us to do—destroying Marxists and developing a free enterprise economy. The war against the Marxists requires exceptional means. You did not hesitate to use them in Vietnam. But you lacked the will to win. You gave up. This is our country. We will not give up. And we will win.

Comparative moderates in the more ruthless regimes justify the demolition of democratic institutions partially on grounds of the obstructions they pose to the anticommunist crusade and partially on grounds of their incompatibility with the pursuit of rapid development. Politicians, it is said, will cater demagogically to the masses, who lack the discipline and restraint required if the country is to be made safe for development. On the other hand, for hardline military and civilian groups in the most violently conservative states, the antidemocratic animus is neither tactical nor temporary. Rather, it is firmly rooted in a contempt for pluralist society comparable in intensity to the feelings of a hardened Stalinist. The fact that the officer corps in which corporatist or fascist views circulate are dotted with men who have studied in U.S. military establishments only contributes to the moral uneasiness of the United States. That unease is further aggravated by the antiegalitarian consequences of laissez-faire development in Brazil, Chile, and many other places in the hemisphere.

Wealth among Nations

While the manifest thinness of the income trickling down to the lower quintiles of the Latin population has cost laissez-faire economic development much of its moral charm, development there has been. In Brazil, which contains roughly one-third of the 300 million citizens of Latin America, there has been explosive economic growth. The average annual increase in the gross national product for the entire postwar period is more than 7 percent, with the annual rate of industrial growth at least 2 percent higher. Mexico's growth, although less dramatic, still has hummed along at an annual rate of 6 percent. The accelerating expansion of industry and large-scale, export-oriented agriculture in these two southern giants and in several other states—albeit on a more modest scale—have brought them into conflict with various U.S. interests experiencing the bite of an intensifying competition for markets.

Having preached the virtues of the international capitalist system, keyed to the theory of comparative advantage, the United States greets the results of its evangelism with restrained enthusiasm. Brazilian soybeans threaten established U.S. markets in third countries. Shoes, textiles, and other labor-intensive products from Brazil, Mexico, and, prominent among the rest, Colombia, in conjunction with comparable products from the more advanced Asian countries now threatening to monopolize the American market, are held tensely at bay by a variety of trade barriers. And the United States shows little inclination to dismantle the barriers despite the fact that Latin America coincidentally provides an expanding market for the sophisticated arms and other high technology products in whose production the United States continues to enjoy a marked comparative advantage.

Within the United States there is not only a clamor actually to toughen the barriers to manufactures and competitive commodities from Latin America but also growing support for restraints on the export of capital, know-how, and technology. For it is feared that if their export continues at the present rate—encouraged among other things by the disciplined, docile, and poorly paid workers to the south—the expanding industries of Latin America will strip the competitive edge from a growing list of traditional U.S. products. At the same time, the principal Latin states, faced with burgeoning populations, suddenly diminished growth rates, ineradicable unemployment, and a massive foreign debt, relentlessly pursue preferential access to markets in the advanced industrial countries, along with easier and less costly access to sophisticated technology.

These contradictions between Latin interests and those of certain influential sectors in the United States lend a new dimension to U.S.-Latin conflict in the economic realm. The traditional concern about limiting U.S. coercive power is still vital, as illustrated by the sharp collective reaction to the U.S. Congress's exclusion of Ecuador and Venezuela, because of their membership in the Organization of Petroleum Exporting Countries (OPEC), from the reduction in tariffs effected by the General System of Preferences (GSP). Beside this negative interest in constraining U.S. power, an affirmative desire to extract positive benefits from the United States has grown to at least equal stature. Not so many years ago, the leading Latin states would have welcomed benign neglect. Now, in their judgment, it is by no means enough.

The effort, led by Peru, to place "collective economic security" on a par with military security as the primary shared objectives of the Inter-American System stems from both concerns. Behind the term lies an elaborate scheme that would commit the United States to affirmative action in the economic sphere and formally subject both its domestic and foreign policies, insofar as they might seriously affect the economic health of other hemispheric states, to their appraisal. In 1975, by a 20–1 vote, its Latin allies trampled over U.S. opposition to an amendment of the Rio Treaty providing that "economic security" shall be "guaranteed" in a "special treaty." The amendment corresponded to a phrase in the Preamble to the Protocol of Amendment, which stated that the parties "recognize that, for the maintenance of peace and security in the Hemisphere, it is also necessary to guarantee collective economic security for the development of the American states." Since the new article was clearly designed to bend the United States toward acceptance of a separate treaty on collective economic security, the United States formally reserved its position, declaring that by signing the Protocol of Amendment it accepted no obligation to negotiate such a treaty. The issue also has arisen in the context of discussions concerning possible amendments to the OAS Charter, where it has practically immobilized the draftsmen.

THE NEW CONTEXT OF HEMISPHERIC RELATIONS

In addition to the shift in the principal themes of hemispheric discourse, two other developments bear significantly on any current appraisal of the Inter-American System. There is first, the epochal change in the whole environment of north-south relations following on the triumphs of OPEC. Third World proposals for a new deal in the distribution of global wealth, once scorned by the developed states, now form the agenda of serious negotiations between parties that for the first time treat each other in a more than ceremonial way as substantive equals.

To convert themselves from mere objects of the historical process into important subjects, the developing countries have striven, not unsuccessfully, for a common front on issues related, directly or indirectly, to the economic realm. In the name of their common economic interests, the southern states bridge yawning ideological chasms. Thus, when democratic Venezuela was excluded from GSP, the most reactionary governments in the hemisphere joined in the chorus of disapproval. Conversely, when the United States voted in the Inter-American Development Bank (IDB) against a loan to the Chilean junta, the Latin democracies voted solidly on the other side.

It is, of course, possible to attribute this display of cohesion simply to traditional Latin sensitivity concerning the exercise of U.S. power. But rather more than that seems to be at work. After all, in contexts other than the IDB, the more moderate Latin states have voted with the United States on human rights issues. Moreover, given the present trends in U.S. policy and the deeper social forces they express, the danger of interventions comparable in character or degree to those that historically obsessed the Latins must seem remote. Finally, there probably has been no time when the leading states of Latin America were as deeply divided on ideological grounds as they are today, a division exemplified by the severing of diplomatic relations between Uruguay and Venezuela.

Strong as it is, the common front of the developing states has its gaps, most notably the special relationship between a cluster of African and Caribbean states, on the one hand, and the Common Market on the other. Codified in the Lomé Convention, it gives these ex-colonies, all of them among the least industrially developed states in the Third World bloc, preferential access to the European market, a commodity price stabilization fund, and certain other advantages.

With that notable exception, the southern states incline generally toward nondiscriminatory global accommodation. At least for the time being, the Latins want improved access to the European market, not a U.S.-Latin analogue of Lomé. They are encouraged in their transhemispheric perspective by the reduced economic role of U.S. capital, goods, and markets and the concomitant growth of economic links with other nations and regions, a second development that bears on the future of the Inter-American System.

European and Japanese multinationals hunt aggressively for an ever-expanding place in the Latin market. Volkswagen has the largest slice of Brazil's auto market. France enabled Peru to break the supersonic barrier by selling Mirage aircraft. Japanese entrepreneurs are tying up big chunks of important commodities in long-term supply contracts. Reflective of their growing role in Latin America, Japan, Canada, Spain, and four members of the European Common Market—Belgium, France, West Germany, and the Netherlands—have joined the IDB and acquired observer status at the OAS.

The United States continues preeminent, in the hemisphere, but more as the first among equals than as an unrivaled economic hegemony.

I

THE SPECIAL RELATIONSHIP AND THE GLOBAL SYSTEM OF POLITICAL ECONOMY

Chapter 1

THE INTER-AMERICAN SYSTEM: DOES IT HAVE A FUTURE?

Richard J. Bloomfield

A study of the Inter-American System might well start by considering this paradox: The chief institution of the System, the Organization of American States, is held in low esteem both by the establishment and its opponents, and for opposite reasons.

The antiestablishment forces—most of whom are found among nationalists of the left and right in Latin America and intellectuals north and south—are inclined to agree with Fidel Castro's caricaturization of the OAS as the U.S. "Colonial Office." At the same time, the OAS is regarded with no little disdain by the establishment whose interests it is presumed to serve. U.S. and Latin American officials, businessmen, and political moderates see the OAS as ineffectual at best and troublesome at worst. U.S. officials in particular have often regarded the OAS as an institution that does little more than afford the Latin Americans an opportunity to bedevil the United States with irresponsible resolutions.

Why the paradox? The explanation lies in the highly transitional state of relations between the United States and Latin America. The OAS mirrors the severe problems that the member states are experiencing in dealing with the U.S.-Latin American relationship in a world that has dramatically changed since the Inter-American System was formally founded 30 years ago.

The label Inter-American System is itself something of a misnomer, as it implies a degree of multilateralism and equality that the System does not in reality possess. The name derives from the apparently mutual rights and obligations assumed by juridically equal states in several treaties, notably the OAS Charter and the Rio Treaty.

These are the formalities, however.

In practice, the Inter-American System has served as a vehicle for dealing with relations between the United States on the one hand and the group of states generally known as Latin America on the other. While the provisions of the treaties that form the legal framework of the System in appearance apply with equal force to all the members, the enormous disparity in power between the United States and the rest of the members means that in fact many of the responsibilities and commitments contained in the treaties and resolutions could only be undertaken by the United States. U.S. officials generally have tried to deny this bipolar character of the Inter-American System, because to admit it gives legitimacy to the collective bargaining that in fact takes place in the OAS—and that U.S. delegations understandably try to avoid.

Once the bipolarism that is the reality of the System is frankly faced, we are in a better position to answer the question as to why the System exists. Put another way, what's in it for the two parties to the System, the United States and Latin America? To answer that question, the System must be examined in the broader context in which the international relations of its 20-odd members have evolved.[1] Finally, can the Inter-American System have relevance for the changing needs and status of the American republics in the last quarter of the twentieth century?

POLITICS VERSUS ECONOMICS

Because so much of the business of the OAS and its subordinate bodies for the past two decades has had to do with economics, there is a tendency to think of the Inter-American System primarily as a vehicle for economic cooperation. Moreover, there is the undeniable fact of the overwhelming importance of the United States to the economies of the Latin American nations. It is at least arguable that the Inter-American System came into being as an attempt to obtain by formal diplomatic process the maximum benefits from the de facto regional economic hegemony of the United States.

It is my contention, however, that to see hemispheric economic relationships as the primary cause of the Inter-American System, or even as its main raison d'être in the future, is to misread both history and the current evolution of the international system.

Yet the notion is very strong among U.S. Latin-Americanists that because economic development is a paramount goal of the Latin American nations, and because the United States still is economically predominant in the area, some form of economic regionalism is not only a feasible but a highly desirable method of improving relations.

But economic regionalism as an issue entered the Inter-American System as an afterthought. The Inter-American System came into being and evolved to its present form because of the assertion by one Great Power, the United States, of a strategic prerogative over the states of Latin America and the Caribbean. The proposition that the independence of the

Latin American states from extracontinental domination was a vital interest of the United States was first put forward in the Monroe Doctrine.

Admittedly, the doctrine remained for almost half a century more of an aspiration than an actionable policy. And there is no denying that the flag and commerce, if they did not proceed hand in hand in the Western Hemisphere, certainly marched side by side. The early proponents of Pan Americanism, like James Blaine, were undoubtedly motivated by a desire for commercial advantage as well as visions of political influence. Indeed, the first Pan American Bureau was largely a trade promotion office.

But it is most unlikely that the evolving economic dependency of Latin America on the United States would have given rise to the Inter-American System of today in the absence of the development of a U.S. strategic doctrine that asserted special prerogatives in the area. After all, American economic power has been predominant in many nations in other parts of the world for about the same period of time. If economic hegemony were the reason for the creation of formal multilateral institutions under U.S. domination, there would have developed an American commonwealth based on commerce rather than geography.[2] Why this particular group of countries?[3] From the U.S. point of view, regional alliances and institutions were not necessary to further U.S. economic expansion. It was sufficient that other Great Powers not be allowed to close off the area to American economic penetration. For this, the Monroe Doctrine would have been enough. Indeed, to an economic superpower, regional economic arrangements are a needless complication.[4]

The United States has assented to regional economic obligations and institutions as a quid pro quo for Latin American acquiescence in its claim to special strategic rights in the Western Hemisphere. Whether U.S. policy in this regard has been prompted by feelings of guilt and idealism or has been merely a hardheaded bargain is beside the point. The truth is probably a mixture. But what has been unique about this group of states has been the assertion by the United States that its national security requires that extracontinental powers not "attempt . . . to extend their system to any portion of this Hemisphere" or intervene in the Americas with a purpose of "controlling in any other manner their destiny."[5] This security doctrine has led the United States to intervene in the internal affairs of various Latin American countries, primarily because of internal political developments that might have given rise to extracontinental interference or influence.[6]

This combination of a security protectorate, economic dependence, and periodic intervention has been defined by James Kurth as a "hegemonial system."[7] Kurth considers the Inter-American System as coming closest to the ideal type. It is, he says,

> among the most formalized, routinized, and institutionalized. Within

> the framework and under the legitimization of the Organization of American States, the U.S. has carried out counterrevolutionary interventions, defense agreements, and the Alliance for Progress; the constitution of United States/Latin America, like the Constitution of the United States of America, is an order among states to "insure the domestic tranquility, provide for the common defense (and) promote the general welfare."[8]

There is, however, a possible source of confusion for our purposes in Kurth's definition. What Kurth is talking about is really the relationship between the United States and the Latin American states in all its forms. This is Kurth's hegemonial system. It is, if you will, the Inter-American system without a capitalized, formal title. The Inter-American System, on the other hand, is the formalized and institutionalized expression of the hegemonial relationship. It is not coterminous with all the elements of the hegemony, such as trade, private U.S. investment, and other transnational relationships (which Kurth uses as criteria to determine hegemony), just as the U.S. Constitution and the U.S. government are not coterminous with all relationships among the 50 states.

In this chapter, both concepts are discussed. The underlying power relationships, which can be called an international "system," are used to explain what the formal "System" of treaties and institutions is capable of accomplishing—and what it is not. In short, Kurth's broader concept of a hegemonial power relationship is crucial to an understanding of why the System exists and what is happening to it.

THE PURPOSES OF THE SYSTEM

Ostensibly, the rights and obligations established by the various treaties and compacts that form the "constitution" of the System apply equally to all members. In reality, these rules are designed to regulate the behavior of the United States toward the Latin American states in certain matters (nonintervention, economic assistance), the behavior of the Latin American states toward the United States in other matters (military alliance), and the behavior of the Latin American states toward one another in certain very limited areas, primarily those affecting the stability of the region and hence the U.S. perception of its security requirements—as, for example, the pledge to the peaceful settlement of disputes. In essence, the purpose of the System is to permit both sides to cope with the enormous inequality in power between the United States on the one hand and the countries of Latin America on the other.

It would be a mistake, therefore, to view the Inter-American System as exclusively an American creation. For the Latin Americans, the System has been of value to the extent it has made the exercise of American power less arbitrary and more benevolent (or less malevolent). At various periods the Latin Americans have been successful in significant measure in making the System work for themselves. This inhibiting function of the System explains why most Latin American governments have not been enthusiastic about proposals to dispense with the Organization of American States, to make it an exclusively Latin American institution, or even to establish a parallel Latin American body.[9]

The System has not, however, supplanted the Monroe Doctrine. It is precisely because the United States continues to adhere to the Monroe Doctrine (a unilateral policy) that the Inter-American System is necessary. As long as the United States asserts special rights in the Western Hemisphere, it has felt that it must assume special obligations. This is the essence of the so-called special relationship with Latin America. And since they have no alternatives, it makes sense for the Latin Americans to try to use the OAS to define as thoroughly as possible the permissible uses of U.S. power. This process is necessarily a dynamic one; as the world changes, so does man's idea of legitimacy. The legitimate use of U.S. power in the Western Hemisphere is in more or less constant litigation. And because the very nature of power has been changing so rapidly in the modern world, the contentiousness of the litigative process within the Inter-American System has reached an unprecedented intensity in recent years.

A HISTORICAL PERSPECTIVE

Clearly the foregoing argument is not a popular explanation, departing as it does from the simpler concepts of hemisphere solidarity based on geography and shared values. To give the argument some concreteness, therefore, the following brief historical summation is offered.

The Central Issue: Intervention

Because they have existed as sovereign states for 150 years, the Latin American nations at times have been thought of as having more in common with the United States and Europe than with the newly independent states of the post-1945 period. But the ex-colonial paradigm provides useful insights into U.S.-Latin American relations.[10]

For Latin Americans, their history for the past 200 years has been a struggle for independence. Barely had the wars of independence ended in 1824 when other states from outside the area began to move into the vacuum left by the retreat of Spanish and Portuguese power. The British were the immediate heirs to the former metropoles, especially economically, and for a time they were paramount in South America. In the late 1800s and early 1900s, however, the U.S. extended its hegemony over the

Caribbean and Central America. By World War II, American influence was preeminent on the southern continent as well.

As was the American way, U.S. hegemony became institutionalized in a body of treaties, resolutions, and charters, a routine of inter-American conferences, and an elaborate multilateral organizational structure, all of which evolved over almost a century.

Although the initiative for the first inter-American conference in 1889 came from the United States in an effort to promote U.S. commerce, the central concern of the System for most of its history has been with two political issues: (1) defining the permissible uses of U.S. power and (2) the closely related problem of devising mechanisms for keeping the peace among the American states.

Even on the eve of World War II, the Latin Americans resisted U.S. efforts to transform the System into a rudimentary collective security instrument against extrahemispheric threats. It was only when Nazi power was unveiled in the 1940 blitzkrieg that the Latin American members of the Inter-American System became willing to cooperate with the United States for their common defense. Even then one state, Argentina, resisted U.S. pressure to join the Allied cause until the very eve of German surrender. And since the late 1960s, the main focus of inter-American debate has once again been the U.S. relationship with the other members of the System.

Seen in this longer historical context, the alliance feature of the System—embodied in the Rio Treaty—is not the essential unifying theme of the System, as it has been in the North Atlantic Treaty Organization (NATO). The collective security treaty is simply a figleaf for the Monroe Doctrine. In the OAS, the theme is the search for a consensus that will legitimize and also restrain the exercise of U.S. power in the hemisphere. A byproduct of any such consensus will be the preservation of the alliance. But collective security is not the motive force for Latin American participation in the System, except when there arises a grave threat that the relatively libertarian U.S. hegemony will be replaced by one more oppressive.

In short, the main business of this particular regional system is that of defining and refining the principle of nonintervention. (Intervention here is defined in the broadest sense of the term, to include economic pressure as well as military incursions or political manipulation.) Hemispheric solidarity historically has been at its apex when U.S. and Latin American views on that issue have coincided most closely.

From this point of view, the most creative period in the history of the System may have been 1930–1940, when U.S. acceptance of the principle of nonintervention was formalized in a series of inter-American conferences. This, not surprisingly, coincided with an innovative phase of U.S. policy toward the region. The Good Neighbor Policy was not, as some have thought, merely a rhetorical conceit. Actually launched under the Hoover Administration, it gave concrete expression to the nonintervention principle by a series of actions:

1. Repudiation of the Roosevelt Corollary to the Monroe Doctrine (1930).
2. Abandonment of Wilson's de jure recognition policy, which was regarded in Latin America as a form of intervention (1930).
3. Withdrawal of U.S. troops from Nicaragua (1933) and Haiti (1934).
4. Abrogation of the Platt Amendment, which had given the United States the right to intervene unilaterally in Cuba's internal affairs (1934).
5. Resistance to pressure from U.S. investors to retaliate when Mexico nationalized the foreign oil companies (1938–40).

This move toward nonintervention undoubtedly reflected internal pressures in the United States and external ones from Latin America, particularly in its initial stages. But ultimately it also obeyed a strategic vision of the Roosevelt Administration, namely, that the threat of Nazi penetration in Latin America required a policy designed to woo the Latin Americans to the U.S. side.

Nonintervention is not a closed chapter in U.S.-Latin American relations. It probably never will be, given that the great disparity in power between the United States and the rest of the countries of the area is likely to continue. Moreover, the nonintervention issue was revived at the height of the cold war by U.S. military intervention, indirect and direct, in Guatemala (1954), Cuba (1961), and the Dominican Republic (1965), and by clandestine operations in several Latin American countries, highlighted by U.S. interference in Chilean politics from 1963 to 1973.

Therefore, it is not surprising that thus far the only notable change wrought by recent efforts to reform the Inter-American System has been a change in the voting requirement for lifting sanctions (a prerequisite for legitimizing reestablishment of relations with Cuba by OAS members). The requirement for a two-thirds vote, written in the heyday of U.S. influence in the area (1948), was designed to prevent the United States from wielding a tyranny of the majority. By the 1970s, with U.S. domination much attenuated, the two-thirds rule was seen as a way for the United States to mobilize a tyranny of the minority. But the essential point is that this reform is aimed at inhibiting U.S. power to interfere with the freedom of action of the other OAS members.

It also is important to recognize that the Latin American response to the "New Dialogue" launched by Henry Kissinger in 1974 at the Conference of Foreign Ministers in Mexico City was very much in the tradition of Inter-Americanism. The issues placed on the agenda of that meeting by the Latin American foreign ministers were concerned chiefly with restraining U.S. public and private power—as the Latin Americans see it, with countering intervention in its newer, more subtle guises as well as in its classical forms.

This theme runs throughout the agenda: in the Latin Americans' strictures against unilateral or discriminatory conditions on economic assistance and their condemnation of "economic coercion"; in their concern over U.S. corporations' interference in domestic affairs, evasion of jurisdiction, and control over technology; in the Latin Americans' espousal of Panama's aspirations for a new canal treaty; in their call on the United States to join Latin American efforts to achieve "radical" changes in the Inter-American System; and in the unspoken item on the Cuban question.

On the U.S. side, however, interventionism was viewed as a marginal issue—something in the past. The U.S. delegation, convinced that the denouement in Vietnam and the revelations of clandestine operations by the U.S. Central Intelligence Agency (CIA) had brought to a close the interventionist chapter in U.S. foreign policy, failed to appreciate sufficiently the concerns of the Latin Americans over the use of U.S. economic power to influence their political process. The U.S. side, with its eyes on the emerging "interdependent" world, called at the conference for a new era of cooperation between the United States and Latin America to confront jointly the new economic and technological problems of modern international life.

But what to the United States was to be an endeavor to form a true "community" (Kissinger's phrase) was seen by the Latin Americans as an effort to reassert U.S. hegemony. The Latins were more concerned with the old issue of interventionism and, as if to confirm their thesis, the U.S. Congress less than a year later excluded members of the Organization of Petroleum Exporting Countries (OPEC) from the generalized tariff out of spite for preferences extended to developing countries in the Trade Act, the stiff increases in oil prices and the Arab embargo. Ecuador and Venezuela, both OPEC members, charged "economic coercion" and refused to participate in further New Dialogue meetings. The other Latin American governments supported their offended colleagues, and the New Dialogue came to a premature end.

The Intractable Issue: Economics

If the dynamic of the Inter-American System is the dialectic of hegemony, what of the emphasis placed in recent times on economic relations? In the Alliance for Progress era, for example, much of the institutional focus of the System was on Latin American development, and currently issues of trade and raw materials prices are said to be central in the U.S.-Latin American dialogue.

In practice, however, the Inter-American System has found it difficult to cope with U.S. economic relations with Latin America, except briefly and in unusual circumstances. For the first half-century of Pan Americanism, the inter-American conferences dealt with economic subjects diffidently and inconclusively. In large part, this reflected the importance of European investment and trade in Latin America up to World War II, and the suspicions of the Latins that the occasional U.S. attempts to raise these subjects masked a desire to capture markets from the Europeans. Only when the war reoriented Latin America's economies almost totally toward the United States did economic cooperation become prominent—even then it was in the main organized bilaterally, with agreements between the United States and individual countries to purchase raw materials needed in the war effort in exchange for the extension of Export-Import Bank loans.

The multilateral codification of the U.S. economic cooperation is a more recent phenomenon, dating from the 1960s. Two developments dictated the introduction of economic issues into the OAS at that point. One was the overwhelming position of the United States in the world economy—because the international economy in the postwar decades was really an American world system, the Latin Americans began in the 1950s to clamor for U.S. attention to their economic problems. This was the beginning of Latin America's growing identification of its interests with those of other developing areas and of its belief that the United States had an obligation to help with the area's economic development. The second factor was the discovery by U.S. policy makers by 1960 of the link between underdevelopment and instability (and hence communist subversion).

The latter point is instructive. The U.S. interest in introducing economics into the inter-American dialogue in 1961 was not intended to deal with the heart of U.S.-Latin American economic relations—trade and investment. Rather, it focused on internal Latin American policies to stimulate economic growth and social justice with U.S. official aid—a form of interventionism, albeit benign in intent.

The reason for U.S. reluctance about attempts by the Inter-American System to establish rules for international economic relations—as distinct from domestic economic policy—is not hard to fathom. The United States as the preeminent world economic power has an overriding interest in a universal economic system. The United States cannot afford to make economic rules for one region that depart from those of the global system.

The United States ignores this fact at its peril. From 1969 to 1971, when it tried to deal with trade issues in the OAS context through the Special Committee on Consultation and Negotiation, the results were little short of disastrous. The failure to get tariff preferences through Congress, the failure to exempt Latin America from the import surcharge at the time of the 1971 devaluation, and the intractability of U.S. import restrictions on products of special interest to Latin America all demonstrated that U.S. economic policy is incapable of according Latin America special consideration.

Nor do the Latin Americans really want preferential economic treatment. A Colombian proposal that the U.S. extend regional tariff preferences was roundly rejected by the other Latin Americans in 1969. Except when stimulated by U.S. rhetoric about the "special relationship," the Latin Americans really want to be full participants in a world economic system that gives preferential treatment to developing countries, not in a Western Hemisphere version of the Lomé Convention. They will, of course, incessantly remind the United States, as a leading actor in the global system, of their aspirations. But the Latin Americans are not anxious to perpetuate a neocolonial relationship through a regional economic bloc. The economic item on the New Dialogue agenda, for example, emphasized the Latin Americans' rights to full participation in the global trade negotiations and the reform of the international monetary system, and to special treatment as developing countries from all developed countries. The Latin Americans' main preoccupation is that they not be left out of these new international arrangements because of their relative affluence.

U.S. rhetoric, on the other hand, has once again been emphasizing the specialness of U.S.-Latin American economic relations, this time as a testing ground or model for solutions to the global north-south issues. But if the United States was unable to make Latin America the hinge of its global economic policy when it dominated the international economic system, it is even less able to do so in a world of many economic powers. We are, in a way, moving back to the pre-1940 situation.

THE FUTURE OF THE INTER-AMERICAN SYSTEM

The hegemony that has undergirded the Inter-American System is under challenge.[11] The Castro regime has successfully violated the Monroe Doctrine. Some states, like Brazil and Venezuela, have the economic and political strength, and apparently the will, to slip out of the System altogether without having to substitute another Great Power's hegemony for that of the United States. They no longer feel a responsibility to preserve the System. Hence Brazil's unconcern over the debilitating effects of the Cuba sanctions issue on the Rio Treaty. Hence Venezuela's cavalier attitude toward the 1975 Kissinger meeting in Buenos Aires. Others, like Ecuador, Peru, and Panama, still weak economically but politically independent, are attempting to broaden and deepen the nonintervention principle—to use the System to shackle Gulliver. In this, they are in the tradition of inter-Americanism. But many small countries are not discontented. They feel too threatened by their neighbors and too dependent economically on the United States to want to change the old ways.

The initiative, however, is is with those who would let the System die or use it to achieve greater independence from the United States. With the former, large parts of the U.S. relationship can no longer be conducted in the inter-American framework. Brazil and Venezuela must increasingly be dealt with as independent actors in the global arena. Bilateralism is the mode of the future with these countries, as it has been for some time with Mexico.

The real challenge in the Inter-American System comes from those who would transform it. Although few in number, these regimes are at the cutting edge of the current struggle to use the Inter-American System to restrain the United States. They will be joined by others as time goes on.

What these states seek is to make effective the existing tenets of the System and to add others so as to neutralize the greater power of the United States. They wish to broaden the principle of nonintervention to encompass indirect as well as direct, covert as well as overt interference with their exercise of sovereignty. They have pushed successfully for U.S. acceptance of the principle of "plurality of ideologies" in the OAS Charter. This would seem to vitiate an interpretation of the Monroe Doctrine that would prohibit a Marxist-Leninist regime in the hemisphere (or a corporativist one?) as incompatible with the dictum against the extension of European "political systems" to the Americas. The revisionists wish to implement Articles 18 and 19 of the OAS Charter so that what the U.S. regards as voluntary economic assistance will become an obligation and thus be free of such strings as the Gonzalez Amendment or the Pelly Amendment.

Until recently, the U.S. response to these challenges has been wide of the mark. In large part, this has been because U.S. policy makers have not understood the nature of the Inter-American System. They have regarded Latin American initiatives to use the System against the United States as peevish manifestations of the hypernationalism of a few regimes rather than the latest episode in the mainstream of inter-Americanism. In their reaction, these U.S. leaders have attempted to revive the "solidarity" of a past era (a solidarity that existed mainly in the rhetoric that sought to make a virtue of necessity). Given the economic determinism that pervades so much U.S. thinking—instead of saying we are all Keynesians, Richard Nixon might have said we are all Marxists—the Ford Administration sought to promote a new rationale for the Inter-American System on the premise of shared objectives in the reform of the international economic order (this was the heart of Kissinger's speech at the Tlatelolco Conference). It also made efforts to revive the Alliance for Progress notion of regional cooperation to promote Latin American development (Kissinger's 1974 Atlanta speech to the OAS General Assembly).

But these efforts are foredoomed to failure. First, because the Latin Americans perceive that, in the short run at least, the interests of the

United States and Latin America in the bargaining about the new international economic order are not the same. They are suspicious that the United States is trying to use the old hegemony for its new goals in shaping the international economic order. Further, many of the problems of Latin American development can only be solved in a global context; regional cooperation is ineffective. Because the Latins use the organs of the Inter-American System to clamor for redistributive policies, one should not be misled into thinking that the issues are susceptible to regional management.

In contrast, the Latin Americans, by and large have been using the OAS and the New Dialogue to raise the intervention issue in its many current manifestations—ranging from Cuba and Panama to corporate political meddling to the Gonzalez, Pelly, and anti-OPEC amendments. They have shown little interest in discussing new forms of regional economic cooperation that include the United States. The result has been that the United States and the Latin Americans largely have been talking past each other.

The System's Value for the United States

If the chief function of the institutions of the Inter-American System is to litigate issues that arise because of U.S. power, and in the process to shrink U.S. hegemony, why should the United States bother to preserve the System at all?

The answer is that the System, as noted previously, provides a legitimizing force for the exercise of U.S. power. This is not to say that the OAS can be used to bless U.S. military interventions, as in the Dominican crisis. Military intervention will no longer be tolerated, and clandestine intervention, if it is uncovered, will be greeted with the condemnation it deserves. But U.S. economic and political power is a fact that cannot be legislated out of existence. As long as U.S. investment, commerce, and technology loom so large, as long as the U.S. power impinges so heavily on the world and on the Western Hemisphere in particular, there will be clashes of sovereignties between the United States and the nations of Latin America. The United States can, as it has in the past, attempt to resolve these conflicts in its favor by resorting to force—if not the force of arms, the force of economic reprisal and political ostracism. But absent violence, which is the ultimate arbiter, these kinds of force are of little avail in the face of a determined, internally united smaller opponent.

Clearly U.S. hegemony in Latin America is on the wane. But the United States need not fear the erosion of its hegemony, as it is not being replaced by that of another outside power. And paradoxically, as U.S. hegemony declines, U.S. influence is likely to increase—provided the United States is seen to be relinquishing the increasingly impotent levers of hegemony in favor of a process of bargaining that more nearly approximates that which is beginning to take place among states in the global forum.

If the United States were to decide to pursue this kind of relationship with the countries of Latin America, the Inter-American System could be an important instrument. It could be used to seek a consensus among the American states on solutions to the problems of conflicting sovereignty that give rise to charges of intervention or coercion leveled against the United States when it takes steps to protect its interests, and to accusations of lawlessness against Latin Americans when they pursue theirs. Used in this manner, the OAS—by breaking new ground in setting standards for the relationship between a Great Power and weaker ones—could promote the rule of law and the kind of international order the United States says it wants.

What objectives, specifically, might the United States pursue in the OAS?

Investment Disputes

Certainly on no other single aspect of the U.S. presence does the clash of sovereignties resound so loudly as the question of jurisdiction over subsidiaries of U.S. corporations operating in Latin America. The Latin Americans adhere to the Calvo Doctrine, which simply asserts that no corporation has any right to invoke the diplomatic protection of its home government and, by inference therefore, that no foreign government has the right to intercede on behalf of one of its companies. The United States has long held the opposite view.

While there are persuasive arguments in favor of the Calvo thesis, particularly in view of the increasing evidence of discrepancy between the U.S. national interest and the interests of the multinationals, it is unlikely given political realities that the United States will embrace the Calvo Doctrine in the foreseeable future. Yet the policies the U.S. government has pursued to protect U.S. investment on the whole have been abysmal failures, relying as they do on the threat of economic sanction and reprisal to induce Latin American governments to treat U.S. firms fairly. Clearly, more diplomacy and less coercion is called for in this situation. In this regard, the OAS could provide a useful forum for discussion of a whole range of issues regarding jurisdiction over the multinationals and corporate conduct.[12] Our eventual goal should be an international agreement for the settlement of investment disputes, but before this can be accomplished a great deal more confidence will have to be built up on both sides.

What the United States would gain by subjecting itself to the undoubtedly difficult process of discussing this subject in a forum in which it would be one against 23 is the creation of a more receptive climate for its bilateral diplomacy in those specific cases in which it has to intercede to settle an investment dispute. Invariably, such quiet diplomatic efforts are the only effective recourse in what is usually a highly charged political controversy. Ironically, the only government that has proven susceptible to the leverage supposedly provided by the Hickenlooper and Gonzalez amendments has been that of the United States, which will go to great lengths to settle an investment controversy by diplomatic efforts in order to avoid the open clash that invoking one of the amendments would provoke.[13] In short, the U.S. government badly needs a more effective means of protecting both the broad U.S. national interest and the corporate U.S. interest. Inevitably, the United States will have to play a more activist role in order to head off intergovernmental clashes over Latin American treatment of U.S. investment. To the extent the United States can create a regional framework of intergovernmental cooperation on these issues, Latin American governments will have more receptivity to the United States as an independent actor in conflicts involving U.S. corporations.

Peacekeeping

The United States also has an interest in a strong inter-American capacity to deal with armed conflict within the hemisphere. There are many old scores in the area and a number of disputes simmering (Chile-Peru, Ecuador-Peru, El Salvador-Honduras, Guatemala-Belize, Venezuela-Guyana). The prospect for peace in Latin America is not bright as more Latin American states acquire modern arms and gain in political and economic strength—and as unilateral U.S. intervention to settle an armed conflict becomes unacceptable to all sides. Strong regional peacekeeping machinery will guarantee the renunciation of unilateral action by the United States. The agreement between El Salvador and Honduras to arbitrate their territorial dispute is the latest example of how the OAS can play a useful role in peacemaking.

Human Rights

There is perhaps no other area in which the machinery of the Inter-American System could prove more useful to U.S. objectives than in the field of human rights. Powerful voices in the U.S. public and Congress are demanding that human rights be accorded a higher priority in foreign policy. Yet there is no foreign policy goal so strewn with pitfalls as this one. The use of economic sanctions to punish governments presumed to be violating human rights is no less interventionism than the use of the same measures to protect U.S. investment from confiscation—and is likely to be equally ineffective.[14]

In the final analysis, the best hope of reconciling U.S. objectives on human rights with a nonintervention policy is the creation of a strong body of international standards and fact-finding procedures. The American states are solemnly pledged, in the OAS Charter, to respect the rights of the individual, even if many ignore these rights in practice. The United States has moved to strengthen the OAS Human Rights Commission by providing badly needed additional funds. Largely through a U.S. initiative, the OAS General Assembly held in Santiago in 1976 established the precedent of openly debating specific charges of human rights violations (in Chile). The United States should continue to strengthen the capacity of the Inter-American System to set standards, to investigate facts, and ultimately to invoke sanctions in this area.

The System's Value for Latin America

If the System's major purposes are the legitimization of U.S. power by collective agreement as to its limits and uses, it is obvious that the OAS will continue to provide the Latin Americans with a forum in which to call the United States to account for its actions in the region. The litigation of the permissible (or desirable) uses of U.S. power will continue, as it has for most of the System's existence.

There are dangers in assuming that the future can be a linear projection of the past, as far as effective use by Latin America of the System, however, is concerned.

In the two periods in which the Inter-American System seems to have played a strong role in hemispheric affairs—the 1930s and the early 1960s—there existed a consensus between Latin America and the United States as to the rights and responsibilities of each party. Both periods, the Good Neighbor era and the Kennedy years, represented a kind of "great bargain."[15] In the first period, the United States forswore military interventions in exchange for greater Latin American support for U.S. security interests; in the second, Latin America rallied to the U.S. side in the cold war (in spite of Castro's attractiveness in his early years to the Latin American noncommunist left) in exchange for U.S. development assistance.

For some time now, the elements of another great bargain have been missing. For one thing, the U.S. government has not been clear in its own mind just what it wanted from Latin America (other than not to cause trouble). On the Latin American side, there has been a vast lack of understanding of what the United States can realistically be expected to do in the region. In part, this lack of Latin American sensitivity stems from a general failure to appreciate how the U.S. political process works; in part, it reflects the unrealistic expectations aroused by U.S. rhetoric ("the special relationship"; "hemispheric solidarity" and the like). But the Latin Americans' insistence in pushing their ideological positions down the United States' throat at every OAS meeting (in the form of resolutions that the U.S. delegations must then try to bend back into minimally acceptable shape) is simply alienating U.S. leaders in the executive branch and Congress who normally would be sympathetic to Latin American concerns. Until the elements of another great bargain are found, the Latin Americans would do well to apply pressure on the United States much more judiciously. As disagreeable as it may be, the Latin Americans will have to accept the fact that they must become participants in the U.S. political process if their collective action to restrain and harness U.S. power is to be effective, rather than only to produce hollow OAS resolutions. What is done and said in the OAS forum will have to be the result of a greater compromise between Latin American aspirations and U.S. capabilities.

In particular, both sides need to recognize the limitations of the regional mechanism for building a new relationship between the rich and poor countries. New approaches to economic relations may be assayed in the OAS framework, but in the final analysis the United States will undertake hard and fast commitments to innovations in the international economic order only after careful consideration of their global implications.

These prescriptions will strike many who are eager to improve the quality of U.S.-Latin American relations as disappointingly austere. But hemisphere relationships are in a state of transition, always a delicate process in international life, and this calls for the utmost care and caution. However, if the United States and Latin America are clear about what the Inter-American System has been and is about, and use its institutional machinery judiciously, there will be a better chance that they will be able to avoid conflict and alienation during the evolution of the U.S.-Latin American relationship from hegemony to something approaching independence within interdependence.

A central issue today is an effort by the Latin Americans (or the "reformists" among them) to make all forms of U.S. economic assistance, both in trade and aid, obligatory and thus free of strings like those embodied in U.S. laws that condition such benefits on Latin American behavior with regard to such matters as expropriations, fishing disputes, and human rights.

Washington should consider whether a new Latin American policy might not consist of giving up some of these sacrosanct but increasingly impotent attempts to exercise leverage in exchange for greater Latin American cooperation in building a new global order. And Latin America might consider diluting some of the purity of its ideology on the global issues in exchange for practical solutions. Only in this manner will the people of the U.S. and their elected representatives become more amenable to giving the Latin Americans the attention they undoubtedly deserve in the shaping of global policy.

NOTES

1. The current membership of the OAS, which is the central deliberative body of the system, consists of 25 American states. Cuba is considered a member but is in suspension. Guyana is not a member, nor is Canada. There are 22 signatories to the Rio Treaty: Barbados, Grenada, and Jamaica are not members of this collective security pact.

2. I realize that it can be said that this is precisely the explanation for the origins of the postwar economic and financial system, the institutional embodiment of which is the GATT, the IMF, the IBRD, and the OECD. But this is exactly my point—these institutions aspire to a universalism that fits the role that American economic power played in the world of the first 25 years of their existence.

3. The fatuous notion that being in the Western Hemisphere and having fought to gain independence from European empires are sufficient reasons for forming a regional association is best reserved for speeches on Pan American Day.

4. For an excellent discussion that bears out this point, *see* S. D. Krasner, *Mercantilism Revived*, WORLD POL. (1976).

5. President Monroe's message to the Congress, Dec. 2, 1823.

6. The right of intervention was formally asserted by President Theodore Roosevelt in his annual message to Congress on Dec. 6, 1904. There also have been U.S. attempts from time to time to influence Latin American politics toward the U.S. model of representative democracy. These efforts have been much weaker than interventions aimed at preventing an extrahemispheric power from gaining a foothold, precisely because the presence of democratic forms of government has not always been perceived as essential to U.S. security.

7. J. Kurth, *United States Foreign Policy and Latin American Military Rule*, in MILITARY RULE IN LATIN AMERICA: FUNCTIONS, CONSEQUENCES, AND PERSPECTIVES (P. Schmitter ed. 1973).

8. *Id.*

9. The difficulties that the recently formed Latin American Economic System (SELA) encountered in arousing more than *pro forma* support among its members is a case in point.

10. For a discussion of anticolonialism as *the* unifying element in Third World ideology, *see* T. Farer, *The United States and the Third World: A Basis for Accommodation*, FOREIGN AFFAIRS (Oct. 1975).

11. *See* A. Lowenthal, *The United States and Latin America: Ending the Hegemonic Presumption*, FOREIGN AFFAIRS (Oct. 1976).

12. An attempt to begin an inter-American dialogue on this very set of issues was made in 1974 as an outgrowth of Kissinger's New Dialogue meetings with his Latin American counterparts. A working group held three meetings in an effort to agree on a statement of principles governing the behavior of multinationals. The working group was disbanded upon the cancellation of the Buenos Aires Foreign Ministers Meeting, to which the working group was to render its report. For a description of this episode, *see* Chapter 6.

13. The IPC case in Peru is an excellent example. See J. EINHORN, EXPROPRIATION POLITICS (1974).

14. There is, of course, another argument for such unilateral measures in the face of human rights violations, which is simply the need to disassociate the United States from the offending regime.

15. I am indebted to Jorge Dominguez for the phrase and the point it makes.

Chapter 2

A NOTE ON THE FUTURE OF THE INTER-AMERICAN SYSTEM

William D. Rogers

Oliver Wendell Holmes once said, "It is revolting to have no better reason for a rule of law than that it was laid down in the time of Henry IV. It is still more revolting if the grounds upon which it was laid down have vanished long since, and the rule simply persists from blind imitation of the past." ("The Path of the Law," reprinted in *Jurisprudence in Action* 276 at 287.)

The spirit that motivated this American Society of International Law study of the Inter-American System was distinctly Holmesian—a quiet skepticism toward the notion that once an international organization is well launched, elaborately staffed, and elegantly housed, as the Organization of American States certainly is, it should be entitled to the perpetual assumption that it is performing useful functions. The study breathed a sense that institutions, like the law itself, must be regularly tested against the contemporary interests and needs of mankind; that the organizations and procedures by which a collectivity functions should be the product of plan and thought, not history and accident; and that the question is not whether the Inter-American System is benignly good but whether it is affirmatively superior to other feasible ways of organizing the common business of the Americas.

Moreover, it is possible that the effort might have significance elsewhere. The Organization of American States, the linchpin of the Inter-American System, is not the only international organization that might be ripe for review. The proliferation of public international entities has become a celebrated fact of contemporary foreign relations. Any of a considerable number might have been taken as a test case. But in many ways the OAS is particularly eligible for inquiry. It is the oldest of the international political entities, antedating the United Nations by decades. Even in its contemporary form, as established in the postwar charter, it is more than a quarter-century old. The major theme of this

ASIL study has been to test whether the broader system, of which the OAS is a central feature, is adequate and appropriate to the needs of the final quarter of this century.

A NEW LOOK AT THE SYSTEM

It is relatively simple to inventory the changes which have occurred within the Americas during the 25 years since the OAS Charter was drafted. There are several major ways in which the hemisphere is different today that are relevant to the future of the organization.

The first change is the increasing divergence among the nations of the hemisphere. In general, it is likely that the members of the Inter-American System are becoming even more different from one another. These differences are benign in many respects. There is an increasing tolerance for differences, not only in cultural and ideological matters but in domestic political preferences as well. Indeed, the Inter-American System has enshrined respect for ideological plurality as a fundamental principle of state relations in the hemisphere. But it would not be correct to assume that this cleavage in the hemisphere is incapable of introducing new and ominous strains into the political relationships. The growing gap between the United States and the Southern Cone countries, for example, has engaged the most powerful nations of the System. On the one hand, Brazil, Paraguay, Uruguay, Chile, and Argentina are now managed by similar regimes. Each is ideologically rightwing. Each is socially conservative. Each is authoritarian. Each is military in character. There is little doubt that their philosophy, posture, and attitude toward the rest of the hemisphere, including the United States, is polarizing.

At the same time, the United States is sharpening its own particular preferences. The increased emphasis on human rights and democracy as objectives consciously to be pursued occurred at the very same time as the United States began to move to the front in the cause of hemispheric detente by publicly opening relations with Cuba.

A second change, as Ambassador Richard Bloomfield pointed out in Chapter 1, has been that to the extent that there still exists a common hemispheric interest, that common interest has been altered radically in recent years. "The Inter-American System," Bloomfield observes, "came into being and evolved to its present form because of the assertion by one Great Power, the United States, of a strategic prerogative over the states of Latin America and the Caribbean." It was original political and security interests in Latin America that moved the United States to exercise leadership in constructing the Inter-American System. Bloomfield, therefore, suggests that the Inter-American System was originally designed to serve the institutional requirements of what was essentially a "hegemonial" system.

For the United States, the original and enduring purpose of the Inter-American System was the security of the hemisphere. That security was the goal of the Rio Treaty, which purported to establish the essential characteristics of an alliance in the hemisphere. "The collective security treaty was simply a figleaf for the Monroe Doctrine," Bloomfield says. Nevertheless, the security concerns of 1948 are no longer the paramount interests of the United States.

Latin America has responded by seeking to add a series of constraints on U.S. action, and to entice the United States into a series of economic commitments; it has been largely successful in that effort. The doctrine of nonintervention, stated in terms so broad as to reach the edge of reality, was enshrined as a centerpiece of the OAS Charter, while the Punta del Este Charter and the recent charter amendment bind the United States to assist Latin American economic and social development. For the Latins, the main objective in the OAS has been to erect a barrier against what they perceived, at particular moments during the last quarter-century, as most threatening to their interests. If the United States was a relatively amicable and libertarian power, it was nevertheless the closest at hand, and the one whose record was the most consistently intrusive in Latin American affairs. Thus, the principal business of Latin America in the Inter-American System has been to perfect the principle of nonintervention, to expand its content, and to make its sanctions increasingly clear and painful. But this objective, too, has fallen far down in the scale of foreign policy goals over the years.

In short, the original purposes of both the United States and Latin America have declined in importance. The U.S.-Soviet conflict has taken on new forms and is bypassing Latin America, and there is no other likely source of external trouble for Latin America. At the same time, the United States is ending its own aspirations to hegemony. The Panama Canal issue, which represented the last pretension of empire, has been resolved. There is every indication that the United States has closed out the interventionist chapter of its own history, and no reasonable prospect that it will repeat such events as the Dominican effort of 1965 or the covert intrusion into the Chilean political process. The original security and political purposes of the OAS have declined radically in significance for both Latin America and the United States.

A third change has been the emergence of economic development issues. These are the commanding interests to the hemisphere today. They are by definition essentially global; it was almost ironic how strongly President Jimmy Carter emphasized that Latin America's fundamental economic problems could not be solved except in the global context, in his speech to the OAS on Pan American Union Day, during his first year in office. (There was no evidence that the irony was appreciated by the authors of the speech.)

Fourth, a number of Latin American nations are breaking out of the hemispheric mold. Brazil and Mexico have assumed a new significance on the world scene. For them, the Inter-American System is by no means the central foreign policy issue. Brazil particularly is now looking to far broader horizons—in the former Portuguese colonies in Africa, and in its relationships with the Arab countries, Europe, and Japan. At the same time, Venezuela has become a vital and active member of the Organization of Petroleum Exporting Countries (OPEC), and its seasoned diplomatic leader, Perez Guerrero, has been the strong man of the Conference on International Economic Cooperation in Paris.

At the same time, a number of issues have emerged between the United States and Latin American nations which can only be dealt with on a bilateral basis. Major U.S. concerns with Mexico, most particularly, are migration and drug control, and these are hardly amenable to treatment in an inter-American mode.

Fifth, it must be said that at the very moment when the original purposes of the OAS have become less important and the member states are looking to new economic issues and opportunities, a number of OAS organs have begun to distinguish themselves by mediocrity. This has been particularly true of the Permanent Council. On the one hand, for a period it fell into the habit of adversarial debate in which the United States was increasingly subject to a barrage of Latin attack so severe as to raise serious questions as to whether the United States wished to subsidize such an entity. On the other hand, the council has fallen into a slough of inconsequentiality matched only by the torpid comings and goings of the overbureaucratized Secretariat. This may account for the fact that there is now a broad agreement in the United States and Latin America that the OAS is entitled to low esteem.

Finally, and beyond all this, is the fact that if development and economic issues are at the top of the agenda for the Americas, there are now, as there were not in 1948, a considerable number of other international institutions prepared, and in fact quite anxious to take on these issues. The United Nations Conference on Trade and Development, as well as the General Assembly of the United Nations, Economic Commission for Latin America (ECLA), Sistema Economicano Latin Americano (SELA), and the Conference on International Economic Cooperation are only a few examples. James Grant, in *The United States and World Development: Agenda 1979* by the Overseas Development Council, has suggested that we are now experiencing a kind of "systems overload" in the international machinery. The multiplicity of mechanisms and objectives is beginning to swamp the carrying capacity of the United States and other nations as well. The demands and pressures of the arrangements of an earlier day for conducting the business of nations are no longer necessarily adequate for those of our age. It is time, in short, to subject the systems of the past to critical scrutiny. The competition among existing institutions for a role is severe.

We are entitled to a polite skepticism about the multitude of international organizations that are springing up around the world. There may even be value to a sunset principle, not merely for the state and federal governments but for international organizations as well. This is an extension into the international arena of some lessons of domestic politics: that we probably ought to think about lessening rather than increasing the number of public agencies; that new entities do not always resolve old issues; and that on occasion less is more when it comes to the management of public affairs.

FUTURE PROSPECTS

The future of the Organization of American States and the Inter-American System is therefore ripe for inquiry. The future issues may be grouped under several headings: the future of security concerns, trade and economic relations, the relevance of the System to the total foreign policy of the emerging Latin powers, and human rights.

Security

As to the first issue, security, it is important to determine whether, after all is said and done, the Inter-American System still has important work to do. Past OAS efforts at peacekeeping have been significant, if modest. But keeping Latin America conflict-free is no small objective, and some will suggest that we ought not to risk diluting such institutions and such incentives toward peaceful resolution of disputes as may exist in this vexed world. The OAS and its constitutive treaties may be just that. In addition, the OAS may have important work to do in respect to arms reduction and the limitation of military expenditures.

For Latin America, there have been two dimensions to the security issue. The first has been the traditional question of exemption from extracontinental forceful intrusions. There is, as noted, some question whether that is an important and relevant consideration today. The second dimension has been the more recent effort to create within the Inter-American System constraints on the United States.

The OAS Charter, along with Article 2(4) of the UN Charter, is the most significant expression of juridical limitation on U.S. international activity. It is not irrelevant or anachronistic; in fact, the principle of nonintervention was at the very heart of the debate over the ratification of the Panama Treaties, which President Carter himself described as "absolutely essential" to his foreign policy. The Senate engaged itself in the most extensive and bitter foreign policy debate since the Treaty of Versailles over whether the United States was prepared to write an end to the era in which Latin America was considered a fit subject for hegemony and intervention.

It will also be important to say something about the recent efforts to reform the OAS by expanding the list of established constraints on U.S. policy and practice to preclude rather untraditional forms of intrusion. The call for a binding doctrine of collective economic security, for example, recently has dominated the internal debate on revising the OAS Charter. That Charter reform drive was in fact directed almost exclusively at such things as the Gonzalez amendments to the IDB legislation and the anti-OPEC provision of the GSP. Are these efforts fruitful? Are they based on false parliamentary analogy? Should the Inter-American System now aspire to a quasi-judicial method of penalizing the United States when it seems to retaliate economically against Latin America by denying it credit or trade opportunities? This is weighty stuff and could have important implications for the north-south relationship in broader terms.

Economic Relations

It is also important to come to grips with the question of the future relevance of the Inter-American System to the future economic relations between the United States and Latin America. Is the institution behind the historic curve? In the 1960s, by common consent, the great issues were cooperation for development and the ways in which the United States could provide bilateral aid to the development process. The OAS was—and remains—the major meeting ground of the north and south within the Western Hemisphere. Hence, it is perhaps natural that it should assume a major responsibility with respect to the organization of U.S. cooperation in the development effort.

But evidently the laws of organizational biology required a major expansion in the size of the OAS to cope with this new issue, and as a result the OAS added massively to its staff and budget during that period. Now, however, there is evidence that the structure of hemispheric relations has changed. As Stephen H. Rogers points out in Chapter 4, "bilateral economic assistance has lost its prominent position." It has, in fact, gone down by a third, and is now targeted only to a few smaller countries. All the major nations of the hemisphere long ago abandoned bilateral assistance. This is a token of the larger change that has occurred.

Multilateral assistance is somewhat larger—about $4.3 billion, split approximately equally between the Inter-American Development Bank and the World Bank and its affiliates. But private capital flows, largely bank loans, are more than double that level. Trade, however, constitutes far and away the largest source of income to the region. Latin American exports are approaching the $50 billion mark. The character of these exports has changed radically in the last two decades. Manufactured products now represent well over a third of the nonpetroleum exports to the United States from Latin America.

Trade, then, is the major point of economic interaction between the United States and Latin America. Thus, the issue that emerges is the extent to which the OAS can make a significant contribution to this increasingly important dimension of the north-south relationship within the hemisphere.

The recent record has not been encouraging. The United States, although it has on occasion claimed that it was prepared to give special solicitude to Latin America's trade interests, continues to act self-interestedly on matters of vital concern to Latin America, such as sugar and meat. The Latin American members of the OAS have attempted regularly to take the United States to task in the Special Coordinating Committee (SCCN), but without much success. Nor has the OAS been able to move smartly forward to hold a special general assembly on cooperation for development. The proposal has been in the mill for several years now, but no serious planning has yet given promise that the general assembly will take place.

Thus, while the Inter-American System reflects the notion that there is a special political relationship within the hemisphere, this has never been duplicated on the economic side. Proposals such as those put forward by the foreign minister of Colombia, Indalecio Liévano Aguirre, for a special economic and trade system within the Western Hemisphere have never moved very far.

For most nations of Latin America, the most significant dimension of the U.S. relationship with them is the extent to which the United States contributes to or impedes development. As noted, it is economics, not politics, that is at center stage at the moment. Thus emerged a critical issue for the Inter-American System—the extent to which that system can make a contribution to the evolution of economic relationships between the north and south. Nor is this a question solely as to the future of U.S. policy. Latin America is part of the upper tier of the developing countries. Its fate is now tied to the export of manufacturers, and to continued access to capital.

The General Agreement on Tariff and Trade (GATT) negotiations will favor the export of manufacturers. As a result, a number of countries in Latin America will in the next several years inevitably join the ranks of the mature manufacturing economies. But Latin America will have all the advantages and none of the obligations of a mature manufacturing economy in terms of its trade relations with the developed countries; it could become another Japan.

We therefore will have to begin to think seriously about negotiating with the nations of Latin America to open their economies increasingly to U.S. exports and to undertake other responsibilities that follow from the success of their development efforts. If the United States intends to compete in the domestic markets of the major countries of Latin America, it will have to urge an increasing dismantlement of the controls, the preferences, and the systems of constraint that now exist there. We must ask, then, whether there is a role for the Inter-American System in defining the consequences for Latin America of its increasing international trade power.

Foreign Policy

The future of the Inter-American System also must be tested against the future foreign policy objectives of the emerging Latin powers. This inquiry must begin with Brazil. The OAS has had a distinctly secondary significance for the managers of Brazil's foreign relations. Their primary foreign policy concern for the last half-century has been the definition of Brazil's borders, the enhancement of its interests in the buffer areas of Bolivia, Paraguay, and Uruguay, and its relative power and influence vis-a-vis Argentina. It has cultivated its bilateral relationship with the United States quite consciously for these ends. U.S.-Brazilian bilateralism has been an extraordinary constant, in fact, in Brazil's modern foreign policy, just as Argentina has been the most prickly of the nations of Latin America for the United States.

Within the Inter-American System though, Brazil has not permitted itself to be seen as opposing the common interests of Latin America as they have found expression in the institutions and proceedings of the System. It might be too much to suggest that Brazil has been gratified to see the United States the object of the pointed attacks of the other nations of the hemisphere when the OAS debates have deteriorated into confrontation. But at the very least it has occurred to more than one Brazilian policymaker that an OAS without the United States would certainly be a regional organization whose national dividing line would be between the smaller Spanish-speaking countries on the one hand and the one remaining foreign-tongued giant on the other. So it has been Brazilian policy not only to accommodate itself to the present structure and pattern of the Inter-American System but in fact to take advantage of it.

What, however, of the future? Will the Inter-American System be more or less significant to Brazil? Is this emerging power, with world pretensions and global interests, prepared to move into a role of leadership, or even dominance, of the Organization of American States and its peripheral machinery, and turn it to its use as a continental base from which to project an intercontinental policy? Or will Brazil instead reject the system even more sharply, particularly if the United States begins to do so?

And what, to take a different case of a Latin nation of world significance, of Venezuela? As Franklin Tugwell makes clear in Chapter

14, Venezuela's foreign policy embraces a series of quite discrete and compatible goals—to defend its oil interests, to consolidate its national boundaries, to take a leadership role in shaping new world institutions, to strengthen ties within Latin America, to play a similar leadership role in global groupings of developing countries, and to help shape and improve U.S. oil policy, most particularly by challenging the exclusion of Venezuela and Ecuador from the U.S. GSP.

This foreign policy mix is highly explicit. Venezuela has been pursuing it with vigor and is unlikely to change radically, although it is possible that some of the intra-Latin American efforts may take a different form. Thus, traditional regional collective institutions, most notably the OAS, probably will continue to be a secondary concern of Venezuela. But should one assume that Caracas will not seek to dismantle inherited institutions of this kind—if only because they again may serve as useful instruments of diplomatic self-protection and protest, and because, perhaps in modified form, they may remain the best forum for the conduct of regional adversarial interaction?

The significance of the Inter-American System for the emerging powers of the hemisphere is, in short, an important area of inquiry.

Human Rights

If there is one accepted item on the common agenda, at least as that agenda is defined in Washington, it is human rights. One State Department Official, when asked to define the three major elements of U.S. foreign policy in Latin America, replied "human rights Number 1, human rights Number 2, and human rights Number 3."

This may be an overstatement, but it is not a distortion. In his Inaugural Address, President Carter devoted more paragraphs to human rights than to any other foreign policy issue—and considerably more than to the international financial crisis, the Middle East, or the Strategic Arms Limitation Talks (SALT).

Furthermore, whatever the significance of human rights for U.S. policy in Africa, the Middle East, Southeast Asia, and with the Soviet Union, in each of those areas the United States has vital strategic interests. Clashes and confrontations with international significance abound. Latin America, on the other hand, is a geopolitical and strategic backwater. It is not, and rarely has been, an arena in which great power politics have been played out. So, while human rights emphasis competes in U.S. concern with protecting the Korean Peninsula against attack, for example, there are not such overwhelming security interests at play in Latin America. For this reason, the human rights issue has occupied center stage in U.S. Latin policy with minimal competition.

The Carter Administration's purpose in giving new emphasis to human rights concerns was authentic and commendable. President Carter made clear in his campaign that he felt himself bound to give a new lift to the U.S. engagement in international affairs. In order to overcome the dispiriting effects of Watergate and Vietnam, it was essential that the U.S. people feel once again, as he said, that foreign policy fairly and authentically represents the genius of the United States in the world. He proposed to speak for those values and traditions in which the United States could take pride.

This effort has been marked with success. There is a new spirit in the U.S. public's attitude about foreign policy. In addition, on balance, human rights behavior, not only in the hemisphere but throughout the world, probably has been measurably improved by the Administration's emphasis. There have been reverses, of course. In the Soviet Union, life has been made more difficult on occasion for the dissidents. But by and large, if all the various evidence at hand can be weighed, the net balance appears to be favorable. Because of the Carter Administration's efforts, human rights behavior is better in the Americas than it otherwise would have been.

But is this the end of the matter? Probably not. There are other considerations at work. First and foremost is the problem of coherence of policy. Human rights are important. They are the authentic expression of the United States in the Americas and in the world. But they are not all, even in this hemisphere. The United States has profoundly important interests in addition to seeing that governments treat their own citizens better. These interests are access to raw materials, the organizing of productive economic relationships, political cooperation, the resolution of regional conflicts. Latin America may be a backwater in world affairs, but it is not irrelevant. Although it has only marginal impact on the front page political crises such as the Arab-Israeli dispute, and although it makes minimal contributions to the strategic balance or the prospects for war, it is nevertheless an important part of the world. Simply stated, Latin America is that group of developing countries that is moving most rapidly toward international economic significance and a breakthrough toward effective industrialization. It is, by the same token, that grouping of developing nations that is a part of the West by culture, tradition, and history. Single issue diplomacy will not serve.

Nevertheless, standards of decency and human rights, and the common commitment to the humane values of Western civilization, represent the single most important thread that ties the nations of the hemisphere together—more important than geography or language or trade or perceived external threat. So by that standard, the human rights issue belongs in the one forum where the nations of the region meet.

How that forum can be organized most effectively to assure the greatest progress in improving human rights in the Americas, while policy toward Latin America remains coherent and manageable, will be a major challenge to the Inter-American System in the years to come.

II

THE CENTRAL ISSUES: AXES OF CONFLICT AND COOPERATION

Section
A

HEMISPHERIC ECONOMIC RELATIONS IN GLOBAL CONTEXT, OR, THE LIMITS OF THE HEMISPHERIC "FIX" FOR NORTH-SOUTH PROBLEMS

Chapter 3

CHANGES IN THE INTER-AMERICAN ECONOMIC SYSTEM

Werner Baer and Donald V. Coes

Economists view the Inter-American Economic System as a network of trade, investment, and financial relationships linking the United States and Latin America. This chapter examines changes in those relationships, both in degree and in nature, as the system has emerged in recent decades. As trade and investment flows within Latin America itself have been a negligible proportion of the region's total foreign trade and investment, the Inter-American Economic System is dominated by U.S.-Latin American relationships. The central focus here, therefore, is on the change in U.S.-Latin American economic relationships since the early part of this century and on the distribution of the benefits of these economic interactions.

HISTORICAL BACKGROUND

The economic development paths of Latin America and the United States differed significantly in the nineteenth century. Latin American economies became fully integrated into the nineteenth century world division of labor as the suppliers of primary products. Their trade ties were principally with Europe, which in turn supplied the capital to develop the primary export sector and to construct an infrastructure designed to integrate the primary sectors of these economies more efficiently into a world trading system whose center was Europe.[1]

The economic development of the United States was more autonomous. Although it also fitted into the nineteenth century world trading pattern as a supplier of primary goods, its economy did not remain as dependent on foreign trade as Latin America. Most regions of the latter were totally geared to the export sector, while major regions in the United States embarked on an inward-oriented industrialization path. By the beginning of the twentieth century, the United States already had evolved into a major industrial power, with a relatively low dependence on trade. Despite the relatively greater autonomy of the U.S. economy, however, its trade, like that of Latin America, was oriented toward Europe and primary exports. Over 40 percent of its exports still consisted of raw materials and food products, and finished manufactures accounted for only 25 percent of exports. By the turn of the century about 70 percent of U.S. exports were shipped to Europe.[2]

When viewed from the United States, the degree of economic interrelationship with Latin America in the nineteenth century was small on both the export and investment side. Latin America accounted for less than 8 percent of U.S. exports in 1880 and was still less than 10 percent at the turn of the century. Until the last two decades of the nineteenth century, U.S. foreign investments were negligible, as might have been expected of a young economy with ample internal uses for its capital. However, it should be noted that there was a stronger link on the import side. In 1880 almost 27 percent of U.S. imports originated in Latin America, and until World War II Latin America's share in U.S. imports hovered around 25 percent. From a Latin American perspective, trade ties with the United States were closer. At the turn of the century over 28 percent of its exports were shipped to the United States and about 25 percent of its imports originated in the United States.[3]

Although U.S. capital began to move into Latin America in the last two decades of the nineteenth century, it was still a small proportion of total investment in the region. At the turn of the century almost 70 percent of foreign investments were owned by British capital and only 10 percent by U.S. enterprises, although this was to change rapidly in the first decades of the twentieth century.

As the United States was more dependent on Latin America for its imports than as an export market, early U.S. investment activities complemented the former. Investments were made principally in primary agricultural and extractive production (for example, sugar in the Caribbean, bananas in Central America, copper mining in the Andean countries). These initial investments were followed by investments in transportation, power generation, and the economic infrastructure necessary to make the primary investments more productive.

As trade and investment relations intensified in the first three decades of the twentieth century, the United States increasingly rivaled Great Britain in the area and gradually assumed the role of the region's principal supplier of manufactured goods and principal buyer of primary products. By the end of the 1920s the share of the Latin American market in U.S. exports had grown to about 19 percent, while imports from Latin America still represented 25 percent of U.S. imports. From the Latin American point of view, the U.S. market accounted for 32 percent of exports in the late 1920s, while almost 40 percent of imports came from the United States.

The emergence of the United States as a premier world economic power at the end of World War I was reflected in an acceleration of U.S. capital flows to Latin America in the succeeding decade. On the eve of the Great Depression the presence of U.S. capital in the region had challenged that of Great Britain.[4]

The destruction and disruption of trade and investment in the Old World as a consequence of World War II reinforced U.S. dominance of economic relationships in this hemisphere. Conversely, the relative importance of Latin America to the United States also increased; in 1950 some 27 percent of U.S. exports went to Latin America and 35 percent of imports originated there. From Latin America's point of view, 35 percent of exports went to the United States in 1948 and almost 63 percent of imports originated there, while the United States represented 51.1 percent of foreign investments in the region by 1950.

The Import-Substitution Era

From this brief description, it can be seen that the Inter-American Economic System that prevailed from the late nineteenth century to the early post-World War II period can be characterized as a center-periphery relationship. The United States increasingly replaced Great Britain as the center country, exporting manufactured goods and investing its capital in the primary and infrastructure sectors, while importing primary products. Since most Latin American economies were totally geared to the export sector, specializing in the production of a small number of primary goods, they were totally dependent on the rate of economic activity at the center, which was increasingly the United States. A decline in U.S. economic activity would be reflected in a decline, often magnified, of economic activity in the Latin American economies, which had few independent means to engage in countercyclical programs.

The Great Depression of the 1930s convinced many Latin Americans in the larger countries that there might be an escape from the traditional dependency relationship with the world's industrial centers. The drastic decline of foreign exchange earnings they experienced in the early 1930s with the fall in center countries' incomes forced them to curtail imports. The resulting shortages of manufactured goods and their increased relative prices provided the necessary incentives for a rapid growth of import-substitutive industries. This, in part, enabled such countries as Argentina and Brazil to recover from the shock of the world depression in a relatively short period of time.[5]

The circumstances leading to industrial growth in the 1930s were not lost on Latin American policy makers in the early post-World War II period. Import substitutive industrialization (ISI) not only was felt to be an essential strategy for development but also was seen as a way to change the dependency relation of Latin American countries vis-a-vis the industrial centers, especially the United States. The ISI drive of many Latin American countries in the 1950s and early 1960s was aimed principally at the reduction of the import coefficient, or the ratio of imports to national income. Most of the major countries emphasized industrialization on an across-the-board basis, with little effort made to identify areas in which scarce resources such as capital and skilled labor would be used most efficiently. Little was done to encourage traditional exports or develop new ones, since the aim was to insulate Latin American economies from the vagaries of the world economy by making them as autarkic as possible.[6]

Post-ISI Dependency

By the mid-1960s it had become clear that ISI had not increased the economic independence of Latin American countries, but had only changed the nature of the link with the United States and a few other industrial countries. ISI had led to a drastic change in the commodity composition of imports. The share of finished manufactured products declined while the import of raw materials (oil, coal, minerals) and capital goods increased.

As the industrial sectors of Latin American economies grew both absolutely and relatively, essential industrial inputs and capital goods imports could not be compressed and the import coefficient actually began to rise again. Thus, despite several decades of ISI, the major Latin American economies were paradoxically more vulnerable to balance of payments difficulties than they had been before ISI, since any reduction in essential imports, unlike interruptions in the supply of imports of consumer goods, was likely to result in severe industrial disruption and stagnation. As most Latin American economies had not changed their export commodity structures along with changes in the internal structure of their economies (they still relied for their export earnings on traditional primary products), the risk of facing industrial stagnation due to import constraints had become very high.

By the mid-1960s most of the large countries of the region were responding to this problem with export diversification programs. These consisted of combinations of exchange rate readjustments in the face of inflation (that is, policies were followed to avoid the overvaluation of their currencies, thus keeping their exports from being priced out of world markets), tax and credit incentives for exporters, and various types of administrative and institutional reforms designed to facilitate exporters' penetration of new markets.

With the industrialization of the major Latin American countries, there also occurred major changes in the structure of foreign investments. For a number of reasons, investments in primary production and public utilities declined. Among them were nationalistic opposition to foreign control of nonrenewable resources, uneconomic but politically popular control over highly visible public utility pricing policies, and the acquisition of foreign technologies in the more traditional sectors by Latin Americans themselves. As a result, new foreign investment after World War II was concentrated in the growing manufacturing sector, where the rewards for foreign technology were higher. It is ironic that, despite the fact that one of the goals of industrialization was to increase the economic independence of Latin American countries, the achievement of industrial growth was based in large part on the attraction of foreign (at first mainly U.S.) capital, which made those countries dependent in a new way.

LATIN AMERICA'S CURRENT TIES WITH THE UNITED STATES: A STATISTICAL SUMMARY

Trade

In the past two decades, Latin America's exports have become increasingly diversified in both their commodity composition and geographic destination (Tables 3.1, 3.2, and 3.3). One of the most striking trends has been the rise of manufactures. By the mid-1970s there was also a greater geographical balance of exports, the U.S. share having declined from 48.3 percent in 1950 to 32 percent in 1975. On the import side one notes the dominance of industrial raw materials and machinery (the imported inputs of industries) and an increased diversification of the sources of imports, although the United States still accounted for almost 36 percent of imports in the mid-1970s.

The tendency toward greater geographical diversification in Latin American exports arises from a number of causes. Among them is the more rapid growth of incomes in developed countries other than the United States in the postwar period, notably in Japan and West Germany. Many Latin American countries have tended to keep their currencies linked in real terms to the dollar, so that as the dollar has declined against the yen, the Deutsche mark, and some other major currencies, Latin American exports have become relatively less expensive in Japan and Western Europe. Still another factor is the potentially greater trade complementarity between some Latin American economies and developed nations other than the United States in comparison with the United States itself.

Foreign Capital

Geographical diversification also is notable in the origin of foreign

TABLE 3.1

Geographic Distribution of Latin American Exports and Imports (percent)

	1950	1960–64	1970–74	1975
Exports				
United States	48.3	36.7	32.8	32.1
Canada		3.3	3.7	4.1
European community		29.4	23.9	20.1
Japan		3.2	5.0	4.6
Latin America		9.6	13.7	14.3
Rest of world		17.8	20.9	24.8
Total		100.0	100.0	100.0
Imports				
United States	50.1	42.0	35.2	35.9
Canada		3.0	2.8	2.3
European community		27.6	23.7	21.7
Japan		3.5	7.2	7.6
Latin America		12.6	17.6	19.4
Total		100.0	100.0	100.0

Source: Inter-American Development Bank, *Economic and Social Progress in Latin America: 1976 Report.*

investments for some of the larger countries. The share of the U.S. investment in Brazil declined from 48 percent in 1950 to 32 percent in 1976, while that share declined from 73 to 54 percent in Mexico between 1950 and 1969 (see Tables 3.5 and 3.6). From a U.S. perspective, moreover, Latin America became relatively less important as a destination for U.S. direct investment, despite its rise in absolute terms, falling from almost 47 percent of total U.S. investment flows in 1929 to about 13 percent in the mid-1970s. However, Latin America is still the principal investment outlet of the United States in the third world. Examining the sectoral composition of U.S. investments in Latin America, one notes a substantial increase of investments in manufacturing with a decline in mining. The share of U.S. investments in Latin American public utilities had fallen to only 2 percent of total U.S. investment in 1976.

Foreign Indebtedness

By 1975 the total public and officially guaranteed foreign debt of Latin America was approximately $50 billion. Taking into account the

TABLE 3.2

Commodity Composition of Latin American Exports (percent)

	Argentina	Brazil	Mexico	Venezuela	Colombia	Latin America
1960–61 exports						
Food	63.1	71.9	38.8	1.3	76.0	46.1
Agricultural raw materials	32.0	16.1	24.6	—	3.3	13.7
Fuels	0.1	1.3	3.5	91.7	18.0	20.9
Minerals	0.6	7.1	9.3	6.9	—	6.8
Manufactures	4.2	3.6	23.8	0.1	2.7	12.5
Total	100.0	100.0	100.0	100.0	100.0	100.0
1970–71 exports						
Food	68.7	57.7	38.6	1.4	72.1	37.6
Agricultural raw materials	16.6	15.3	8.2	—	6.3	8.1
Fuels	0.4	0.7	2.8	91.0	10.4	29.0
Minerals	0.3	9.9	7.8	5.7	—	7.2
Manufactures	14.0	16.4	42.6	1.9	11.2	18.1
Total	100.0	100.0	100.0	100.0	100.0	100.0
1974—Latin America						
Food, tobacco, beverages	29.1					
Raw materials	12.2					
Fuels	38.7					
Chemical products	2.9					
Manufactures	16.6					
Other	0.5					
Total	100.0					
1976—Brazil						
Coffee	21.					
Sugar	3.					
Soybeans	17.					
Iron ore	10.					
Semi-processed manufactures	8.					
Manufactures	26.					
Other goods	15.					
Total	100.					

Sources: IDB, *Economic and Social Progress in Latin America, 1976 Report*; Banco Central do Brasil, *Boletim.*

TABLE 3.3

Commodity Composition of Latin American Imports (percent)

	Argentina	Brazil	Mexico	Venezuela	Columbia	Latin America
1960 imports						
Food and raw materials	26.7	26.9	17.1	27.8	23.1	22.7
Fuels and lubricants	12.5	19.2	2.4	1.1	2.7	16.0
Machinery and equipment	43.9	35.7	51.6	36.0	42.8	35.1
Other manufactures	16.9	18.2	28.9	35.1	31.4	26.2
Total	100.0	100.0	100.0	100.0	100.0	100.0
1973 imports*						
Food and raw materials	36.5	19.0	20.8	16.9	23.3	19.2
Fuels and lubricants	4.7	13.5	4.8	—	1.1	12.6
Machinery and equipment	30.7	39.8	48.4	50.0	46.5	39.1
Other manufactures	28.1	27.7	25.8	33.1	24.1	29.1
Total	100.0	100.0	100.0	100.0	100.0	100.0

*Figures for Argentina and Colombia are for 1970.

Sources: Inter-American Development Bank, *Economic and Social Progress in Latin America: 1976 Report*; *World Tables 1976* (Washington, D.C.: The World Bank, 1977).

TABLE 3.4

U.S. Exports to and Imports from Latin America as Percentage of U.S. Totals

Year	Percentage of U.S. Total
U.S. exports to Latin America	
1945	14.1
1950	27.9
1960	17.4
1970	13.8
1976	13.5
U.S. imports from Latin America	
1945	42.1
1950	35.0
1960	24.1
1970	12.0
1976	10.9

Source: U.S. Statistical Abstract: United States: Historical Statistics, Colonial Times to 1970.

TABLE 3.5

U.S. Direct Investments in Latin America as a Percentage of Total U.S. Investments Abroad

Year	Percentage of Total
1929	46.7
1950	37.7
1960	23.5
1970	14.7
1975	13.2

Source: *U.S. Statistical Abstract* and *Survey of Current Business,* U.S. Commerce Department.

TABLE 3.6

U.S. Share in Geographical Origin of Foreign Direct Investments in Latin America (percent)

	1950	1969	1976
Argentina	44.5	65.8	
Brazil	48.0	45.0	32.0
Chile	87.1	82.8	
Mexico	73.3	54.0	
Latin America	51.1		

Source: CEPAL, *Tendencias y Estructuras de la Economia Latinoamericana* (Santiago: 1971), Table 18; for Brazil, data from Banco Central do Brasil, *Boletim.*

TABLE 3.7

U.S. Direct Investment in Latin America, by Sector (percent)

	Total	Mining and Smelting	Petroleum	Manufacturing	Other*
1929	100	21	17	7	55
1950	100	15	28	17	40
1960	100	14	35	18	33
1976	100	7	12	39	42 (2)†

*Includes agriculture, trade, public utilities, finance, and miscellaneous nonmanufacturing industries.

†Number in parenthesis refers to percentage investment in public utilities.

Source: Richard S. Newfarmer and Willard F. Mueller, *Multinational Corporations in Brazil and Mexico: Structural Sources of Economic and Noneconomic Power* (Washington, D.C.: Report to the Subcommittee on Multinational Corporations of the Comm. on Foreign Relations, U.S. Senate, August 1975), p. 35; U.S. Commerce Department, *Survey of Current Business,* August 1977.

total debt, which would include loans made without public backing, the estimate stood at about $67 billion in 1975, at year's end.[7] In the mid-1970s about 51 percent of the public debt was owed to private financial institutions and suppliers, 22 percent to multilateral agencies (like the World Bank), and 27 percent to individual governments. Although there is no official breakdown on the specific geographic origin of the debt, it is fairly certain that more than half the private debt is owed to U.S. institutions, while more than half the bilateral governmental debt also is owed to the United States. The debt owed to multilateral agencies also is sensitive to U.S. influence, since in most of them the U.S. representative has proportionately the greatest influence.

TABLE 3.8

U.S. Aid to Latin America: Official Loans and Grants (percent of total U.S. foreign aid)

Year	Percent of U.S. Total
1961–65	23.4
1966–70	23.8
1971	13.5
1972	14.7
1973	20.4
1974	16.1
1975	15.8

Source: Calculated from data in *Survey of Current Business*, Commerce Department.

THE CURRENT NATURE OF U.S.-LATIN AMERICAN ECONOMIC RELATIONS

Trade

The increased commodity and geographic diversification of Latin America's trade have contributed toward strengthening the region's position vis-a-vis the United States. The commodity diversification of exports has increased the possibilities for more rapid growth in foreign exchange earning capacity and decreased the risks associated with over-dependence on just a few export commodities. The geographic diversification of the region's exports and imports has diminished its dependence on the level of U.S. economic activity and increased its bargaining strength.

The necessity for export diversification in the post-ISI era, however, and the dependence of the new industrial sectors on imported inputs have made Latin America more interdependent with the industrial centers than was envisioned originally by the policy makers who conceived the ISI programs. The exports of manufactured goods, like those of primary products, are dependent on the level of economic activities in the United States, Europe, and Japan. To the extent that these economies fluctuate independently, Latin America's geographic diversification will have paid off in softening the transfer of the business cycle; the more the cycles are synchronized, as they appear to be in the contemporary world economy, however, the less isolated from center fluctuations will the Latin American economies be.

Multinationals

Since many of the most dynamic industries of Latin America are owned or controlled by multinational enterprises, a new type of interdependency between the region and the center countries (notably the United States) has emerged. First, in pursuing export diversification, Latin American governments have relied on, and often encouraged, the subsidiaries of multinationals to export a certain proportion of their production. Second, in a number of Latin American countries a significant portion of the exports of multinationals consist of semifinished products, increasingly integrating these economies into a vertical division of labor. For example, some automobile companies produce engines in Brazil or Mexico for cars assembled elsewhere, while plans are being made for joint ventures to produce semifinished steel products in Brazil.

It remains to be seen how much decision-making autonomy is thus sacrificed within Latin America as it becomes a more integrated piece of an international system of production. The level of production of the subsidiaries of multinationals, especially those vertically integrated on an international level, thus depends on decisions of multinationals concerning their world production objectives, such as the international division of their activities.

International bargaining for shares in the international production scheme of multinationals is still in its infancy. On the Latin American side, the multinationals increasingly are feeling the pressure of governments interested in pushing their export diversification programs. They are feeling the political pressure of the governments but also are attracted by tax incentive schemes designed to increase exports. In the United States, on the other hand, there has been a mounting pressure by labor unions and other interest groups to limit the expansion of overseas production facilities of U.S.-based multinationals, on the grounds that such operations in effect "export" American jobs.

It has become increasingly clear in the 1970s that one cannot view U.S.-Latin American economic relations as consisting of one group of

U.S. interests versus another group of united Latin American interests. On each side one can identify conflicting interests. For instance, pressured by labor unions and some multinationals, the U.S. government in 1977 demanded the abandonment of export incentive arrangements by Brazil on the grounds that these incentives were in violation of GATT rules. It also demanded the reduction of import barriers that hindered the import of capital goods, replacement parts, and other production inputs used by U.S. multinationals. In 1977 Brazil managed to eliminate its trade deficit, reducing its large current account deficit, partly as a result of its export incentives and import restrictions. Abandonment of these measures would once again open up a substantial trade gap. Given Brazil's large debt, this would work to the detriment of the country's creditworthiness and, due to Brazil's size, jeopardize the portfolios of its creditors, many of whom are U.S. banks. This is an example of the type of split in U.S. economic interests—labor unions and some multinationals versus banks—which make contemporary relations most complex.

Another aspect of the presence of multinationals in complicating economic and political relations can be found in the conflicting goals of multinationals and host governments, on the one hand, and groups dissatisfied with the current functioning of Latin American society and the distribution of the benefits of economic growth. The presence of multinationals in some of Latin America's most important industries, for instance, may give them a vested interest in the existing production profile of the region. They either will resist efforts to redistribute income, which could threaten their markets, or they will use advertising, credit arrangements, and other sales tools to "distort" the demand profiles of lower income groups, persuading them to buy products (consumer durables) that are not necessarily in the interest of those groups. Although North Americans might reject this argument on the basis of "consumer sovereignty," in Latin America the relative unfamiliarity of large sectors of the population with both the opportunities and complexities of modern markets suggests that the problem cannot easily be dismissed.

As most multinationals do not develop their technologies in their foreign subsidiaries, industrialization has led to a substantial increase in Latin America's dependence on foreign technologies. Against the positive effect of the transfer of technologies that might have been considerably more difficult to acquire independently, one must include the additional burden on the balance of payments created by the need to pay for the new technology. Although these costs are sometimes direct and clearly identifiable, as when the payment is in the form of royalties, license fees, or service contracts, they also may appear in the form of overpriced inputs imported by the subsidiary from its parent or underpriced exports sent to the parent. As neither the technology nor its true cost are usually well defined, the payments generated by technology transfers are likely to continue to be a growing bone of contention between host governments and the multinationals, as well as involving the United States and other countries in which the multinationals are based.

Closely related is the issue of adequacy of the technology transferred. Few adaptations to local conditions have been attempted by multinationals and, more important, most multinationals have a policy of developing new technology in the home country. Since control of technology gives these firms their basic bargaining power with host governments, they are reluctant to carry out basic research away from home. This is in direct conflict with the desire of Latin American countries to increase their share of frontier research in technological development.

Related to the issue of payments for technology transfers by multinationals is the larger question of the net balance of payments effect of the multinationals' presence. Although the abstract, static models of economic theory tend to present investment and other factor movements as a substitute for trade flows, a growing and increasingly interdependent world economy appears to offer little empirical support for this argument. Indeed, it is ironic to note that U.S.-based multinationals have defended themselves against the charges by American labor and allied groups that they export jobs by arguing that they in fact increase the demand for American exports by the countries in which they invest. Despite the lack of conclusive empirical evidence for or against this argument,[8] if it is true, it is small consolation for Latin American countries with balance of payments problems to hear they are stimulating developed countries' exports.

The Implications of Latin American Indebtedness

Accompanying the rise in direct foreign investment in Latin America in the post-World War II era has been an equally massive, nonequity financial capital flow of both private and public lending. This trend has accelerated in the last decade as the larger Latin American nations, led by Brazil and Mexico, have gained increasing access to world capital markets. Such capital flows, from the receiving countries' point of view, have the advantage of permitting them to retain management control of the investment, especially when it is undertaken by a public or government-backed enterprise. In addition, such borrowing actually may be cheaper. Larger countries like Brazil have paid up to 2 percent above the London Inter Bank Official Rate (analogous to a world prime rate), giving a net rate of between 9 and 12 percent. Rates of return on equity capital, however, have been estimated to range between 12 and 20 percent. Although its validity is compromised by the elements of greater risk inherent in equity investments, as well as their implicit payments for potential technology transfers and management services, such a comparison suggests that loans may be preferable from the receiving countries' point of view.

Whatever its merits, however, there is little question that the large indebtedness of Brazil, Mexico, Peru, and Argentina has a number of costs. Substantial proportions of the foreign exchange earned by these countries must now be used to finance the debt. To the extent that new financing is required, the price of new debt is higher due to the large amount already outstanding. The debt places these countries at a bargaining disadvantage with the major creditor countries, as well as with institutions dominated by these countries, such as the IMF and the World Bank. This disadvantage may be translated into a certain degree of foreign interference in domestic policy making, such as the tying of new loans to specific internal credit or exchange rate policies. Finally, the increased indebtedness may make the borrowing countries more vulnerable to pressure by creditor nations. This might take the form of requests for more lenient treatment of multinationals operating in the borrowing countries, or even in pressure for an increasing share of foreign capital in indebted local firms.

One might argue, however, that the indebtedness of countries as large and important as Brazil (whose debt in early 1978 was U.S.$32 billion), Mexico (debt in early 1978 was over U.S.$25 billion), or even Peru (debt in late 1977 about U.S.$6 billion) gives their governments some bargaining strength. The large stake of both multinationals and the larger banks in the United States and other developed country financial centers in the economic growth and balance of payments strength of the borrowers is an obvious consequence of their past financial commitments. It is probably no exaggeration to state that the continuing ability of the larger Latin American nations, notably Brazil and Mexico, to service their external debt is essential to the solvency of many of the principal members of the international financial community. For this reason, their past borrowing and receptivity to foreign direct investment has given the major Latin American nations a group of allies in their effort to obtain favorable trade policies and expanded credits from the developed world.

The Impact of the Energy Crisis

Even without the quadrupling of petroleum prices in 1973-74, the economic growth of the major Latin American economies would have been affected by limitations in energy availability. With the exception of Latin America's two members of OPEC, Venezuela and Ecuador, and possibly Mexico, which may benefit from recently discovered reserves of petroleum, the radical changes in the world petroleum market have had a severe impact on the Latin American economies. In two of the leading petroleum importers, Argentina and Brazil, nationalistic traditions in the petroleum sector have been broken, as the state oil companies, YPF in Argentina and Petrobras in Brazil, have been joined by foreign companies allowed to explore for petroleum under "risk contracts." Under these arrangements, a foreign company finding petroleum in its designated area would share the proceeds with the state company.

On the demand side, the developing automobile industries of Brazil and Argentina have been dealt a severe blow by higher gasoline prices. In addition to rationing, attempts are under way in Brazil to supplement the meager gasoline supply with alcohol produced from Brazilian sugar cane.

Concern for access to energy and raw materials also is creating new subregional dependency relationships. Brazil's drive to increase ties with Paraguay and Bolivia, for instance, is motivated primarily by such considerations. The building of the world's largest hydroelectric dam between Brazil and Paraguay on the Parana River at Itaipu as a joint venture of these two nations will make Paraguay the world's largest exporter of electricity and contribute substantially to the energy needs of Brazil's center-south. There can be little doubt that it will make Paraguay's economic system extremely dependent on Brazil, as well as making Paraguayan political stability and cooperation a major national security concern of Brazil. Argentina also has worked out plans with Paraguay, however, to build one or possibly two joint hydroelectric projects. Similarly, Brazil's large-scale investments in Bolivia are designed to bring that country's abundant natural gas and other raw materials to the industrial center of Brazil.

To assure itself of petroleum supplies, a subsidiary of Brazil's Petrobras, Braspetro, has made technical assistance and prospecting contracts with Middle Eastern, African, and South American countries. There has been an increase in bilateral trade with socialists countries for the same reason.

Concern with energy also has been a motive for nuclear development in both Brazil and Argentina. American worries that the type of nuclear technology chosen by Brazil could be used for weapons production as well as energy production led to opposition to Brazil's agreement with West Germany, the supplier of the technology, and precipitated one of the most severe crises in U.S.-Brazilian relations in this century.

LATIN AMERICAN TRADE POLICIES FOR INDUSTRIAL EXPORT EXPANSION

It has been argued here that the ISI strategy for the development of the major Latin American economies was both a success and a failure. It did succeed in inducing a substantial degree of industrialization, although this was sometimes accomplish with scant concern for economic efficiency. The ISI policy failed, however, in the sense that it did not reduce external dependency but only changed its nature, since it made many Latin American nations more dependent than ever before on imported inputs to maintain, equip, and fuel their industrial sectors. Viewed in retrospect, this outcome was perhaps inevitable, given the lack of certain basic raw materials. But reliance on certain key sectors, notably the automobile industry in the ISI process in Brazil, Argentina, Mexico, and Chile, made these countries unnecessarily vulnerable and dependent in a world of high petroleum prices.

This dependency has been heightened by the vertical integration of Latin American industry, especially enterprises that are subsidiaries of multinationals, into a larger international system. In this sense it is more accurate to speak of interdependence rather than dependence, since the degree to which this development can benefit the Latin American economies depends largely on the skills of the region's policy makers and economic diplomats. Trade diversification, both in the variety of exports and geographically, as well as in diversification of investment sources, has expanded the room in which policy makers may maneuver.

The objectives of Latin American trade policies in today's post-ISI era vary with the size of the economy and the degree to which it is industrialized and export-oriented. There is a common concern, however, with the possibility that the Latin Americans will find the markets for their manufactured exports limited by what they perceive as increasing protectionism in the developed countries. Brazil has already faced this type of response to its export drive in the United States, where it has been accused of "dumping" or unfairly subsidizing footwear, and in Western Europe, where similar charges have been leveled against its exports of pig iron.

The question of developing countries dumping in U.S. and European markets is likely to continue as a major irritant in the relations of Latin America with the United States. Existing international trade agreements, as embodied in the GATT (General Agreement on Tariffs and Trade), leave much room for argument.[9] Strictly and traditionally defined as selling the export product below its cost of production, dumping by Latin American producers is rare. The fact that a pair of Brazilian shoes may sell for less in Chicago than in São Paulo is due principally to the high internal sales and value-added taxes that are not assessed on export sales.

The policies that have aroused the ire of U.S. producer groups, in other words, are more the result of tax and subsidy policies designed to stimulate exports than they are the decisions of individual producers to drive out domestic American competition. There is ample precedent in the gradual extension and relaxation of GATT rules to accommodate "border tax adjustments" and other policies used in the European Common Market to offset the price effects of domestic taxes. U.S. critics of the Latin American export policies, however, have argued that these policies go beyond a simple offset.

From an economist's point of view, much of the debate is of questionable value since it ignores the effects on the consumer of the adjustments and subsidies, as well as the retaliatory "countervailing duties" that may be imposed by the importing countries. Both critics and proponents of the export incentive policies have concentrated their attention on the effects of these policies on producers. It is clear, however, that the American consumer can benefit from lower prices of imports, and if domestic American workers in the affected industry can obtain more productive employment in other activities, U.S. welfare actually may be raised by Latin American manufactured export incentives. From a national welfare point of view, rather than a producers' perspective, it is the Latin American nations themselves that might benefit most from an examination of the allocative efficiency effects of their export policies.

PRIMARY COMMODITY AGREEMENTS

Accompanying their efforts to enlarge markets for their growing industrial exports, most Latin American nations have attempted to secure and extend their capacity to import foreign goods with income generated by their more traditional exports of primary commodities. Included in this group of countries are a number of the smaller ones that have few prospects for any significant export of industrial products and often are highly dependent on one or two primary commodities.

Regional efforts to fashion common policies affecting primary product trade, however, are complicated by many countries' ambivalent roles as both producers and consumers. The Central American countries, for example, have had a common interest with other coffee producers in the International Coffee Agreement, yet as consumers of oil they have been severely affected by OPEC, which was founded in part through Venezuelan efforts. Brazil is the dominant force in the world coffee market, as well as the second largest exporter of soybeans, with a vital interest in maintaining high prices for these products. As a net importer of copper, wheat, and several other important exports of other Latin American primary products, however, it would look with disfavor on cartelization efforts in these areas. For this reason, it is unlikely that any common Latin American policy in primary commodities will emerge, due to the disparity of national interests. Worldwide associations organized along product lines, however, are attractive in a number of cases: Peru and Chile with Zaire and Zambia in the copper market, or Bolivia and Malaysia in tin.

Prospects for the successful negotiation of commodity agreements are further diminished by ambiguities in the objectives of potential participants. Price "stabilization" is a rallying point for both producers and consumers, an objective endorsed by many European nations and at least paid lip service by the United States. Beneath the apparent unanimity, however, is a fundamental divergence. Producers have naturally viewed possible agreements as a means of providing some security against temporary but potentially disastrous declines in price, while they have understandably shown little interest in agreements as a defense against quick price rises. The support of consuming nations, however, is contingent on their expectation that commodity agreements will provide some protection against sudden increases in price, which may tend to ratchet up the cost of living to the extent they enter the downwardly rigid general price level in the consuming countries.

Although there is some theoretical and empirical support for the argument that reduced price variation about the same average is desirable, this feature of a commodity agreement alone is unlikely to satisfy either producers interested in eliminating periods of depressed prices or consumers attempting to avoid high prices. Even if agreement on the objectives of stabilization arrangements were attained, however, a number of problems remain. First, the costs of managing a buffer stock, production quota system, or price support and price limiting system may be considerably greater than potential benefits. Second, temporary success in the short run may lead to long-run imbalances. The International Coffee Agreement created conditions favorable to the entrance of many new producers, resulting in an oversupply that induced Brazil to make unilateral production cutbacks, thus reducing its market share. Finally, the competence and administrative ability of those responsible for a marketing agreement must be considered, as well as the political power of participants to deal with nonparticipant attempts to exploit opportunities that the agreement may present.

CONCLUSION: IS THERE A BASIS FOR COOPERATION?

The emergence of the major Latin American economies from a period of relative economic isolation, and their reintegration into the world economy as industrial economies as well as primary producers, has profoundly altered their former economic ties to the United States. The increase in diversity of both their exports and the markets in which they are sold, as well as the growth of capital inflows from other sources besides the United States, might be interpreted by some as a decline in the Inter-American System. As should be clear from the first part of this chapter, however, this fall in the relative importance of Latin America and the United States to each other is more apparent than real, due to the rapid and sustained growth of the Western European and Japanese economies in the post-World War II period. Latin America today is more than ever dependent on the growth of the world economy as both a source of essential imports and a market for the region's exports. Latin American stakes in open, internationally efficient world trade have thus brought their national interests closer to those of the United States and other major trading and investing countries.

We have identified a number of areas in which contention exists and may grow: the role of multinationals, the effects of export promotion policies, primary commodity agreements, energy policies, and the role of external debt in Latin American development. What is striking, and perhaps encouraging from either a North American or Latin American perspective, however, is the complexity of interests and objectives.

Older views of a monolithic United States facing a group of weak, dependent economies on the periphery of the world economy are obsolete and misleading. Today it would be presumptuous and certainly naive to attempt to identify a U.S. interest in this complexity. As we have argued, the interests of U.S. labor, multinationals, U.S. consumers, and New York banks are separate and, if not in conflict, certainly not identical. In a similar sense, it would be disingenuous to seek a single Latin American position on many of the issues that dominate economic discussions in the Inter-American Economic System.

NOTES

1. For detailed description and analyses of the nineteenth century integration of Latin America into the world economy, *see* W. GLADE, THE LATIN AMERICAN ECONOMIES chs. 7-9 (1969); S. STEIN and B. STEIN, THE COLONIAL HERITAGE OF LATIN AMERICA ch. 5 (1970); C. FURTADO, ECONOMIC DEVELOPMENT OF LATIN AMERICA chs. 4-5 (1976); chs. by R. Harbison, D. Coes, F. Norbury, in TROPICAL DEVELOPMENT 1880-1913: STUDIES IN ECONOMIC PROGRESS (W. Lewis ed. 1970).

2. For further details, *see* D. NORTH, THE ECONOMIC GROWTH OF THE UNITED STATES 1790-1860 (1968).

3. U.S. data were obtained from U.S. DEP'T OF COMMERCE, BUREAU OF THE CENSUS, HISTORICAL STATISTICS OF THE U.S.—COLONIAL TIMES TO 1957 (1960), while Latin American data were taken from GLADE, *supra* note 1. THE LATIN AMERICAN ECONOMIES.

4. U.N. DEP'T OF ECONOMIC AND SOCIAL AFFAIRS, FOREIGN CAPITAL IN LATIN AMERICA (1955).

5. For a general analysis of import substitution industrialization in Latin America *see* BAER, *Import Substitution Industrialization in Latin America,* LATIN AM. RESEARCH REV. (spring 1972); specific country experiences in the 1930s can be obtained in the following books: C. DIAZ ALEJANDRO, ESSAYS ON THE ECONOMIC HISTORY OF THE ARGENTINE REPUBLIC chs. 2 & 4 (1970) and W. BAER, INDUSTRIALIZATION AND ECONOMIC DEVELOPMENT IN BRAZIL ch. 2 (1965).

6. The intellectual support for these policies stemmed mainly from the writings of Raul Prebisch and his aides at the U.N. Economic Commission for Latin America. W. BAER, THE ECONOMICS OF PREBISCH AND ECLA, ECONOMIC DEVELOPMENT AND CULTURAL CHANGE (1961-62), reprinted in ECONOMIC POLICY FOR DEVELOPMENT (I. Livingstone ed. 1971).

7. INTER-AMERICAN DEVELOPMENT BANK, REPORT ON ECONOMIC AND SOCIAL PROGRESS IN LATIN AMERICA (1976).

8. G. HUFBAUER and F. ADLER, OVERSEAS MANUFACTURING INVESTMENT AND THE BALANCE OF PAYMENTS (1968).

9. For a discussion of the evolution of GATT and subsequent modifications of the system, *see* K. DAM, THE GATT: LAW AND INTERNATIONAL ECONOMIC ORGANIZATION (1970).

Chapter 4

TRADE RELATIONS IN THE INTER-AMERICAN SYSTEM

Stephen H. Rogers

The emphasis placed on economic and social development by all Latin American and Caribbean countries assures that economic relations will be a major focus of bilateral and multilateral attention within the Inter-American System for some time to come.

In practical effect, this largely means U.S.-Latin American economic relations (references to Latin America from here on are taken to mean Caribbean members of the Inter-American System as well). For questions of economic relationships among themselves, the Latin Americans have regional and subregional organizations without the United States. These include the four major economic integration schemes in the region—the Latin American Free Trade Area and the Andean, Caribbean, and Central American common markets, which among them cover most but not all countries in the region. In addition, the Latin American Economic System (SELA), launched in 1975, includes virtually all Latin American countries but not the United States. Indeed, it was for the purpose of bringing together that membership for consultation, coordination, and cooperation that SELA was created.

Thus the United States is involved, through the organs of the Inter-American System and bilaterally, when its help is deemed needed or, typically, when the Latin Americans wish jointly to influence U.S. actions or policies in some particular manner that affects Latin American interests. On occasion, the United States itself has taken the initiative in consulting Latin America on trade questions.

THE EVOLUTION OF U.S. ECONOMIC RELATIONS WITH LATIN AMERICA

The U.S.-Latin American economic relationship has many aspects—financial assistance, loans from private capital markets, private equity investment, technical and scientific cooperation, and services (shipping, aviation, insurance, and the like)—as well as trade in basic and manufactured products.

A striking element is that bilateral economic assistance has lost its prominent position in these relationships. In money terms, bilateral assistance is about one-third of what it was at its high point in the 1960s. It is now devoted principally to the smaller countries of Central America and the Caribbean, and remains important to them. Mexico has long since abandoned bilateral assistance, most other large Latin American countries have renounced or never had aid programs, and after 1980 under present plans and policies only Bolivia, Paraguay, and Peru in South America would have bilateral U.S. aid programs.

Multilateral official capital remains important to most Latin American countries. The Inter-American Development Bank (IDB), an element of the regional system, is the source of about half of the current flows of multilateral official capital; the World Bank and its affiliates are responsible for approximately an equal amount. Most of that assistance is at close to market interest rates and considerably longer than commercial maturities.

But the private capital market now accounts for the vast majority of Latin American capital acquisition—an estimated $10 billion in 1976, compared to $4.3 billion in bilateral and multilateral official capital. Direct investment from the United States, by comparison, amounted to a net of about $1 billion in 1975, the latest period for which figures are available.

The more important source of U.S. and other foreign currencies to support development plans is trade. Latin American countries exported $45 billion in 1976, of which about 76 percent was to hard currency areas. Latin American countries acquired $17.1 billion from exports to the United States. The composition of exports to the United States has changed significantly. Manufactured products now account for about 37 percent of Latin America's nonpetroleum exports to the United States. In volume terms, the change is even more dramatic. U.S. imports of oil from Latin America have dropped sharply in volume since 1973, but value figures are distorted by the sharp increase in the price of oil in 1973–74, and oil now accounts for about 45 percent of U.S. imports from Latin America by value.

This evolution of relationships, from aid to private capital borrowings and export earnings, reflects several factors: the sharp decline of U.S. foreign aid appropriations relative to Latin American imports, the congressionally mandated emphasis on assistance to the poor in the foreign aid program (which effectively reduces Latin America's claim on aid funds relative to less advanced developing countries in other parts of the world), and the greatly expanded capital needs of Latin America resulting from deterioration in the terms of trade for nonpetroleum exporters from the favorable levels early in this decade. Even with the substantial increase in U.S. foreign aid projected by President Carter, and the Administration's new look at means of assisting middle-developing countries, there is no doubt that transfers from private sources will continue to be much larger than official flows of resources.

This evolution is widely regarded as appropriate both in the United States and in Latin America, in view of the substantial momentum of economic growth built up by 1974, the substantial development of industry and particularly of exports of industrial products, the relatively high per capita levels of income, and Latin America's increasing interactions with other parts of the world. Latin America is distinct from most developing areas in its relatively advanced capability for relying on private market mechanisms for the goods, capital, and technology that it needs for development.

Trade holds the greatest attention in intergovernmental relations between Latin America and the United States. Repeatedly, official visitors to different parts of Latin America have found that trade is the economic subject of primary interest. Furthermore, it is peculiarly subject to joint Latin American consideration—and sometimes confrontation—with the United States within the Inter-American System.

Along with the evolution of Latin American exports away from noncompeting commodities such as coffee and oil toward increasing amounts of manufactured products, it is probably safe to say that the opportunities for friction in trade policy will multiply. Recent evidence includes the attempts to establish protection for the U.S. shoe industry and to remove leather wearing apparel from the generalized system of preferences. For both reasons, then—Latin American concern and the likelihood of increased conflicts—it is appropriate to review U.S. trade policy with Latin America, current proposals, and considerations to be taken into account in evaluating the principal options.

The Trade Act of 1974

When the U.S. Congress passed the Trade Act of 1974, including authority to give special attention to the needs of developing countries in the multilateral trade negotiations (MTN) in Geneva and to establish a U.S. generalized preference system (GSP), most members of the legislative and executive branches probably thought that the framework for trade relations between the United States and developing countries had been established for a long time to come.

Admittedly, much remained to be done in the Geneva negotiations to carry out the pledge in the Tokyo Declaration of 1973 that a new trade system would be devised that would give special and differential treatment to developing countries in the application of the rules and procedures of the GATT. And in fact "S and D" remains an objective of the negotiations that continue in Geneva. U.S. proposals for handling subsidies and countervailing duties and for safeguards have contained explicit recognition of the S and D principle, as have the proposals of others.

In no place did the Trade Act of 1974 single out Latin America for any kind of special treatment, although section 502(b) excludes from the benefits of GSP Cuba and other communist countries that do not receive MFN treatment, and Venezuela and Ecuador as well as other members of the Organization of Petroleum Exporting Countries (OPEC). The latter exclusion continues to affect U.S. relations with all of Latin America and other developing countries—not just those directly affected—on the grounds that it constitutes coercion and violates the sovereignty (that is, the right to raise prices of commodity exports in an oligopolistic situation) of the exporting countries. Furthermore, the act does not distinguish between OPEC members that embargoed oil shipments to the United States during the 1973 Mideast war and those—like Venezuela and Ecuador (as well as Iran, Indonesia, Nigeria, and Gabon)—that did not.

A number of events since the Trade Act was signed have shown that the implementation of GSP and continuation of the MTN would not suffice to end trade controversies in the Inter-American System.

The GSP was in fact implemented as of January 1, 1976, for all of Latin America except the three excluded states. It was widely recognized as a generous and promising system. Imports of Latin American products under GSP increased by 25 percent in 1976 compared to 10 percent for other products. While other factors were important, and traders have not taken full advantage of the duty-free possibilities, preliminary analysis indicates GSP is having its intended effect of increasing developing country exports.

Nevertheless, Latin Americans have pressed for improvements both in product coverage and in reducing the limitations and uncertainties of the system. They have shown intense interest in the current Administration review of GSP; the OAS Special Committee for Consultation and Negotiation (SCCN), which brings the United States together with its Latin American trading partners, seriously examined Latin American proposals on GSP at its May 1977 meeting in Buenos Aires. Most agricultural and semiprocessed goods are excluded because of sensitivity of U.S. producers to competition from abroad, as are by law textiles, shoes, and other products that are of particular concern to Latin Americans. Furthermore, the system excludes products from countries that have in the previous year—under the "competitive need criteria"—demonstrated their competitiveness in the U.S. market by shipping quantities above certain arbitrary limits.

In a related development, two Latin American governments, Colombia and Costa Rica, in 1976 floated explicit plans for a completely new approach to trade relations within the Inter-American System, based in part on a special preferential relationship with the United States that would not apply to developing countries in other regions. (These proposals are discussed below.)

The United States, in Secretary of State Henry Kissinger's June 1976 speech on cooperation for development to the General Assembly of the Organization of American States, recognized the primacy of trade as an element in U.S.-Latin American relations with a set of proposals for handling the issues within the Inter-American System—but stopping well short of "super-preferences" for Latin America.

On the other hand, the United States has taken certain actions—notably on sugar and meat imports—that have been seen as injurious to Latin American as well as other producers. The Latin Americans reacted in the trade subgroup of the SCCN by accusing the United States of reneging on its obligations by failing to consult prior to increasing the duty on sugar. (In fact, the 1976 sugar action helped some and hurt some—marginally. The action on meat was taken early in 1975 and was changed in form—from voluntary restraints to imposed quotas—but not in substance in the fall of 1976. For 1977, the United States again negotiated voluntary agreements with meat exporters, this time with a very marginal extra benefit for developing country suppliers, all of which are in the Western Hemisphere.)

At the same time, the MTN in Geneva slowed to barely perceptible movement for an extended period, in part because of disagreements within the European Community. The Carter Administration, however, gave the negotiations a new impetus with its pledge to accelerate the MTN, an objective the Latin Americans endorsed at the June 1977 meeting of the OAS General Assembly. European agreement on the new impetus has given hope for more rapid progress.

The OAS has pursued, although somewhat fitfully, its preparations for a Special General Assembly on Cooperation for Development; if and when it takes place, trade is expected to be a prime subject.

Recent Proposals

Recent proposals for U.S.-Latin American trade relations fall into three categories: (1) those related philosophically to global attempts to legislate substantial changes in the international economic order; (2) specific ambitious plans for liberalization of U.S. trade barriers and import rules as they apply to Latin American exports; and (3) a limited pragmatic approach emphasizing negotiated improvement on a global basis but including supplementary features in the Inter-American System.

As members of the Group of 77, Latin Americans have supported the action program of the new international economic order and the Charter of Economic Rights and Duties of States. The basic thrust of these documents is to require the developed countries to grant substantial benefits to exports of developing countries and to limit the freedom of action of the developed countries in this area. Specifically in the trade field, Brazil has been a major source of proposals for radical changes in the world trading system for the benefit of developing countries.

Philosophically related is an attempt in the OAS to draft a treaty for collective economic security. The treaty would establish a system under which a country—presumed most often to be the United States—within the Inter-American System could be collectively judged for economic actions against the welfare of others. A country so judged and found deficient would be required to take compensatory actions.

The proposed treaty implies a degree of external jurisdiction over trade policy that many countries would likely find unacceptable. The United States has opposed the treaty and indicated it would not sign even if all other OAS members do so. In fact, it is likely that some others within the Inter-American System would be easily reconciled to the loss of the treaty for similar reasons.

At the June 1976 meeting of the OAS General Assembly in Santiago, Foreign Ministers Indalecio Liévano Aguirre of Colombia and Gonzalo J. Facio of Costa Rica submitted memorandums for the consideration of the members on an inter-American trade system. The two proposals differ in a number of respects, but fundamentally they reflect the same kind of concern about Latin America's position in the world trading system, and the solutions suggested are similar.*

The Liévano and Facio memorandums were not considered at the Santiago meeting. However, they were incorporated by reference in the resolution on a Special General Assembly on Development.

The essence of the two memorandums can be discussed under four headings: the stimulus and philosophy for the preferential element; the specific trade problems that are reflected; the regional preferential element in the proposed solutions; and the nonpreferential regional elements of the proposals.

Some 49 developing countries have a special trade relationship with the European Community under the Lomé Convention that goes beyond the EEC's general preference scheme.

This relationship provides to the associated countries of Africa, the Caribbean, and the Pacific (ACP countries) unlimited duty-free entry for

---

*The idea of proposals for strengthening trade relations was discussed during Secretary of State Henry Kissinger's February 1976 visits to Bogotá and San José. On his arrival in San José, he told Foreign Minister Facio and the press that he had at his previous stop heard extremely interesting proposals from Foreign Minister Liévano concerning the Inter-American Trading System that the United States would wish to pursue with the Latin Americans. Facio concurred in the importance of the proposal. The two memorandums to the Santiago General Assembly followed.

their manufactured products and, through the exchange earnings stabilization scheme (STABEX), a measure of assurance that their foreign exchange receipts from a specified list of commodities will not suffer because of changes in the world market. The United States, on the other hand, grants to Latin America only its GSP, from which most of the ACP countries can benefit as well. Thus Latin America competes in the European Community market at a disadvantage with the ACP countries, while the latter have the same access to the U.S. market as Latin Americans have. There is an asymmetry, according to Liévano and Facio, that should be corrected.

Specific trade factors in the U.S. market that are addressed in the memorandums include the legislated exclusion of certain products (especially textiles) from benefits under GSP, and the absence of others by Administration decision; the constant (although rarely implemented) threat of restrictions to protect U.S. producers from competitive or subsidized products from abroad; the absence of any preference for Latin America where quantitative restrictions are necessary; and certain technical problems with the GSP.

In order to correct Latin America's disadvantageous position and resolve the practical difficulties noted, it is proposed that the United States agree to eliminate or reduce barriers to imports of Latin American commodities and manufactured products. Where restrictions must be maintained or imposed, they would be implemented so as to minimize the impact on Latin America. These benefits would not be available to ACP countries unless, in the Liévano memorandum, the European Community extended ACP benefits to Latin America.

The Liévano memorandum suggests a study of the trade opportunities and problems of each of the Latin American countries in the OAS. The Facio memorandum adds a proposal for a fund or funds to support trade, earnings and development in Latin America.

The United States has consistently placed primary emphasis on benefits to be gained from the MTN by the Latin American countries. It has not accepted or proposed preferential treatment for Latin American exports to the United States. At Santiago, however, the United States included a regional element that consisted of two parts. First, it pledged that the U.S. Administration would take into account the interest of Latin American exporters in any area of trade policy in which it has discretionary powers. Second, it proposed the establishment of a new mechanism for consultation within the OAS, a special high-level group for trade cooperation, and announced that the United States would intensify consultations on the MTN with Latin American countries. The Carter Administration has continued the emphasis on the benefits to the region from the MTN and has vigorously restated the commitment to consult with Latin American countries on global economic issues, including the MTN.

THE BASIC OPTIONS

Distilling from recent proposals and policies U.S. options are to establish a regional preferential arrangement for imports from Latin America analogous to the Lomé arrangement for the ACP countries or to maintain its traditional nondiscriminatory treatment for imports from all developing countries that receive the benefits for GSP.

If the latter option is accepted, the United States might or might not wish or be able to include special features in its policy that would have substantive meaning for Latin American exports.

The system analogous to Lomé would of course be the clearest expression of U.S. interest in Latin America and determination to assist Latin American economic development.* It would balance Lomé politically and could be seen as a means of bringing pressure on the European Community and ACP countries to negotiate elimination of specialized preferences. It might be seen as a means of giving Latin America an alternative to its close ties with other members of the Group of 77.

Furthermore, specialized preferences going beyond GSP would mean the United States was maximizing trade opportunities for the countries in the best position to use them, with less impact on the U.S. economy than if the same preferences were extended to essentially all developing countries.

On the other hand, the Lomé analogy is not completely valid. All of the ACP countries are former colonies of one or another member of the European Community. The Lomé arrangement therefore is to some extent a continuation of long-standing trade relations between colony and metropole. Thus adjustments have been made in the importing economy. No such colonial relationship has existed between the United States and Latin America. It is doubtful that more than a very few Latin American countries would endorse a substantial preferential arrangement with the United States. (That does not mean, however, that many of the Latin American countries would actively oppose such an arrangement if it were offered or if it were pressed by several other Latin American countries.)

Even more to the point, Latin American economies are collectively larger, more advanced, and more industrialized than those of the ACP countries and therefore could have much more of an impact and cause more of an adjustment problem. The U.S. GSP provides duty-free treatment up to certain limits, unlike the European Community import

---

*The "Inter-American Lomé System" option is not identical to the proposals of the foreign ministers of Colombia and Costa Rica. Although special preferences are a significant element of the latter proposals, both of them are concerned with specific real trade problems facing Latin Americans in the U.S. market. Those trade problems can be dealt with on a nondiscriminatory basis.

tariff, which gives preferential duty cuts to all developing countries but gives zero duties only to the ACP countries. A substantial preference for Latin American imports into the U.S. market would more likely be created by withdrawing some of the present GSP benefits from other developing countries than by expanding benefits to Latin America. A few Caribbean countries are both signatories of the Lomé Convention and members of the OAS, adding a minor complication to the Lomé analogy schemes.

The Lomé policy would contrast with the traditional U.S. view of a single world economic system. The United States has opposed trade blocs such as that of the European Community with the ACP countries (which is tolerable to the United States because it continues a relationship that antedates the GATT, is essentially now a one-way arrangement, and is limited in its trade impact on the United States). The traditional U.S. view is reflected in the emphasis on the MTN and on U.S. encouragement of Latin American economic relations with other parts of the developed world in addition to the United States.

Latin America is, of course, not the only "left out" area. In fact, the ACPs, although numerous, account for only a small percentage of developing country trade, while Latin America by itself is responsible for some 28 percent of developing country exports. Furthermore, the ACP countries outside the Western Hemisphere trade very little with the United States, while Latin America exports substantially to the European Community. Thus there is little evidence that the asymmetry in trading relationships has a significant impact on trade flows or export opportunities, and the perceived disadvantage to Latin America is more political than economic.

Alternatively, future U.S. trade policy toward Latin America might theoretically be identical to that toward other developing countries.

Such an approach would demonstrate most clearly U.S. belief in a single world economy. It would show concern with development not only in the Western Hemisphere but also in Africa and Asia, and that the United States has no intention (as President Carter stressed in his March 14, 1977 speech to the OAS) of trying to split Latin America from the rest of the world by economic means or for political purposes.

This approach also would recognize that several of the Latin American countries are real factors in the world economy. Some of them are already close to the levels of industrialization, urbanization, and trade of some Western European countries in the post-World War II period. Brazil is now, in terms of GNP, the world's eighth economy. Venezuela is the ninth in terms of foreign exchange reserves, and Mexico is the fifth country of the world in trade with the United States.

Such a policy would leave Latin America still benefiting from U.S. (and others') generalized preferences and from the special and differential treatment being negotiated in Geneva. Economic relations between Latin

America and the United States could develop in healthy fashion and to mutual benefit under these global arrangements. And this option obviates the need to seek a waiver in the GATT.

In the long run, the absence of special arrangements for Latin America likely would minimize friction between Latin America and the United States. In any case Latin America has turned toward the rest of the world in its economic relationships. The United States might wish actively to encourage a broadening of the responsibility for Latin American trade opportunities, much as it sought to share responsibility for Japanese export opportunities with Europe in an earlier period.

But this approach appears to suggest that the economic relationship between the United States and Latin America is less important than the political and security relationship, a suggestion that most Latin Americans and many in the United States would reject.

A variation would acknowledge that economic and social development is the highest priority objective of most Latin American countries and that the U.S. contribution to that development—through trade, aid, capital availability, and technology—is the most important aspect of the U.S.-Latin American relationship to most countries in the hemisphere. It would, however, stop short of discriminating between Latin America and other developing countries in access to the U.S. market.

This essentially is the approach to U.S. policy toward Latin America enunciated by the Ford administration in Secretary of State Kissinger's presentation to the OAS General Assembly in June 1976. In effect, the United States said it would, while maintaining nondiscrimination between Latin America and other developing countries, give special attention to the needs of Latin America in considering possible action on commodity trade, in administering provisions of U.S. trade legislation where the president has discretion, and in developing U.S. positions for the Geneva multilateral trade negotiations.

This policy was not explicitly or broadly endorsed by the Carter administration. Relevant expressions of the administration's view include President Carter's emphasis in his United Nations and OAS speeches on the global character of Latin America's problems, his commitment to consult with Latin America on such problems, and—most important—the evidence in words and actions that the administration intends to pursue a liberal trade policy with special consideration for developing countries.

The element of consultations may be more substantial than it seems, especially if it is regularized and contains an element of balanced interests. The proposal at Santiago for a new trade consultative group in the OAS reflected in part the limitations of the present OAS mechanism, the SCCN, which is concerned exclusively with U.S. trade policy that affects Latin America. A more balanced trade mechanism would give an opportunity to consider U.S. problems in Latin America as well as Latin American problems with the United States, recognizing that the extent to which the United States politically can be forthcoming toward Latin American exports depends in part on consideration by the Latin Americans of U.S. export problems. Such a mechanism would provide an opportunity for analysis of and consultation on Latin American exports to other developed areas, and ideally on trade within Latin America, although it must be recognized that Latin America may prefer to focus on intraregional trade in bodies that do not include the United States.

Better mutual understanding of trade needs and possibilities through such a mechanism and through improved bilateral and multilateral trade consultations could pay dividends. Policy officials who know firsthand the views of their counterparts in other governments—and who know further that they will have to face those same officials under regular and frequent consultation procedures—are likely to give greater attention to the impact of their decisions and recommendations on those exporting countries.

The trade relationship under this variant of the option becomes analogous to that between the United States and the other members of the Organization for Economic Cooperation and Development (OECD), under which U.S. trade policies are influenced, and the U.S. can influence those of others, through institutionalized, regular, multilateral consultations. In some respects—such as the "trade pledge" developed to help cope with the sudden increase in the price of oil at the beginning of 1974—the obligations within the OECD go beyond those of the GATT. The multilateral arrangement is supplemented by regular bilateral consultations between the United States and some of its major OECD trading partners—the European Community and Japan. This latter element has been replicated in Latin America in the regularized trade consultations with Brazil.

Under either version of this second option (pure global policy or special attention to Latin America within a global policy), the emphasis is placed on dealing with issues of U.S. trade policy in the global framework. Latin Americans complain about the U.S. countervailing duty law. So do others, and the United States has made proposals for a new code on subsidies and countervailing duties in the Geneva negotiations. Similarly, the United States has proposed that a new safeguards code be developed in which developing countries would get special treatment.

Special and differential treatment is the objective of the Latin American and other developing countries in the MTN. The United States has resisted the suggestion that this treatment is so important that it should be allowed to interfere with liberalization on a most-favored-nation basis. The United States has based this policy on the belief that general liberalization measures and bound tariff reductions are more valuable than preferences, which are not bound, and that overall trade liberalization is in the interest of all.

CONCLUSION

The United States and Latin America are in search of a productive trade relationship. Trade is more important than ever to Latin American development, and the hemispheric system should take that factor into account more effectively than it does now.

The important objective is to work to understand and deal with mutual trade problems and to seek opportunities for expansion of Latin American exports on a pragmatic basis, within a framework of mutual interest in Latin America.

If the United States continues to oppose the establishment of a general regional trade preference system, it still will have to deal with pressures resulting in part from resentment at the special treatment given to the ACP countries by the European Community. A realistic appraisal of the significance of this discrimination against Latin America could help to contain the understandable resentment. This might be a good subject for multilateral examination, for instance in the type of trade cooperation mechanism the United States proposed in Santiago.

More important, however, will be the opportunities for export earnings that are presented to Latin America. These opportunities will of necessity be in the European Community and Japan as well as in the United States. But there also will be opportunities within Latin America through regional and subregional integration schemes that the United States has offered to assist. Trade opportunities will depend in part on the success of the multilateral trade negotiations in Geneva, but above all they will depend upon prosperity of the developed countries.

Chapter 5

TOWARD REGIONAL ACCOMMODATION: IS THERE ANYTHING TO NEGOTIATE?

Tom J. Farer

THE SPECIAL RELATIONSHIP

By their very existence, the institutions of the Inter-American System help to sustain a feeling that within the global framework, the United States owes something extra to Latin America. Annually rekindled by bibulous North American encomiums to the Pan American dream, hope of special treatment is as regularly disappointed by new evidence of deadlock over substantive issues. The pulsing alternative of hope and disappointment, to the extent it aggravates the always delicate emotional relations between the United States and Latin America, can narrow the real grounds for pragmatic accommodation. As north-south issues came to dominate the OAS agenda, lending special acrimony to U.S.-Latin discourse, this concern fueled proposals for U.S. withdrawal from the OAS. The misleading idea of a special relationship is so bound up with the present set of institutions, it was argued, that it is impossible to liquidate the former without first burying the latter.

Intended, one suspects, more as a stimulant to reformist thought than a program for action, the proposal made little appreciable headway within the policy-making apparatus. Opponents of fundamental change massed themselves behind the putative value of the present institutional structure, particularly in the realm of security and peacekeeping. Furthermore, despite the increasingly acerbic tone of multilateral diplomacy, they foresaw the special relationship ultimately yielding benefits even in connection with north-south issues.

Precisely how this joyful phenomenon would occur was not always made clear to the jaundiced auditor. But the general notion seemed to be that institutionalized consultation and the resulting personal ties among diplomatic personnel, the continuing experience of collaboration on other matters, and the gentling emotions induced by the symbols of Pan Americanism would facilitate agreement on "moderate" reforms that could serve as a model for or add momentum to global negotiations. In this vein, enthusiasts also cited the virtues of forum size, in comparison to institutions like UNCTAD (United Nations Conference on Trade and Development) with global membership, and the commitment of leading Latin states to the theoretical essentials of the existing international economic order. With Cuba excluded, there was no consequential country in the OAS—comparable, for instance, to Algeria in UNCTAD or UN Special Sessions—to organize confrontation by tabling revolutionary demands and then marshaling support for them under the banner of Third World solidarity.

All that sounded fine until one asked oneself just what the United States was willing and able to negotiate in this agreeably cozy forum. Certainly not trade preferences or commodity price stabilization. The former are plainly incompatible with the campaign for freer trade worldwide. Furthermore, under present conditions there is neither an economic nor a political basis for reverting to the long-discarded idea of a closed, hemispheric trading system. The latter requires participation by producers and consumers from outside the region. So what is left?

Principally five issues remain: investment disputes, the control of transnational corporations (TNCs), the transfer of technology, concessional lending (access to capital on terms more favorable than those dictated by the market), and debt.

Debt cannot make it onto the regional agenda, first because any regional settlement would merely become a point of departure for further demands in global forums. It therefore would undermine the northern negotiating position and aggravate relations between the United States and some of its European allies, which are even more reluctant than the United States to yield anything beyond the proposed writeoff of some of the outstanding official debt of the world's poorest countries. Moreover, the issue has no appeal to the major Latin states, which fear the effect of blanket debt relief on their own credit standing.

Concessional lending could go on the agenda. Patterns of unequal disbursements by developed states to regional funds and banks seem to be accepted by the developing countries. But once on the agenda, what could be negotiated? Foreign assistance is close to the bottom of political priorities in the United States. Inter-American Development Bank (IDB) replenishments had to be dredged out of a reluctant Congress. Political support might with difficulty be marshaled for an improved balance-of-payments safety net, particularly if the net could be defended as part of an overall north-south package and there were substantial contributions by other developed states. But for the time being, at least, even that may go beyond congressional tolerance. Without a great deal more confidence about its ability to deliver the goods, no U.S. administration can prudently enter expectation-raising negotiations.

And so we are left with the overlapping issues of investment disputes, regulation of transnational corporations, and the transfer of technology. At the time of Kissinger's call for a "New Dialogue" in 1973, these were indeed the issues around which hopes for substantive agreement coalesced. Regional understandings would not conflict with later global ones and need not establish a mere base point for more onerous claims, in part because on these issues the Latin states were the principal Third World parties in interest, in part because agreements on these issues do not readily submit to a simple calculus of gain and loss. It is not a zero-sum game. There are points of common interest.

The hopes aroused by the inauguration of substantive negotiations did not survive. It was immediately apparent that the two sides disagreed both on basic substantive principles and on the methodology of negotiations. The two were integrally related. Latin participants sought agreement on general principles; their counterparts had a mandate for technical discussions, a mandate designed to circumvent the foreseen disagreement on general principles. After a few sessions, the negotiating initiative more or less spontaneously aborted.

At the root of its failure is an endemic conflict over the rights of sovereign governments in relation to foreign investors. Latin governments still adhere to the view first enunciated by the distinguished Argentine scholar-diplomat, Carlos Calvo. Sovereign states owe foreign investors only one thing: equal application of national law. Since national courts are the best interpreters of national law, there is no reason to transfer investment disputes to international tribunals. And since there is no international minimum standard above national law, there is no basis for diplomatic intervention on behalf of investors. It also follows from this conception of investor rights as a function of national law that international codes of conduct for transnational corporations (TNCs) should define only their obligations, not their "rights."

A second and not unrelated difference concerns the role of the state in economic life. Liberal views about the supremacy of private interests never achieved the kind of formal hegemony in Latin America that they have enjoyed in the United States. On the contrary, the dominant intellectual traditions, both of the right and the left, emphasize the subordination of private to national interests, that is, to the interests of the state. Hence, on ideological grounds alone, there can be difficulties on such questions as technology transfer. After all, most of the technology in our society is in private hands. According to the U.S. view, it is no more susceptible to public appropriation than any other form of property. Hence U.S. proposals must be limited to measures designed to correct deformities in the market—for instance, inadequate information about competitive technologies—or to facilitate the slow process of building up indigenous capacities for technological innovation. And the United States is driven by ideology and interest actively to resist any doctrinal formulation that would facilitate the expropriation of privately developed technology.

Multilateral negotiations possess a peculiar capacity to highlight these differences. Perhaps it is because, even where every effort is made to keep them private, concrete, and informal, they invariably slide back toward formality, abstraction, and well-advertised pronunciamentos.

Differences on the basic issues of principle are real and powerful and show no signs of abating. In fact, as William D. Rogers, former assistant secretary of state for inter-American affairs, has written, "the current probabilities are in the opposite direction. Latin America in recent years has bent its efforts to convert the Calvo doctrine into positive international law, binding on all states."[1] The effort culminated in approval by an overwhelming U.N. General Assembly majority of the Mexican-drafted Charter of Economic Rights and Duties of States, which frankly endorses the Calvo concept.

The tide flows away from compromise on principle. And yet, constantly recurring disputes between U.S. investors and Latin governments over alleged expropriatory acts are regularly resolved without inflaming diplomatic relations. The U.S. government stands stoutly behind the "international minimum standard" and the associated claim that the compensation required under it must be equivalent to "fair market value" or, in the absence of any real market, to the discounted value of projected earnings. In practice, however, it acquiesces in or even directly negotiates settlements that are substantial, reasonably satisfactory to the investor, yet fall short of claimed fair market value. For their part, Latin governments yield not an inch on their claim that any nondiscriminatory compensation standard contained in national law discharges their legal obligations. But at the same time, except in the case of Chilean nationalization of the copper mines, they have refrained from using national law to deny levels of compensation conceivably acceptable to investors. In the judgment of most observers, they have pursued compromise settlements, not primarily to avoid collision with the U.S. government but rather to maintain their credibility as borrowers in northern financial markets and as sites for new foreign investment.

The system works. Its only casualty is principle. Attempts in regional forums to rehabilitate principle will magnify its deformities—and thus complicate the workings of the system.

Principle also obstructs agreement on what to do about TNCs. More effective monitoring of their operations can serve U.S. as well as Latin interests—for example, in facilitating taxation of these elusive giants and in limiting their capacity to restrain trade. The United States could work out information-sharing agreements with individual Latin countries. Proceeding bilaterally will be more expeditious. In addition, since bilateral agreements can be quite informal, the United States would more easily retain the option of reducing or terminating information flows in cases where the other party exploited information sharing for unreasonable ends.

If mutual confidence grows through the experience of bilateral cooperation, potentially useful multilateral arrangements could become negotiable. For instance, a hemispheric corporation code, under which all companies of a certain size or proposing to invest in a number of states would be incorporated, might some day facilitate equal treatment and reasonable regulation of TNCs. That or any other ambitious scheme awaits the dissolution of antagonistic principles and the coincident growth of a felt community of interest.

As long as the OAS remains a general-purpose regional organization, rather than a mere security alliance along the lines of NATO and the Warsaw Pact although somewhat looser, the United States cannot and the Latin states will not exclude north-south issues from its agenda. Discussion need not aggravate the tensions naturally incident to a contest over wealth and power. Discussion can even be marginally useful if it is frank and conducted without the polarizing dynamic of formal resolutions and contested votes in the classic parliamentary mode.

To be frank is to concede publicly, without flinching, that the special relationship, whatever reality it may retain in other fields—defense, peacekeeping, human rights, culture—can have very little substance in connection with north-south issues. But there is one important exception. For the foreseeable future, dominant capitalist elites in both North and South America will retain a powerful shared interest in preventing breakup of the liberal international economic system. Thus U.S. and Latin governments might welcome a mechanism for coordinating their efforts to resist higher tariffs, trade blocs, and all the other insignia of neomercantilist economics.

Once having stabilized Latin expectations at the appropriate low level, the United States then can outline the very limited subjects, such as means for disseminating information about competitive technologies, concerning which neither global commitments nor hostile principles prevent agreement. Finally, it should endorse continued discussion of broader issues as part of the global search for north-south accommodation.

Parliamentary institutions encourage the decline of colloquy into confrontation. Awareness of this tendency no doubt informed the proposals advanced by the U.S. government at the OAS General Assembly in 1977. Secretary of State Cyrus R. Vance urged integration of the three OAS councils (education, science, and culture; economic and social; and political) into a single body and replacement of "much of the standing bureaucracy" by arrangements calculated to assist informal consultation, which should take the form of temporary committees or ad hoc meetings, preferably of ministers of finance or trade rather than of ambassadors to the OAS.

Having nothing else to discuss, a separate economic and social council, conducted with formal resolutions and recorded votes, falls inexorably into a pattern characterized by Latin demands on the United States in relation to north-south issues and an essentially negative U.S. response. But even an integrated council will slide toward U.S.-Latin conflict over "high principle." Being generalists, ambassadors to the OAS find defense of principle a good deal more congenial, as well as newsworthy, than painstaking, narrowly focused discussions of markets, money, and technology. Yet if there is any meat on the regional version of the north-south bone, it will be found in just such esoteric consultations. Ambassadors also suffer from a lack of authority and sustained foreign office interest. Serious negotiations are best launched by senior officials and conducted by technicians acting under their direct supervision, provided that initial negotiations have produced an adequate consensus. But the failure of the consultations, precipitated by Kissinger's New Dialogue, on transfer of technology and regulation of the TNC, illustrates that the most favorable format cannot bridge enduring conflicts of interest. When countries are so divided, one chooses a forum largely for its damage-limiting potential.

FUTURE LIMITS ON OAS

Secretary Vance's proposals have that considerable virtue. They deserve support, insofar as it is prudent to maintain a general-purpose regional organization. But just how far is that, even if the United States and the Latin states agree to evade insoluble differences and to dissolve conflict-generating institutions? A regional organization conceived as this one was, and dedicated to the equal rights and privileges of its members, inhibits discrimination in the dispensation of political and economic goods. Such discrimination is the normal stuff of diplomacy. With force largely circumscribed, it is the surviving instrument of traditional bilateral diplomacy.

For three decades the security issue imposed a measure of homogeneity on U.S. relations with the Latin states. Fearing subversion by contagion, soliciting their votes in the United Nations and the OAS, the United States acted as if all were equally deserving, intimate friends. Nothing approximating equality of treatment was achieved, but the allocation of incentives and sanctions by the United States was not closely tailored to real economic interests and natural political ties. Now that security obsessions no longer impose a patina of uniformity upon U.S. interests, bilateral diplomacy with all its inevitable discrimination presses multilateralism to the wall. And so it must be. Even the most liberal global economic policy, for instance, will allow room for adjacent states to negotiate preferential arrangements. The health of the Mexican economy is so important in so many ways to the United States that special advantageous relations cannot be excluded.

Mexico is only the most extreme illustration of the necessary centrality of bilateral diplomacy in U.S.-Latin relations. Time promises to intensify the differences among Latin countries and thus their relative significance to U.S. diplomacy. When, as seems almost inevitable, the leading Latin states formally join the ranks of the developed—for example, by inclusion in existing or recruitment to some new organization of the rich—the principle of nondiscrimination will become trivial. In the meantime, it nags at strategies for gradually co-opting the most developed Latin states to the ranks of the north.

NOTE

1. W. Rogers, *Of Missionaries, Fanatics, and Lawyers: Some Thoughts on Investment Disputes in the Americas,* 72 AM. J. INTL L. 5 (1978).

Chapter 6

THE NEW DIALOGUE WITH LATIN AMERICA AND THE WORKING GROUP ON TRANSNATIONAL ENTERPRISES: CALVO VERSUS HICKENLOOPER

Richard J. Bloomfield

GENESIS

The Meeting of the Foreign Ministers Working Group on Transnational Enterprises had its origins in the first "New Dialogue" meeting at Tlatelolco in Mexico City in February 1974. The Latin American foreign ministers had drawn up an agenda for this encounter with U.S. Secretary of State Henry Kissinger that included the following topic:

> There exists a deep concern in the group of Latin-American countries because of the attitude of the TNEs that have intervened in internal matters of the countries in which they carry out their activities and presume to exempt themselves from the legislation and the jurisdiction of the competent national courts.
>
> The TNEs constitute a suitable factor in Latin-American development so long as they respect the sovereignty of the countries in which they operate and adjust themselves to the plans and programs of development.
>
> Latin America considers it necessary to have the cooperation of the United States for the purpose of overcoming the resulting difficulties or frictions and of avoiding such difficulties and frictions that might originate from the conduct of the TNEs that may violate the principles set forth here.

This statement was a thinly-veiled reassertion of the Calvo Doctrine, by which the Latin Americans have traditionally opposed the policy of the United States of siding with its corporations in disputes, for example, by threatening to cut off U.S. aid to offending governments (Hickenlooper and Gonzalez amendments).

In his public address at Tlatelolco, Kissinger did state that the United

States would be prepared to attempt to reconcile the conflicing positions represented by the Calvo Doctrine on the one hand, and Hickenlooper and Gonzales amendments, on the other-hand. Somewhat to the surprise of the U.S. delegation, the spokesman for Latin America, the Venezuelan foreign minister, said that the Latin Americans preferred to deal with the issue of the conduct of TNEs in the United Nations framework rather than at the hemispheric level.

The foreign ministers met again for the second and what proved to be the last New Dialogue meeting in April 1974 in Washington just prior to the meeting of the OAS General Assembly. The April meeting continued discussion of the Tlatelolco agenda. The issue of TNEs came up in the context of the agenda item on investment disputes and the triggering of U.S. sanctions for expropriation.

In his reply, Kissinger assured the Latin American foreign ministers that the United States strongly opposed the intervention of U.S. corporations in the political affairs of host countries. But he went on to say that rather than resting on his personal guarantees, the United States would be prepared to establish a working group that would develop certain principles relating to the behavior of transnational corporations for the consideration of the next conference.

There was considerable reluctance on the part of a number of Latin American ministers to set up any working groups at all. The U.S. delegation on the other hand felt that there was little chance of making progress on the Tlatelolco agenda without staff work between the periodic foreign ministers' meetings. This difference in attitude really was symptomatic of a fundamental difference in viewpoint that plagued the entire New Dialogue. From the Latin American point of view, the agenda was a list of demands that the United States take certain actions. It was up to the U.S. government to respond to these proposals; there was no need for multilateral discussion. From the U.S. point of view, each of the agenda items implied a certain degree of sacrifice of U.S. interests, or at least changes in current U.S. policy, and therefore it was essential that there be some tradeoffs worked out with the Latin Americans. At the April meeting the United States prevailed to some extent and two working groups were established, one to deal with the agenda item on transfer of technology and the second to deal with TNEs.

THE WORKING GROUP BEGINS

The first preparatory meeting of the working group took place in Washington on August 19-21, 1974. The U.S. delegation proposed that there be two special sessions of the working group to examine the role and impact of transnational enterprises in Latin America. The first special session would deal with the general topic of "Transnational Corporations and the Economic Order," including such subtopics as "Transnational Enterprises—How They Operate and the Variables They Consider in Making Their Decisions" and "The Impact of the Transnational Enterprise on the Process of Development." The second special session would be dedicated to the interaction between governments and transnational enterprises. It would cover such matters as legal and ethical conduct, problems relating to tax jurisdiction, transfer pricing, restrictive commercial practices, and differences between governments that arise as a result of the operations of transnational enterprises. Outside technical experts would be invited to present papers on these topics.

The Mexican delegation broke with the Latin American tactic of speaking with one voice in response to the United States, a tactic that had begun in Tlatelolco and had carried over to the April meeting. The Mexicans proposed that the working group get on with the job of drafting a code of conduct and proceeded to set forth nine principles that would make up such a code.

After the Mexican intervention, the Latins regrouped and responded to the U.S. suggestion for two special sessions at which technical experts would expound on various aspects of TNEs by saying that the Latin Americans considered that a sufficient amount of research already had been done on these matters and that the working group should begin to discuss principles for proposals to the March meeting of foreign ministers. The Latin Americans did agree with the United States that there should be two further preparatory meetings: one to discuss the principles of conduct that TNEs should observe in their development role, and the second to consider principles that pertained to TNEs as a result of political problems resulting from their activities—including problems between states. The principles suggested in the Mexican declaration could serve as a reference point for the group's discussions. The United States accepted the Latin American proposal, and two further meetings to take place in Washington were scheduled for November and January.

FURTHER DELIBERATIONS BY THE WORKING GROUP

The U.S. delegation decided from the outset that Mexico's nine principles inevitably would become the reference points for future meetings of the working group. Rather than fight for a different set of agenda items, the United States prepared to comment on the Mexican formulations and to try to alter them so as to be acceptable to the United States. The Mexican Principles were as follows:

1. Obligation to obey the laws and courts of the host country.
2. Abstention from any political activity and from the exercise of any kind of pressure or coercion on the government of the host country.

3. Adaptation to the social and cultural conditions of the country and observance of national development policies.
4. Adequate and unrestricted technological contribution, as well as collaboration to create autonomous technology for the benefit of the host country according to forms and procedures suitable to its economy and needs and in line with the national development policies.
5. Training of local personnel to occupy managerial positions in the administration of transnational or other enterprises.
6. Financing of TNE activities so as not to affect the host country's balance of payments adversely.
7. Abstention from transfer pricing and other mechanisms that might be used to evade national tax provisions.
8. Abstention from restrictive business practices, in both the domestic and international markets.
9. Prohibition against the TNE serving as an instrument of the foreign policy of another state and as a means of extending legal provisions of the home country to the host country.

The United States included on its delegation a number of experts on TNE operations such as Jack Behrman of the University of North Carolina, Gary Hufbauer of the Treasury Department, and Seymour J. Rubin of the American Society of International Law.

In the course of the two meetings, the Latin Americans made a successful attempt to pin the U.S. delegation down as to what it would be prepared to accept in precise language. This was summed up in a document submitted by the U.S. delegation on January 16, 1975, entitled "Summary of U.S. Position on Latin American Principles." The text of that document, which represents the distillation of the series of preparatory meetings, is attached as an Appendix.

At the closing sessions there was an illuminating dialogue between the United States and the Latin Americans. The debate demonstrated the fundamental difference in the approaches of the two sides. The U.S. delegation pointed out that the Latin American insistence upon principles relating to the effect of TNEs on relations between states (Principles A, C, and D of the U.S. summary document) was tantamount to asking that the U.S. government commit itself as to its behavior without a reciprocal commitment on the part of the Latin American countries. The spokesman for the U.S. delegation pointed out that the Latin Americans had insisted all along that the terms of reference of the working group be limited to the conduct of corporations and not extend to the question of governmental action. Yet the Latin Americans were attempting to introduce, albeit indirectly, the issue of governmental action by cloaking the question in terms of the effect of TNE operations on relations between states. The U.S. delegation said that it was quite willing to discuss interstate obligations and rights if the Latin Americans would agree to broaden the scope of the terms of reference for the working group.

By the end of the working group therefore, the positions of both sides were sharply delineated. The moment of truth was to come at the substantive meeting called for by the communique of April. This meeting was set for February 10–14. In the meantime, however, larger events intervened. The U.S. Congress had passed the Trade Act in December 1974 with the offensive exclusion of Ecuador and Venezuela from the GSP. By the end of January both countries had informed Argentina that they would refuse to attend the Buenos Aires meeting of foreign ministers as long as the offensive legislation was on the books. The Argentine government called off the Buenos Aires meeting indefinitely. When the question arose as to whether the working groups on transnational enterprises and the transfer of technology should continue to function, the United States declined to carry on those negotiations. The New Dialogue, at least in its formal phase, came to an end.

CONCLUSION

The TNE working group experience supports both the opponents and proponents of regionalism. Given the original U.S. objective, which was largely to dispel certain political obstacles to a better working relationship with Latin America, the working group did indeed make progress. By the end of the third meeting there was at least a 50–50 chance that the foreign ministers would agree on a document embodying a limited number of principles. There also was the possibility that the life of the working group would be extended beyond March to discuss the political questions at the root of the issue.

On the other hand, the principles that both sides were able to agree upon had little significance in terms of shaping the conduct of the corporations themselves. It was clear that the United States was not prepared to agree to binding principles but only to hortatory guidelines, and the principles themselves were phrased so vaguely as to have little operational usefulness.

It is interesting that the principles advanced and developed by the Latin Americans in the working group have since surfaced in the United Nations forums as the Third World position on a code of conduct.

Again, both the opponents and proponents can draw their own conclusions. The opponents would say that the Latin American experience merely served to help the Third World develop a code much more quickly than it otherwise would have. The advocates of the regional approach would argue that the code that the Latins developed probably was more moderate than one that might have been developed in a Third World grouping of the nonaligned.

APPENDIX: SUMMARY OF U.S. POSITION ON LATIN AMERICAN PRINCIPLES FOR THIRD PREPARATORY MEETING OF THE WORKING GROUP ON TRANSNATIONAL ENTERPRISES OF THE MEETING OF FOREIGN MINISTERS (Submitted by the U.S. Delegation)

A. *The TNEs shall be subject to the laws and regulations of the receiving country and, in case of litigation, they should be subject to the exclusive jurisdiction of the courts of the country in which they operate.*

The United States Delegation agrees there should be a principle recognizing that every state has the right to prescribe the conditions under which TNEs operate within its jurisdiction and that such corporations must respect the sovereignty and laws of the nation in which they operate. The United States Delegation believes that appropriate reference should be made to international law in this principle. Further, the United States could not support language which asserts the exclusive jurisdiction of the courts of host countries with respect to the operations of transnational enterprises, and which purports to exclude the normal jurisdiction of other tribunals.

B. *The TNEs shall abstrain from all interference in the internal affairs of the states where they operate.*

The United States Delegation is in agreement with this principle, on the understanding that "interference" does not include legitimate activities by TNEs, including normal contacts with governments.

C. *The TNEs shall abstain from interference in relations between the government of a receiving country and other states, and from perturbing those relations.*

The United States Delegation recognizes that this principle touches on one of the most important and difficult issues relating to the activities of transnational enterprises in Latin America. All our countries have an important interest in finding means of preventing investment disputes from becoming problems in relations between states. However, the United States Delegation believes that this problem cannot properly be dealt with in terms of transnational corporation activity alone; any serious discussion of it must necessarily deal with questions of state as well as TNE activity. The United States Delegation is prepared to discuss the question in the broader context of intergovernmental arrangements.

D. *The TNEs shall not serve as an instrument of the external policy of another state or as a means of extending to the receiving country provisions of the juridical order of the country of origin.*

As the United States Delegation understands this principle, it deals with two different issues, certain alleged political activities of TNEs ("instrument of the external policy of another state") and the extraterritorial application of national laws and regulations ("extending to the receiving country provisions of the juridical order of the country of origin"). The United States Delegation believes the first point is covered by point B, which we support, and thus need not be treated separately.

The second point, the extraterritorial application of laws, raises the issue of action by states, not by the enterprises. It is, in this respect, analogous to point C, above. The United States delegation is prepared to subscribe to a principle calling upon states, with full regard for their sovereign rights, to cooperate in good faith with other states in exercising their right to regulate TNEs and to resolve conflicts of jurisdiction in the application of their laws to foreign investors, due regard being paid to the interests of both states.

D.bis *The TNEs shall be subject to the exercise by the host country of its permanent sovereignty over all its wealth, natural resources and economic activities.*

The United States Delegation is prepared to attempt to work out a mutually agreeable principle on the question of permanent sovereignty over natural resources, recognizing the difficulties of reaching agreement on this issue as reflected in recent efforts in other forums.

E. *The TNEs shall be subject to the national policies, objectives and priorities for development, and should contribute positively to carrying them out.*

The United States Delegation is prepared to accept a principle to the effect that TNEs should be responsive to the policies, objectives, and priorities for development of the countries in which they operate.

F. *The TNEs shall supply to the government of the host country pertinent information about their activities in order to assure that these activities are in accord with the national policies, objectives and priorities of development of the host country.*

The United States Delegation recognizes that all countries need adequate information on the operation of TNEs in their countries in order to formulate sound economic policy. The question of access to information from company operations beyond a country's borders is a complex one currently under study in the United Nations and other forums. The United States Delegation is prepared to discuss the problem in this forum as well.

G. *The TNEs shall conduct their operations in a manner that results in a net receipt of financial resources for the host country.*

The United States Delegation could support a principle indicating that TNEs should provide a net contribution to the economic development of the host country and that they should avoid practices that distort financial flows.

H. *The TNEs shall contribute to the development of the scientific and technological capacity of the host country.*

The United States Delegation can agree to a principle that TNEs should contribute to the development of the scientific and technological capacity of the countries in which they operate.

I. *The TNEs shall refrain from restrictive commercial practices.*

The United States Delegation is prepared to support a principle to this effect that TNEs should observe business practices in domestic and international markets that permit competition and foster the free flow of goods, services and capital.

J. *The TNEs shall respect the socio-cultural identity of the host country.*

The United States Delegation can support a principle along these lines.

Section
B
HUMAN RIGHTS

Chapter 7

HUMAN RIGHTS AND ECONOMIC REALITIES IN DEVELOPING NATIONS

Sylvia Ann Hewlett

Public discussion on the issue of human rights in the Third World has generated more heat than light because it has failed to recognize the large scale economic costs of more humane policies. There is no natural affinity between economic growth, political freedom, and social justice in capitalist systems. Nothing shows this more clearly than recent economic development in the underdeveloped world. The high growth rates typical of the last two decades in the more mature developing nations have done little to relieve the miserable poverty that is the lot of the vast majority of citizens in these countries, and have gone hand in hand with authoritarian and repressive political systems.

These juxtapositions raise a number of extremely important questions. Perhaps the most fundamental issue is whether the social and political accompaniments of modern economic development are functional or coincidental. In other words, were the high growth rates of the recent period dependent upon massive poverty and political repression, or would this economic performance have been possible under democratic governments with more egalitarian economic policies? If it turns out that the denial of a whole series of basic political freedoms and human needs has been a necessary condition for rapid economic growth in Third World nations, there are obvious and rather disturbing lessons to be drawn. This conclusion implies that in developing capitalist nations there is a tradeoff between growth and political freedom and between growth and social justice; and that policy makers have to choose between helping and involving the mass of the population and achieving rapid economic growth.

But it is clearly not enough to establish the presence or absence of a growth/equity tradeoff; it also is necessary to examine the questions of degree and longevity, and to determine the precise nature of the chain of causality that links inequality and repression to economic success in the Third World.

ISSUES IN HUMAN RIGHTS

Degree

This point can be illustrated by addressing the question of degree. If a successful capitalist growth strategy is contingent upon massive poverty, it is crucial to determine how much poverty. To put this in concrete terms: Does the growth imperative of inflation control or labor discipline require the suppression of wages rates and rule out the possibility of decent health care for the mass of the people, or is one of these items discretionary, representing a welfare goal that could be pursued concurrently with the growth strategy if the government so desired?

One can examine the issue of political rights in a similar vein. Does the economic requirement of resolving a balance-of-payments crisis or balancing the budget necessitate the suspension of elections and the imposition of torture, or are some elements of many authoritarian scenarios merely the voluntary preference of a specific military regime? In short, how much social injustice or political repression is functional to an economic strategy, and how much is the gratuitous imposition of a particular power elite, constituting options that are not functionally related to the growth dynamics of that nation?

This question of the degree of social injustice and political repression compatible with a successful capitalist growth strategy is central to any discussion of policy alternatives in poor nations. With the proliferation of authoritarian regimes in the Third World, it is increasingly clear that while none of them resemble representational social democracies responsive to the needs of the mass of the people, they differ somewhat in the degree to which they transgress social and political rights.

Take the social welfare issue. On this front there appears to be a rather narrow range of policy alternatives—and results—within the general category of capitalist developing countries. The great majority of governments have pursued development strategies that have permitted very little "trickle down" of the fruits of economic growth to the bulk of the population. Indeed, in a study of growth and social equity in 74 developing countries, Adelman and Morris came to the conclusion that "millions of desperately poor people throughout the world have been hurt rather than helped by economic development."[1] Available evidence points overwhelmingly to the fact that, in underdeveloped capitalist nations, growth has been accompanied by a massive concentration of wealth and a drastic increase in inequality.[2] However, there does seem to be some difference in degree between, for example, the social equity impact of economic strategies in Colombia and Brazil—the former being slightly less inequitable.[3] Since even a small difference in the degree of trickle down literally can constitute the margin between life and death for those at the bottom of the heap in poor countries, it becomes vital to address the issue of how much social injustice is functional to a given growth path and how much is avoidable.

In the sphere of political participation and civil liberties, there seems to be a wider range of policy alternatives. Some regimes are wildly and fearsomely repressive, with Argentina and Chile being perhaps the most glaring contemporary examples of systematic governmental brutality in Latin America. Others, such as Mexico and Brazil, have less repressive authoritarian regimes with fewer flagrant violations of basic political and civil rights. At first glance, it would seem that many of the repressive extremes are at best but distantly related to economic strategies and have more to do with, for example, the particular nature of bourgeois reaction to Salvador Allende's rule in Chile. However, one should not overdraw the importance of specifics for political systems; the appearance together of political repression and capitalist growth strategies is one of the more convincing and conspicuous associations of the contemporary developing world, and it is my contention that this association is neither arbitrary nor accidental. The great majority of economically successful Third World nations have found the systematic denial of political freedoms an essential tool in their struggle for takeoff into sustained economic development. As with the social welfare issue, the question to be addressed is how much political repression is functional to a given growth strategy, how much is avoidable, and what the tradeoffs are at the margin.

Longevity

A second dimension of the costs of growth issue in the developing world is the longevity of these critical social and political tradeoffs. Many theorists, particularly economists, have advocated uninhibited capitalist growth in the short run, whatever the costs, on the assumption that this is the efficient and perhaps the only way to acquire a bigger pie that can and will be more equitably divided at some point in the future. This begs all sorts of questions as to the structural, institutional, and political impediments to growth that may be created by the development process itself. For example, who says when and how the cake is going to be divided? For there would seem to be no compelling or obvious factor that would prompt a military dictatorship in a labor surplus economy to spontaneously divide up the spoils of economic growth.

The only way of explaining the origins and persistence of this item of conventional wisdom—that the costs of growth are short term—is to look at the specific historical experience of advanced industrial nations.

THE HISTORICAL ANALOGY

When one examines the economic histories of Western Europe and North America, the coincidence of rapid industrialization and social injustice during the takeoff period is both dramatic and convincing.

Thomas Carlyle's complaint that "in the midst of plethoric plenty the people perish" and Friedrich Engels's moving and tightly documented account of the suffering of the English poor date from 1843 and 1852 respectively.[4] These studies reveal the social welfare consequences of half a century of both growth and astonishing structural transformation, which the poor financed with their bodies and the bodies of their children, but from which they appear to have gained no improvement at all in living standards. Machines were scarce and the capitalists who owned them well rewarded; laborers, forced off the land by agricultural modernization, competed for urban jobs and kept wages down. Yet this scenario was essentially temporary; after 1850 the workers' standard of living began to improve. The capitalist class, although strengthened by the fruits of past growth, was driven toward concessions as the increasingly organized urban proletariat gained both political and economic muscle. During the twentieth century, periodic labor scarcity, the end of mass unemployment (by 1946), and governmental welfare measures all increased the share of national product going to workers. Although there has been some variation in the details of the process, a similar strengthening of working-class economic and political bargaining power followed the early phases of industrial development in most advanced capitalist nations. Simon Kuznets accurately describes the secular income trends in today's rich countries as constituting a long swing: "widening in the early phases of economic growth when the transition from the pre-industrial to the industrial civilization was most rapid; becoming stabilized for a while; and then narrowing in the later phases."[5]

In other words, before the exhaustion of excess rural labor and the advent of effective collective bargaining, and before the implementation of governmental welfare measures, industrialization did exacerbate income inequality and poverty in the currently developed nations. It is interesting to note that Kuznets's third phase of narrowing income differentials has not been cumulative. Despite convictions about the strongly egalitarian effects of social and economic policies pursued by most Western European and North American governments since World War II, trends have been rather ambiguous. For example, in Britain and the United States the very wealthy have indeed suffered a relative decline in their income shares, but the beneficiaries have been the middle class rather than those at the bottom of the heap.[6] However, even allowing for these refinements, it is undoubtedly true that the lower income groups in the advanced industrial nations have enormously increased their absolute living standards and greatly improved their relative living standards over the last two centuries. But it is unwarranted to go from this specific set of circumstances to a generalized expectation that economic growth, in all contexts and at all times, will enhance earnings opportunities across the board. Kuznets himself is careful to emphasize that his findings are specific to the advanced industrial countries. He warns of the dangers of simple analogies and poses the question:

> How can either the institutional or political framework of the underdeveloped societies or the processes of economic growth and industrialization be modified to favor a sustained rise to higher levels of economic performance and yet avoid the fatally simple remedy of an authoritarian regime that would use the population as cannon-fodder in the fight for economic achievement?[7]

And this was an ominous premonition of what was to occur subsequently in many capitalist developing nations.

In order to demonstrate how misleading it is to extrapolate from the experience of advanced nations, it is useful to spell out, in theoretical terms, the nature of the interaction between growth and equity in the now affluent countries of Western Europe and North America; this makes it possible to see the ways in which conditions in the contemporary developing world diverge fundamentally from this historical analogy.

Let us first take the conventional raison d'être for the growth/equity tradeoff. Economists, drawing on the experience of the advanced world, normally have grounded their tolerance for a short-run worsening of equality in developing countries on the conviction that an extreme distribution of income generates the savings requirement for fast rates of economic growth. This notion is an established part of the conventional wisdom, witness a statement by Harry Johnson: ". . . There is likely to be a conflict between rapid growth and an equitable distribution of income; and a poor country anxious to develop would probably be well advised not to worry too much about the distribution of income."[8]

The argument runs as follows: A highly skewed distribution of income promotes savings because a large chunk of disposable income is in the hands of an elite group with a high marginal propensity to save. High rates of savings are translated into high rates of investment, which lead to rapid rates of economic growth.

But this theory is logically flawed and inconsistent with the available evidence. It ignores the possibility that high income groups in developing countries may indulge in conspicuous consumption rather than save; it neglects the growing importance of corporate savings and public sector savings in modern growth processes; it forgets that private savings may be channeled into Swiss bank accounts rather than domestic investment; and it overlooks the fact that the empirical evidence shows no correlation between inequality and high rates of savings and investment in developing countries.

It is true that private savings did play an extremely important role in the initial industrialization of Britain and America, and this saving was the result of frugal behavior on the part of entrepreneurs—an elite group within an extremely skewed distributional picture. But this dynamic reflected a unique set of historical circumstances that will never be duplicated. In the contemporary Third World, inequality is functional to both stability and growth, but as we shall see, the role it plays is quite different from that outlined above.

Let us now turn to the evolution of these critical social and economic tradeoffs through time. Three elements in the economic histories of Western Europe and North America conspired to make the growth/equity tradeoff a temporary phenomenon and made long-run economic development compatible with a better deal for the mass of the people. None of these crucial factors exists in today's developing world.

Take discrepancies in the economic sphere. The extent and pace of change in economic structures over the last two centuries is often underestimated. Capitalism in the latter half of the twentieth century is an entirely different animal from what it was in the seventeenth and eighteenth centuries, when the presently developed countries entered their takeoff phase. Today the process of capital accumulation is more highly concentrated, more internationally integrated, and much more technologically advanced. Developing nations entering the industrial phase today have few alternatives but to adopt a capital-intensive, technologically sophisticated production function, which often has little to do with their own factor endowment because of its evolution in a context of labor scarcity. This type of industrialization often coincides with, or closely follows, the transfer of another type of technology from the developed world—that of medical know-how. Within a few years killer diseases are wiped out, death rates fall drastically, and population growth rates assume explosive proportions.

The coincidence of these types of technological transfer has obvious implications for income distribution in developing countries. Industrial growth rates often are quite high by any historical standard but, given an imported capital-intensive technology and an acceleration of population increase, the rate of growth of industrial (that is, well-paid) employment is often less than the rate of population growth. This results in a situation where the modern work force is a declining proportion of the potential labor pool. Industrial workers become a small, privileged, protected minority, a labor aristocracy that is quite distinct from the mass of the population in both political and and economic terms.

This obviously contrasts quite markedly with the structure of early industrialization in the advanced nations. In Western Europe and North America during the eighteenth and nineteenth centuries, there was a gradual and mostly indigenous evolution of the technological base of society that went hand in hand with a much slower and milder demographic transition. Over the course of a century first death rates and then birth rates fell, and population growth rates had stabilized in most industrial societies by the beginning of the twentieth century (North America is an exception because of large-scale immigration throughout the first quarter of this century). Also, the simple technologies of the original industrial revolution were relatively labor intensive and absorbed large quantities of unskilled as well as skilled workers. The net result of these trends was the eventual elimination of surplus labor; the bulk of the potential labor pool was absorbed into the modern industrial sector with predictable effects on the standard of living of the mass of the populace.

A second economic discrepancy that serves to differentiate the advanced from the developing world, revolves around the demand dynamics of early as opposed to late development.[9]

Since the end of the nineteenth century, Western Europe and North America have been reliant on mass production and mass consumption for the maintenance of their growth rates, and the major threat to prosperity has been recurrent crises of effective demand. In simple terms these crises have been caused by the lack of balance between the increased output of a growing economy and the capacity of the mass of consumers to buy the additional output.

This demand constraint on growth, and the realization by the capitalist class that low wages meant low demand and thus low profits in the long run, produced a gradual softening of business attitudes toward trade unionism and ultimately increased money incomes for workers. This softening of attitudes was helped by the concomitant trend toward oligopoly. In the late nineteenth century, the structure of industry was becoming increasingly concentrated and consequently businesses were freed from the need to pay very low wages in order to remain price competitive. They could therefore "afford" to play a part in bolstering demand, and they had a collective incentive to do so.

In the contemporary developing world, this important incentive for wage increases is almost totally lacking. Poverty in developing countries is not caused by a surplus of production and a deficit of money wages. Rather it is caused by insufficient production capacity and inelasticities in the supply of the various factors of production. Therefore, raising wages will only cause inflation, because supply—of capital, of skilled labor, of energy—is inelastic. In short, poverty in Latin America, Africa, and Asia is caused by the lack of means to create wealth, not by the superabundance of such means and the absence of demand.

A final discrepancy hinges on the nature and effects of governmental intervention. Given the link between income levels, effective demand, and the health of mature industrial economies, governments increasingly have taken upon themselves the task of regulating demand via various social welfare and tax programs. In essence, in an effort to regulate the demand crises of capitalism, governments in advanced countries have intervened progressively, with results in the social equity solidarity sphere.

However, the smoothness of this process should not be overemphasized; even in the advanced world, capitalists and governments have not always swallowed the logic of this particular item of enlightened self-interest. The appalling social costs of the Great Depression obviously were exacerbated by governments refusing to reflate via the costly and drastic method of deficit-financed public works. But this aberration does not deny the fairly steady growth of governmental intervention in advanced economies from the 1850s to the present day. Historians gradually are revealing the nineteenth century origins of social welfare legislation—in Disraeli's Britain, Louis Napoleon's France, and Bismarck's Germany. In setting income floors below which the poor could not fall, not only did governments meet a clear human need but these measures also dampened the decline in purchasing power during downturns in the business cycle. It should be stressed that crisis control, demand management, and income equalization have gone hand in hand. Unemployment relief, social security benefits, progressive income taxation, a growing public sector—which, unlike private industry, does not deepen depressions by cutting investment and employment—all reduce the depth of economic crises and thereby transfer resources from the rich to the poor.

Almost all of these economic incentives for increasing social justice via welfare state measures are missing in developing countries. In the contemporary Third World, deficit demand is not the cause of poverty, nor is the welfare state a sure prescription for high profits. In developing countries, instability often is caused by fluctuations in climate and in agricultural production, in foreign demand for exports, and in the external supply price of manufactured inputs—fluctuations that no single government can control. And, as already noted, the long-run causes of poverty have far more to do with low productivity and shortages of machines and human skills than with manipulable deficiencies of home demand. In short, the economic pressures facing governments in the developing world are not met by giving priority to social welfare measures, and regimes in these countries are correct in seeing stability and equality as separate issues, that cannot be tackled together by social welfare programs designed to put a floor under domestic demand as was and is the case in advanced nations.

It is now time to turn to the politics of government intervention. One would have to be an extremely hard-nosed economic determinist to imagine that all governmental action was prompted by economic considerations. True, the maintenance of domestic demand did encourage governments in the advanced countries to adopt policies of enlightened self-interest, but the issue is more fundamental than this. In order to understand the emergence of political freedom and social justice in advanced capitalist countries, it is necessary to confront head-on the ideological frameworks of nations.

In analyzing the development paths of developing as opposed to advanced countries, economists (and other social scientists) often ignore profound differences or discontinuities in the evolution of systems of values. It is forgotten that all rich capitalist countries are effective democracies that accord the broad mass of their populations an extremely wide range of political and civil liberties, and possess an array of public programs explicitly geared toward diminishing inequality between social classes and between regions. In many cases such "democratic" attributes are neither novel nor ephemeral but are firmly rooted in a tradition and a philosophy that predate the emergence of modern representational democracy; they go well beyond the requirements of economic strategies.

Political freedoms seem to have preceded social justice in the modern evolution of Western Europe and North America. The eighteenth century doctrines of the natural rights of man hinged on notions of freedom and liberty. The American Revolution was a prime example of these new convictions; it was in essence a struggle against tyranny and oppression (rather than exploitation and poverty) fought in the name of such tangible civil liberties as freedom of movement, of expression, and of assembly, and freedom from "taxation without representation."

It was the French Revolution that first focused on basic human needs and turned "the rights of man into the rights of the Sans Culottes,"[10] By the end of the nineteenth century, Marx had elevated the welfare of the mass into a key doctrine of the modern age. Life itself became the highest goal, and the

> role of the revolution was no longer to liberate men from the oppression of their fellow men, let alone to found freedom, but to liberate the life process of society from the fetters of scarcity so that it could swell into a stream of abundance. Not freedom but abundance became now the aim of revolution.[11]

Leaving aside the future evolution of Marxian thought and turning back to the development of Western democracies, one can trace successive periods during which three types of rights were conferred on the broad mass of the populace by governments: civil rights (equality in the eyes of the law, freedom of movement, of expression, and of assembly); political rights (universal suffrage, political parties, trade unions); and finally certain social welfare rights (old age pensions, unemployment benefits, public health facilities).[12]

These successive stages, were, of course, related. An initial civil right of assembly greatly strengthened the chances of successful trade unionism; collective bargaining while in its turn was an important ingredient in the struggle toward a higher standard of living and enhanced social welfare provisions for the bulk of the population.

By now it should be obvious that both the economic constraints and the political conditions of early development in Western Europe and North America interacted in a cumulative fashion so as to permit, or indeed foster, the coexistence of growth, freedom, and justice. Both the intention and the effect of state action came to be the amelioration of the harsher aspects of capitalist takeoff, particularly its unequalizing tendencies. Where the state did not intervene directly, the individual was armed with a limited number of tools to protect personal interests. These economic constraints and political conditions have existed only erratically in the contemporary Third World; as a result, the state is extremely unlikely to perform a similar countervailing function.

Before leaving this analysis of the crucial differences between early and late development, two social factors should be noted to strengthen the case against simple-minded analogies.

First, many traditional props of inequality—feudalism, serfdom, clan, and caste—had been drastically reduced in most advanced countries by violence or edict before the advent of modern industrialization. These traditional social structures rest on ascribed roles rather than achieved functions and are extremely prone to channel the fruits of progress to a nonproductive elite. They still prevail in many developing countries, often as a legacy of the colonial era, and do much to reinforce the inequitable trends within late development.

Capitalism in most developing countries has never confronted traditional social structures as it did, for example, in Cromwell's England or late eighteenth century France. In Europe, the new inequalities of capitalism—to some extent nonhereditary—replaced the relics of feudalism, while in today's developing world they often reinforce a still thriving traditional social structure. In concrete terms, the landlord class often has been co-opted rather than destroyed. This clearly impedes the evolution of a political system that will direct the benefits of development toward the mass of the population.

A second social factor revolves around the attributes of the working class in early as opposed to late developing countries. As noted, an important reason for the gains of the working class in Europe and North America include the fact that labor began to organize in trade unions and political parties. The precondition was obviously an organizable working class, in the sense of a mass of urbanized and substantially literate workers. There are 15 advanced countries with fairly reliable estimates of the beginning of modern economic growth; all except one (Japan) had over 35 percent of the labor force outside agriculture at that time and a greater than 50 percent literacy rate. A very different situation prevailed in most developing countries when they entered their takeoff phases. Generally speaking, only 10 to 35 percent of workers were outside agriculture, a similar percentage were literate, and the gap between their output (and hence income levels) and that of agricultural workers was far greater than in developing nineteenth century Europe or North America.[13]

Primarily due to the technological and demographic factors described earlier, modern industralization in developing countries has confirmed rather than countered this previously existing differentiation. The industrial work force has emerged as a labor aristocracy with more to lose than to gain from sharing the benefits of economic growth with the mass of the people, and the trade union movement has grown up as an instrument to protect the interests of this elite group. The net result is that "organized labor" in the Third World is likely to fight against equalizing measures. In yesterday's developing nations, it spearheaded them.

In summary, the really poor in contemporary developing countries are excluded from the dynamics of modern economic growth. They are minifarmers, landless laborers, and recent migrants to the cities. In political terms, they constitute a voiceless, largely illiterate, dispersed, unorganized mass that is incapable of combining, articulating its needs, or backing them up with effective political or trade union power.

The Western European and North American analogy is false. There is nothing in the contemporary structure of Third World nations to lead one to suppose that the grand dynamics of the original industrial revolution will repeat themselves. The conditions for growth and development to go hand in hand with enhanced civil liberties, increased political participation, and a much higher standard of living for the bulk of the population—conditions established in most of Western Europe and North America in the early nineteenth century—are highly special. They involve the cumulative interaction of a specific set of economic, political, and social factors. The original conditions of transition to capitalist industrialization, the contemporary structure of class relations and political power, and the underlying value systems of Western Europe and North America all served to turn growth from a process in which the wealthy gained both the political power and the economic surplus into a process in which the mass of the people shared. Conditions in the modern developing world do not support a reasonable expectation of replicating these trends. The same set of factors is simply not at work.

It is important to stress the coincidence of political and economic incentives for greater equity in the advanced world. The wretchedness and exploitation of the English, European, and immigrant U.S. working classes in the early and middle nineteenth century stemmed from low wages and permitted high rates of capital formation. But these social costs were short-lived; there was a gradual accumulation of civil and political rights by the laboring classes and increased state activism on behalf of these classes, and furthermore economic imperatives came to the fore. The drying up of the pool of surplus rural labor gave the emerging trade union movement some solid bargaining power, and at the same time the capitalist class was discovering that it needed both a mass market for its products and an increasingly skilled and literate work force to keep the industrial structure running and improving. The result was an increasingly prosperous and increasingly powerful working class. Capitalist self-interest seems to have determined the development path of advanced nations as much as capitalist humanity.

Contemporary Brazil or Mexico or Chile present a rather stark contrast. In the political sphere repressive, autocratic regimes are increasingly dominant. Authoritarian governments generally are not concerned with the eradication of poverty and inequality, and they are rarely enthusiastic supporters of workers' rights. To use Kuznets' apt phrase, few of these regimes have avoided the fatally simple remedy of using "the population as cannon fodder in the fight for economic achievement."[14] In addition, the rather special and exclusive trade union movements of many Third World countries often have been co-opted by governments. Frequently the trade union structure becomes a government-sponsored interest group designed to buy off the industrial work force with material goodies and ensure that workers do not join with the mass of the population. This tends to complete the differentiation of the lower classes in developing nations; in essence, the evolution of an official and exclusive trade union structure breaks the identification between "the laboring classes" and "the dangerous classes,"[15] and in so doing prevents the mass from acquiring this important type of political muscle.

In the economic sphere, conditions also fail to provide any incentive for egalitarian measures. Industry is not a mass employer, nor does it confront an impoverished but largely urban and literate work force. Rather, most industry in most poor countries is an exotic, fragile, and artificially nurtured plant. It is exotic in much of the Third World because it is dominated by an inappropriate capital-intensive technology and by multinational firms. It is fragile due to its dependence on a whole range of imported basic inputs—raw materials, energy, capital goods—that cannot always be imported in sufficient quantities given balance-of-payments constraints. It is artificial since it survives largely because governments grant it permanent and prohibitive protection against imports.

Above all, almost everywhere in the Third World the growth dynamics of the modern industrial sector do not impinge upon the vast mass of the population at all. The capital-intensive nature of industry, which absorbs a small (and often decreasing) proportion of the urban work force, and the composition of production, which normally emphasizes consumer durables or "rich country goods," mean that it is possible to have a flourishing industrial sector and high average rates of growth while the vast mass of the population remains miserably poor and in a state of increasing relative deprivation.

In summary, the distinctive pattern of industrial growth typical of the capitalist Third World tends to create a situation where there is no economic incentive for improving social equity; the vast masses of the populace are redundant to the development process both as workers and as consumers. Indeed, the situation is more extreme than this: the growth strategy is not merely indifferent to equity considerations but actively prefers a less equal and more repressive "solution" to the social question. As will be explored below, modern capitalist growth processes have their own sets of tradeoffs with both political freedom and social justice.

Given this economic scenario, it would seem that the burden on political systems in developing countries to counter widespread and deepening poverty is huge, much greater than was the case in the advanced world. However, despite the severity of this burden, the autocratic governments of most developing nations are singularly unprepared to shoulder it. An authoritarian state will tend to reinforce rather than counter the disequilibrating and polarizing effects of modern capitalist growth, and one certainly cannot rely on the emergence of a strong, independent labor movement of the type that played such an important role in obtaining a better deal for the broad spectrum of workers in the advanced industrial countries; in the developing world, the trade union movement has, as noted, been co-opted or bought off. In short, the prospects seem bleak for developing nations to find their own paths to growth, freedom, and justice in the not-too-distant future.

In concluding this section, a word on borrowed assumptions is useful. The coincidence of rapid growth and increasing poverty in contemporary developing nations has repeatedly been justified, by theorists and by governments, on the grounds that it is a time-honored, inevitable, and temporary cost of growth highly reminiscent of the experience of advanced countries. The implication is that Third World regimes need only concentrate on growing, since in the not-very-long run the equity issue can and will be resolved.

As noted above, this is a facile and erroneous train of thought. For a variety of deeply seated economic, political, and social reasons, developing nations are not about to repeat the grand dynamics of the original industrial revolution of Western Europe and North America. Contemporary social science is rife with these kinds of false analogies, which can be extremely dangerous in policy-making circles when they are used to justify and obscure grim social reality. As Paul Streeten puts it, "The paradigms of 'western' social science serve as blinkers or escape mechanisms preventing scholars and policy-makers from seeing and acting upon strategic fronts."[16]

It is important to stress how pervasive has been the expectation that it is "the history of advanced or established industrial countries which traces out the road of development for the more backward countries."[17] This has given rise to a belief in a linear, evolutionary dynamic that spreads beyond the economic sphere and pervades the theories of political scientists and sociologists. In simple terms, this has meant a faith in a smooth, continuous, and cumulative progression from various states of economic and political backwardness to representational democracy and high mass consumption for all.

During the 1960s, the rhetoric and part of the reality could be made to support this upbeat theme. In Latin America, for example, the Alliance for Progress, LAFTA (the Latin American Free Trade Area), high growth rates, and a veneer of democracy spawned a brand of academic euphoria, and Rostowian theories of continuous development emerged in several disciplines:

> David Lerner, Karl Deutsch, Gino Germani and Gabriel Almond all taught us how societies develop from tradition to modernity, from isolation to communication, from reduced to expanded political participation, from national isolationism to international integration.[18]

This doctrine of continuous progress naturally left little room for repressive dictatorship or increasing poverty, two of the most conspicuous facts of life in the Third World during the 1970s.[19]

TOWARD A NEW MODEL

Having demolished the underlying analogy, on both empirical and theoretical grounds, we can discard the notion that developing nations are becoming well-behaved representational democracies responsive to the needs of the mass of the population. It is time to move on to the development of a more convincing conceptual framework that will begin to describe the raison d'être of stable, reactionary, autocratic regimes in the Third World and the exact nature of the chain of causality that links late capitalist growth with social injustice and political repression.

First, some definitions. Before one can make sense of the relevant tradeoffs in the Third World, it is necessary to be explicit about the phenomenon in question. What do we mean by economic growth, political freedom, or social justice in these contexts?

The Facts of Growth

In the first instance, it is true that over the last three decades poor countries have experienced unprecedented economic growth. Accepting the UN definition of a developing country—annual income of $500 per capita in 1960 prices or $750 per capita in the higher prices of 1974—real income per head rose by 75 percent in the 1950–70 period. Indeed, the years since World War II in most developing nations have seen more growth in real output per person than the previous 20 centuries. The recency of sustained growth in the developing world can be demonstrated by some arithmetic examples. Income per head for at least half of the world's poor people (those in China, India, Pakistan, Indonesia, and Nigeria) averaged below $50 per year in 1950, and at least half of these populations were receiving less than $25 a year; such elemental levels simply cannot have grown from a much lower base. A further example: Even if the average Indian at the birth of Christ enjoyed only $25 worth of goods (at 1960 prices) yearly, growth at only 0.5 percent per year would have brought him/her up to $318,000 per year by 1950. Indeed, historical reconstructions suggest that income per head in the Indian subcontinent probably stagnated between 1600 and 1900 and fell between 1900 and 1950. The fact that it has risen by over one-third since 1950 demonstrates a fantastic change in economic tempo, and many poor countries have grown much more dramatically in recent years.

Second, this is not growth without development if one interprets development as modernizing structural change or transformation. The most striking manifestation of structural change has been the dramatic movement toward urbanization and industrialization in Third World nations, but perhaps a more fundamental indication of how poor nations have radically and permanently expanded their productive capacity lies in their vastly increased stocks of physical capital (machinery, plant, infrastructure) and human capital (education, skills). How this extra productive capacity is used—whether it is converted into rising living standards for the mass of the people or channeled into enriching an elite group—is a problem not of development but of social justice.

Human Rights

One sad result of linear evolutionary theories and the borrowed assumptions of contemporary social science is that they have prevented clear thinking in and around such concepts as political freedom and social justice. As economic, political, and social enlightenment in the Third World were and are supposed to progress hand in hand, very little attention has been paid, either by scholars or policy makers, to distinguishing between these various ideological and humanitarian ideals or to tracing their separate relationships with the growth process. In the recent past, there has been a pronounced tendency to lump them all together under the singularly woolly label of human rights. Although the basis of these rights (granted by some abstract deity or by a specific government?) and the nature of the identity among them (what do systematic torture, press censorship, and a guaranteed subsistence wage have in common?) is often left quite vague, human rights are now in the forefront of foreign policy making. Let us attempt to clear up this gray area.

It makes practical sense to break down the category of political freedoms into (1) civil liberties—equality in the eyes of the law, habeas corpus, freedom of speech, of religion, of the press, of assembly; (2) individual integrity—freedom from governmental violation of the person through torture, arbitrary arrest, or imprisonment; (3) political participation—the right to vote, to form political parties, to organize independent trade unions, to take part in government.

Social justice constitutes a completely different bundle of goods. It involves the elimination of the more desperate states of poverty and a narrowing of the gap between the rich and the poor. It is important to remember that poverty in developing countries is on a qualitatively different scale from poverty in rich nations. It is a state of "constant want and acute misery whose ignominy consists in its dehumanizing force." It "is abject because it puts men under the dictate of their bodies."[20] It is crucial to note that social justice in poor countries encompasses an absolute and a relative dimension; both are relevant to explaining levels of deprivation in the Third World.[21]

Political freedom and social justice both have been prominent goals of European-based civilization and hinge on such values as Christian doctrines of brotherly love, Rousseauian notions of the dignity of man, and Marxian convictions that poverty is a product of exploitation. During this century they have been given a certain international legal status through such declaratory acts as the Universal Declaration of Human Rights of 1946 and the three 1966 human rights covenants.[22]

One interesting difference between these two main categories of rights is that they demand contrasting types of behavior from governments. Political freedom involves a deliberate restraining of arbitrary and coercive state power. Freedom of speech essentially denies the state the right to limit what citizens say, while habeas corpus prevents the state from incarcerating an individual without a prompt and fair trial. Social justice, on the other hand, requires that the state step in and actively redress the balance between classes; in advanced democracies the state, as both regulator and participant, has become a major economic actor with the ability and the will to ensure that the weak and underprivileged improve their lot. All this serves to emphasize the point that it can be extremely misleading to muddle the issues of political freedom and social justice and lump them together under the vaguely defined umbrella of human rights.

MODERN CAPITALIST DEVELOPMENT

It is a basic contention that contemporary growth strategies do not go hand in hand with political freedom and social justice, as was eventually the case in the advanced countries of Western Europe and North America. Instead, there is a series of tradeoffs that drive poor nations to sacrifice these political and social goals in the name of economic development. Previous sections of this chapter have considered key economic, political, and social discrepancies between early and late development. Specifically, growth strategies in the contemporary Third World are conditioned by the following factors: industrialization processes are markedly more capital intensive; population growth rates are incomparably higher; governments lack both the economic incentive and the political motivation to spearhead far-reaching social welfare measures; trade unions are elitist organizations co-opted by government; and traditional social structure often are intact particularly in the countryside.

Using Latin America as the primary focus, let us put these various elements together and construct a dynamic portrait of modern capitalist development that will explain both the origins and functions of social and political inequities.

Stages of Economic Development

The first and most fundamental element in the conceptual framework is that contemporary growth patterns are intimately linked to the successive, historical stages of late capitalist development. The economic evolution of most developing countries in Latin America can be divided into three stages:

1. A primary exporter (and often colonial) economy, based on agricultural cash crops and mining; this period lasted until the Great Depression and was characterized by long run domestic stagnation and a highly differentiated social structure.
2. The phase of "easy" import substituting industrialization, which in some Latin American countries started as early as the 1930s and lasted through the 1960s; this phase was marked by rapid industrial growth, recurrent inflation and balance-of-payments problems, and a rigidifying of the highly skewed distributional pattern inherited from the previous period.
3. The recent period of stabilization and export-oriented growth, which in many countries has seen the juxtaposition of renewed economic growth with deepening poverty.

Despite the dramatic changes in economic structure, all three eras witnessed a steady and cumulative differentiation of Latin American nations into a privileged elite and a poverty-stricken mass.

Political Framework

Second, each stage of development is associated with a specific political framework: The primary-exporter economy with colonial government and a trade-oriented domestic oligarchy; the easy import-substituting period with modernizing and often populist regimes; and the recent period with repressive military governments. Generally speaking, the exhaustion of each stage of development has precipitated structural crisis and internal political change. These changes normally have encompassed a regrouping of political actors and a significant redirectioning of policy. For example, the structural crisis of the 1930s—precipitated by the Great Depression and the collapse of the primary commodity market—provoked in Latin America the ousting of the landed oligarchy and the coming to power of modernizing urban-based regimes that had marked populist overtones and self-consciously co-opted the emerging industrial work force.

One also can detect common threads in the political reaction to the end of easy import substitution. In countries as diverse as Brazil, Argentina, and Peru, mounting inflationary and balance-of-payments problems were resolved by resorting to more or less repressive forms of authoritarianism that tended to exclude the articulate urban classes as well as the masses from the political process. However, one should not overdraw the differences between regimes in the modern period. They all have tended to emphasize developmentalism and nationalism; none has constituted government by and for the people. In certain countries during certain eras, discrete population segments have been rewarded with a rather limited set of civil and political freedoms. But such "rights" rarely have been universally applied (the rural masses have been the most conspicuous losers) and generally have been withdrawn when they have come into conflict with the imperatives of economic growth. In short, political differences in the modern era of industrial growth have been of degree rather than kind.

Ideology

Third, it should be stressed that one cannot go from economic crisis to the political solution of that crisis without talking about motivating forces. There is nothing automatic or inevitable in the link between economic cause and political effect. But given a driving force—in this case the prime emphasis given by the majority of Third World regimes to national economic success—a strong repressive state has become a necessary component of the answer to structural crisis in many developing nations. The dominant ideology of Latin American leaders since the 1930s and 1960s, whether oligarchic or autocratic, has comprised a mixture of developmentalism and nationalism, and this image of the future has left little time for political freedom and social justice as ends in themselves.

Economic Actors

The final element in this conceptual framework is the balance of power between the various economic actors in the growth process. The timing of industrial takeoff, together with the nature of the political response, has largely dictated the roles played by national, state, and foreign capital—the ménage à trois of contemporary economic development. This balance of power has important implications for social equity.

Developing nations are latecomers to the industrial game, and as a result national private capital has been unable to capture the dynamic sectors or commanding heights of industrial development. Multinational corporations, the industrial giants of the advanced world, have a multifaceted technological edge and privileged access to finance; they therefore have preempted the most profitable areas of final goods production while the state has become increasingly dominant in basic industry and infrastructural investment. This fact is also a function of late dependent development and the economic facts of life in the twentieth century. Economies of scale, "indivisibilities," and long gestation periods make the state rather than the private investor the natural agent for certain types of industrial growth.

Political factors undoubtedly have exacerbated this structural tendency in favor of the multinational corporations and the state. Throughout the modern period, the national project of most Latin American countries has involved the maximization of the rate of GNP growth. This has necessitated a reliance on the most efficient producers and a progressive strengthening of the multinational corporations and the state. During certain stages, the multinational corporations have advanced faster than the state; at others the state has advanced faster, depending on the nature of the economic cycle. Most stages have featured the co-optation or assimilation of national capital, which has become an increasingly shadowy member of the ménage à trois. If the national project of these countries had been defined differently—if, for example, the ideology of the state had been dominated by such issues as employment creation—the scenario might have been different and private national capital utilizing more labor-intensive techniques might have been significantly subsidized by the state.

In summary, the current constellation of economic actors in Latin American countries, with the dominant roles played by the state and the multinational corporations, is a result of late industrialization where the political project is national economic success defined in terms of growth rates per year.

With these bare bones of a theoretical framework, one can begin to understand some of the conspicuous juxtapositions of contemporary capitalist development in Latin America: that it has achieved fast economic growth rates and yet has exacerbated poverty for the mass of the population; that it is firmly nationalistic but has linked these countries firmly to foreign capital; that civil liberties and political freedom are admired but, the institutionalized regimes often are autocratic and repressive; and that it prefers free enterprise and yet has created in practice something akin to state capitalism.

It should be clear by now that there is no simple or one-dimensional explanation of social and political inequities in the Third World. We are in an arena of circular and multiple causation where the historical evolution of economic structures, domestic power relationships, the ideologies of regimes, and the balance of power between the various economic actors interact and feed on one another to produce the contemporary pattern of economic development.

Conspiracy theories simply do not work; they are too linear, too monocausal, and have no historical perspective. Take, for example, U.S. multinationals. In radical literature, they often are put forward as the bête noire, solely and directly responsible for the ills of developing nations.[23] It is true that the product mix and employment propensities of multinational firms tend to exacerbate inequality in poor countries, but in no simpleminded sense do multinational corporations cause poverty. We are in a complex world where changing one factor—in this case, controlling or even eliminating foreign capital—would be fruitless without change in other spheres such as domestic industrialization strategies. Multinational corporations entered Latin America, not in a self-conscious effort to warp national development, but in response to the industrialization policies of the regimes. In the years of easy import substitution, successive governments in the developing world threw up protective barriers (tariffs, import licenses) that gave the greatest protection to goods that previously had been imported—luxury items for an elite group. As the production, managerial, and marketing technologies required to manufacture identical products effectively were monopolized by the giant international oligopolies, this strategy led to a situation where the dynamic sectors of industry in Latin American countries came to be dominated by foreign capital and multinational firms with predictable effects on employment patterns and social welfare.

Complex as the interaction is between domestic industrialization strategies and multinational corporations, one must probe deeper. The fundamental factors determining the choice and viability of a particular development strategy revolve around previously existing social structures and power relationships. In the first place, the primary exporter or colonial phase of late development created a highly differentiated social structure and an extremely skewed distribution of income. The wealth generated by international trade was appropriated by a planter-exporter elite that used it to buy imported luxury goods. Second, when these countries began to industrialize, the new modernizing regimes primarily wanted to grow—and the easiest and most expedient route to rapid industrial growth was to internalize extant (that is, elite) demand. Hence, import substitution strategies encouraged the multinational corporations to produce "rich country goods" within the domestic economies of Latin America. The interest groups that might have promoted industrialization strategies more in keeping with the employment and consumption needs of ordinary citizens were, quite simply, not present in the corridors of power.

In figure 7.1 I have attempted to formalize this circle of multiple and cumulative causation that is responsible for contemporary growth patterns in Latin American countries. This figure should serve to emphasize the complex interrelationships that account for the coexistence of rapid growth with deepening poverty and political repression. None of the inputs to this process should be viewed independently; all are caused by the interplay of other factors, and in their turn combine to cause the cumulative effect.

Take the familiar example of the multinational corporation. The advent of multinationals was a response to a demand dynamic emanating from an elite group and was encouraged by the policies of a national government controlled by the same elite. The effect of the multinationals was to reinforce the highly differentiated social structure of many Latin American nations and to bolster an elitist system of power.

Similarly, successive governments in Latin America have been part of this chain of cumulative causation. The power elite that initiated the import substitution process was a product of a highly differentiated class system inherited from the primary exporter economy. The chosen industrialization strategy reflected the needs of this elite; hence its reliance on sophisticated consumer goods and the multinational corporations, which both rigidified and exacerbated the previously existing distribution of income.

Meanwhile, the state in its role as producer advanced the growth goals of government by providing infrastructural items (road networks, electricity grids) and basic industrial goods (steel, chemicals). It also directly promoted the profitability of multinational corporations by subsidizing the important inputs to their manufacturing processes.

It should be stressed that the chain of cumulative causation interacts in multiple ways. A government may affect the multinational corporation directly, perhaps through a specific tax incentive meant solely for foreign capital, or it may influence multinational corporations indirectly via a generalized development policy such as export subsidies available to most segments of industry. Conversely, multinational corporations may affect government directly through support for a specific regime (1964 in Brazil, 1973 in Chile) or they may influence government indirectly via the domestic social structure. An example of the latter effect involves the

FIGURE 7.1

The Circle of Multiple and Cumulative Causation in Modern Capitalist Growth

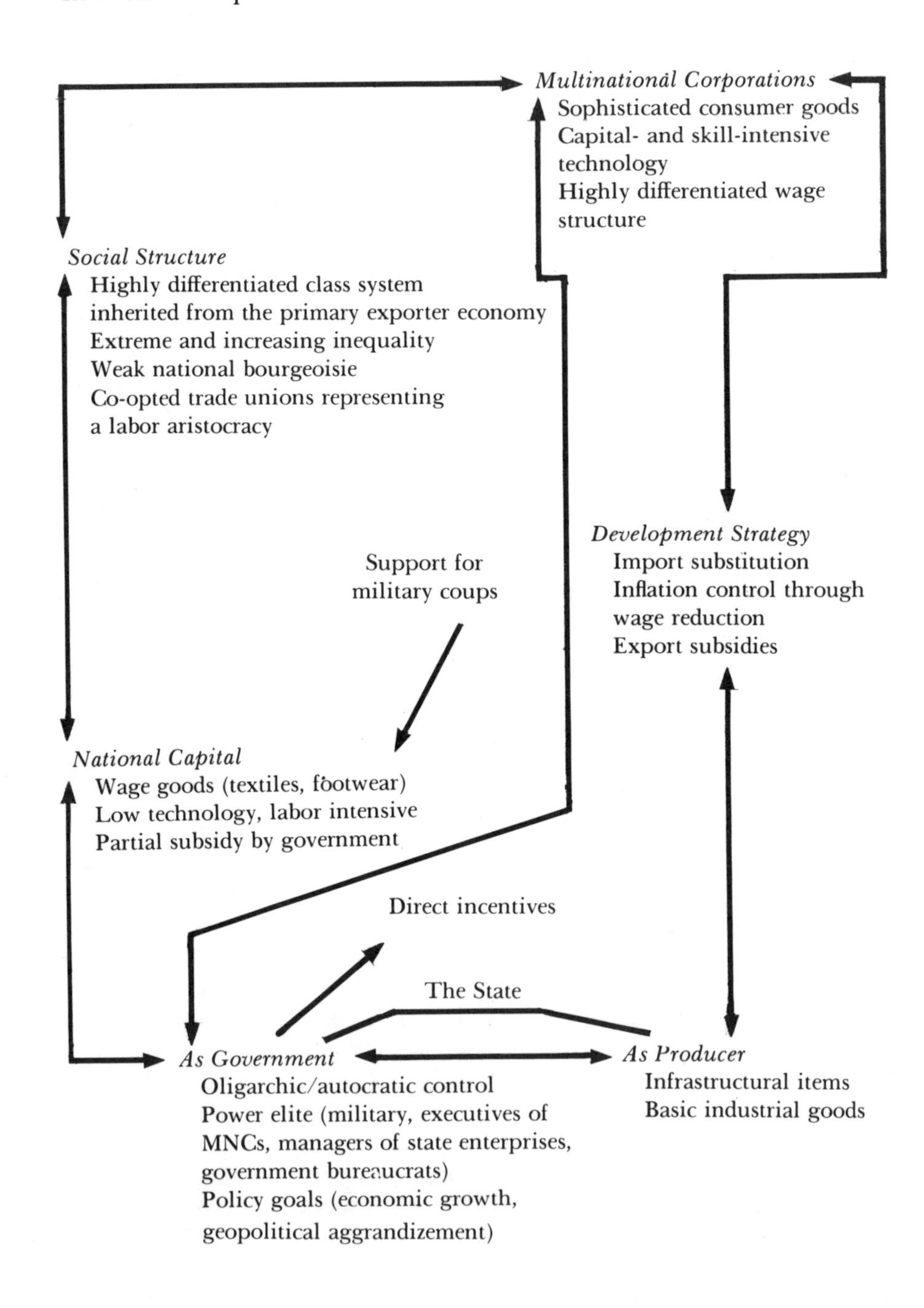

employment propensities of multinational firms, which tend to enrich and strengthen the well-educated segments of the urban upper classes, who subsequently wield greater influence in the political arena.

In summary, the circle of multiple and cumulative causation in contemporary development processes results in a situation where several decades of rapid industrial growth have bypassed the vast mass of the population in Latin America. It is as though a vicious circle of wealth were operating between and among the top 25 percent of people. An elitist power structure inherited from an earlier epoch promotes an industrialization strategy that employs and sells to a restricted and privileged group within the population. Succeeding cycles of development rigidify and exacerbate this process as the imperatives of maintaining the growth conditions (namely inflation control and balance-of-payments contraints) require that segments of the urban work force as well as the rural masses be excluded from the fruits of economic progress and from the political arena.

Particularly important in this regard is the inflation control imperative. Import substituting industrialization via the multinational firm in heavily protected small markets is a high-cost business. Above-normal profit margins, operation at less than full capacity, and inelasticity in the supply of skilled labor and basic industrial goods all contribute to this picture. As a result, these countries are plagued by chronic inflationary distortions and balance-of-payments difficulties, which are ultimately resolved (or at least tackled) by resorting to a ruthless set of stabilization measures. Brazil, Argentina, and Peru in the 1960s, and Chile, Argentina, and Peru in the 1970s have all tried, with varying degrees of success, to institute drastic stabilization policies.[24] All these programs have tended to include the reduction of real wage levels, a tightening of domestic sources of credit, budget cutting, and a concerted attempt to increase the rate of effective taxation. Such programs are inherently unpopular and often have necessitated the suspension of various political freedoms—for example, the emasculation of the trade union structure is a predictable and usually fairly immediate consequence of such policies. Where stabilization programs have been successful, it has proved possible to rescue the development strategy and move forward into a post-import substitution era of export-oriented growth.[25]

Widespread poverty and political repression are indeed functional to the growth dynamics of capitalist nations in Latin America, but in ways that are complex and reach back into the past. As a result, there is no simple remedy and no easy way to point a finger and accuse a single actor of being the evil genius responsible for the unhappy juxtapositions of contemporary development. One particularly dramatic point to emerge from the preceding analysis is that Latin American countries are a long way from the "stabilization measures equal enhanced social welfare" calculus of the advanced world. Modern industrial takeoff is not dependent upon mass demand and governments are not presented with economic incentives to reduce poverty and inequality; instead, successful growth strategies seem to require the active suppression of the majority of the population.

A final word on questions of degree and longevity is useful here. First, how much social and political injustice has been functional to growth strategies in the capitalist Third World? The vicious circle of wealth seems to have excluded roughly 75 percent of the population from the fruits of economic progress—this includes the rural masses and the under- or unemployed lower echelons of the urban population. Apart from this fundamental dynamic, the stabilization policies of many contemporary regimes have reduced living standards among industrial workers, particularly the unskilled. The net result is that all strategies have increased the degree of inequality, and in many cases discrete groups within the urban population actually have received an absolute cut in their living standards.

On the political front, contemporary growth strategies have relied upon considerable repression. Specifically, the more ruthless aspects of stabilization policies have resulted in the indefinite suspension of key political and civil liberties—open elections, independent political parties and trade unions, freedom of speech and press—all these "rights" have proven incompatible with the severe and extended belt tightening associated with stabilization programs.

There is an interesting point of comparison here. Although social justice and political freedom coincide in the fact that both impede growth, they are not functionally synonymous. Social justice and political freedom are separate phenomenons that interact somewhat differently with the growth dynamics of Latin American nations and affect different groups within their populations. Social inequity is a result of the fundamental way which modern capitalist development has built upon and exaggerated the highly unequal patterns of a colonial past, producing a vicious circle of wealth that enables two decades of vigorous economic growth to bypass 75 percent of all citizens. Recent stabilization policies have worsened the situation, but in a fundamental sense the social welfare issue reaches way back into the past and is first and foremost an issue of the masses. Political freedoms and civil liberties, on the other hand, constitute a set of rights that are most relevant to the elite (the 25 percent of the population that is integrated into the modern urban economy), and these rights have been most conspicuously violated in the recent past. True, colonial regimes were not generous in their allocation of political and civil freedoms, but in the 1940s, 1950s, and 1960s many Latin American countries did institutionalize a type of democracy that gave the normal menu of political rights and civil liberties to their articulate urban populations. As we now know, the structural crises of the

1960s and 1970s made a new and more ruthless form of political repression a necessary condition for continued economic success.

Let us now turn the question of longevity. How durable are these social and political costs of growth in Latin America? Two factors lead to rather pessimistic conclusions in the social welfare sphere. First, the origins of modern development processes are both complex and deeply rooted in the historical evolution of these countries—economic structures, power relations, and ideologies all played a part in the creation of a highly polarized society. Second, the specifics of industrial takeoff and the emergence of a vicious circle of wealth have created a situation where rapid economic growth is a self-contained and exclusive process that seems capable of permanently bypassing the bulk of the populace.

In the sphere of political freedoms and civil liberties, the outlook is a little less gloomy. Many of the more repressive measures have been linked to the ruthless stabilization programs of the 1960s and 1970s. It is at least conceivable that various Latin American nations will enter periods where their growth strategies are less prone to inflationary and balance-of-payments difficulties. But we must remember that even when favorable has probably delayed the coming of an easier era, but capitalist growth is a cyclical phenomenon and balmy days will return, at least for a while. At such a time, it might prove possible to relax political controls and allow the population a greater measure of political freedom and civil liberty. It is as though these political rights were luxuries in the capitalist Third World, affordable when economies are booming and when growth strategies are not threatened by the twin evils of inflation and balance-of-payments difficulties. But we must remember than even when favorable economic circumstances permit such luxuries, they tend to benefit elite groups. Freedom of the press is after all of rather limited significance to most citizens in countries where only a tiny percentage of households read newspapers. For the majority of the people in Latin America, many of whom are struggling with basic survival issues, social justice has to be of more immediate concern than political freedom and civil liberty.

POLICY OPTIONS FOR THE UNITED STATES

By now it should be clear that recent discussion in American foreign policy circles on the issue of human rights in Latin America has failed to take into consideration the massive economic and political costs of more humane policies.

Widespread (and in some cases deepening) poverty and political repression are much more than the idiosyncratic preferences of a few military leaders and are rarely susceptible to "jaw boning" by well-meaning leaders of advanced democracies. The problem of human rights in Latin America can only be tackled on a much more fundamental plane and involves such basic issues as the design and goals of development strategies. But what role can the U.S. government play at this deeper level of causality? Once again, it is useful to distinguish between the social and political spheres of human rights.

On social justice, it should be clear from the argument spelled out above that the massive poverty and increasing inequality typical of so many Latin American nations is a deeply rooted, phenomenon. Unequal development became entrenched during a colonial, primary exporting era and was exacerbated by the import substituting strategies of the modern period. Changing such a highly inequitable pattern of growth involves a profound restructuring of the economy and of society. For example, a more egalitarian development trajectory could imply a mix of large-scale land reform (to equalize incomes in the rural sector) and labor-intensive industrialization (to provide employment and a reasonable standard of living for the urban masses).

But it is not at all obvious that it is either possible or likely that the United States would foster such a program. True, U.S. aid could be (and indeed sometimes is) tied to particular schemes deemed to have a positive social welfare effect—primary school education is a popular target. But it is difficult to imagine the United States lending wholehearted support to something as fundamental as thoroughgoing land reform. For the crux of the matter is that the United States, and the advanced capitalist world in general, has a great deal of vested interest in maintaining stable, pro-growth regimes in Latin America that are sympathetic to such crucial concerns as foreign investment. Large-scale land reform is intrinsically destabilizing and almost inevitably means a lurch to the left in the domestic balance of political power. This is an excellent example of the way in which economic self-interest can fly in the face of equity considerations.

In the sphere of industrialization policies, the potential conflict of interest is even more stark. Let us take the example of multinational corporations operating in Latin America. These firms are rational economic actors that would be quite willing to experiment with more labor-intensive production techniques if they had a sufficiently compelling incentive to do so, but there are severe barriers involving both production and consumption.

Of all industrial research and development, 98 percent has been undertaken in advanced nations and is geared to the factor endowments of these rich countries.[26] It therefore makes sense for a multinational corporation to capitalize on this accumulated vested interest and to transfer well-tried, rich country products with their sophisticated capital-intensive technologies to Latin America. This type of industrialization has many negative social welfare repercussions for the host country but nevertheless is generally the one that prevails because it involves zero marginal costs for the firms concerned. However, if some international agency, or the Carter administration for that matter, were to step in and provide a massive subsidy for research and development in labor-intensive technology, industrialization strategies could begin to change.

But a stickier problem would have to be solved before industrialization in capitalist developing countries would benefit the masses; this problem revolves around the question of effective demand. As stated earlier, multinational corporations moved into Latin America in the modern period in order to satisfy the demand for sophisticated goods emanating from an elite group. It thus becomes apparent that without the initial step of income redistribution it is difficult to change the product mix and the production technologies of multinational firms. At the present time, income in many Latin American nations is so highly concentrated (the top 10 percent of the population often appropriates one half of national income)[27] that the elite market in these countries is capable of reproducing the demand characteristics of the mass market in rich countries. In short, effective demand calls for the very group of sophisticated products already manufactured by the multinational firm, and there is very little incentive from consumers to change the status quo. However, if income were redistributed so that the most significant demand for goods in Latin America was generated by the masses clustered around the national average income (generally $700 to $1,000 per year) demand would tend to be for a range of wage goods (textiles, furniture, footwear, utensils) characterized by labor-intensive production techniques. Such large-scale employment creation obviously would reinforce the egalitarian aspects of the initial redistribution.

To sum up this complex picture, a crucial cause of uneven and unequal growth in Latin America is the vicious circle of wealth set up by capital-intensive industrial structures that produce sophisticated consumer goods for an elite market. One way for an external agent to break into this circle and increase social welfare in Latin America would be to subsidize massively the development of more appropriate technologies (in particular, more labor-intensive technologies). However, this would not be enough; a reorientation toward a low technology, labor-intensive industrial structure would only make sense in a context of income redistribution and the emergence of a mass market for wage goods.

How can the US government (or any other external political force) advance the cause of income redistribution? Moral suasion clearly is not enough. The autocratic leaders of Latin America are unlikely to be convinced that income redistribution is a necessary step in their national development programs, for the very simple reason that few of them attach any weight to the social welfare dimension of economic growth. Their primary aim is to grow, as rapidly and as expediently as possible, and the last thing many of them want to do is to stir up a hornet's nest in the form of a more prosperous and more demanding lower class. At best, the political rhetoric of Latin American authoritarian regimes has stressed that equity considerations can be worried about at some future time when the national pie is larger. Many have borrowed the false historical analogy discussed earlier. For example, in the early 1970s Delfim Netto, the finance minister of the Medici administration, excused Brazil's poor performance in the equity sphere on the grounds that this was a short-run and inevitable cost of growth reminiscent of the experience of advanced countries. In a famous statement, he proclaimed that at present redistributional policies would only serve to "divide up the misery more equally."[28]

If so little headway can be made with the contemporary set of military dictatorships in Latin America, there remains the route of regime change. The U.S. government could attempt to force a shift to the left in domestic power structures—toward more democratic governments that might be expected to place greater weight on redistributional policies.

But this scenario raises serious problems. In the aftermath of Vietnam, it is extremely unlikely that the United States would or could contemplate that degree of interference in the internal affairs of any nation. Second, even if this role were feasible, the economic costs and political risks of such a route would be prohibitive. To speculate on a few: Leftwing regimes and redistributional policies would mean the drying up of the market for U.S.-style goods and an expensive redesigning of the technology used by multinational firms; a much more nationalistic stance on such questions as the role and terms of entry of foreign capital; and more restrictions on the control and use of natural resources. In addition, there would be the ever-present threat of a further swerve to the left, the emergence of a socialist state, and the consequent expropriation of foreign interests (Cuba in the post-1959 period is of course the prime example, although post-1968 Peru partially followed this route).

We may safely say that no U.S. administration has been or is willing to incur these types of costs and risks in the name of enhanced social welfare for the citizens of Latin America. Indeed, in recent decades the most conspicious examples of U.S. interference with the internal politics of Latin American nations have involved the encouragement of shifts to the right. In several cases—Brazil in 1964, Chile in 1973—such policies were triggered by the apparent need to counter the leftwing and redistributional threat posed by João Goulart and Salvador Allende. In essence, these interventions constituted an attempt to avoid the economic costs and political risks outlined above, particularly those implicit in pro-worker and pro-peasant programs. Thus, despite the U.S. commitment on the level of principle to alleviating poverty in Latin America (which certainly was present long before the Carter initiative), the hard facts of political and economic self-interest have, and most probably will, determine the formulation of policy.

In the sphere of political rights and civil liberties, the realistic scope for U.S. foreign policy initiatives is greater, primarily because the issues involved are considerably less fundamental. As we now know, the recent history of many Latin American nations illustrates that for considerable periods of time it has proved possible to award the normal menu of political and civil rights to discrete groups within the population—generally the articulate urban classes. This was particularly true during the phase of easy import substitution, before mounting inflationary and balance-of-payments problems made populist politics an unaffordable luxury. Effective stabilization means suppression of wages, budget cutting, credit restrictions, and higher taxation. All these measures are inherently unpopular and in many Latin American contexts can be carried out only by repressive authoritarian governments that are both willing and able to suspend many political rights and civil liberties. To illustrate these interconnections, significant wage suppression often means sapping the strength of trade union structures, imprisoning the more active labor leaders (without trial), and a degree of press censorship. In the same vein, eliminating public sector jobs and increasing effective taxation rates—both of which are essential steps in controlling inflation via a balanced budget—are rarely feasible policy options in Latin American nations if the government of the day has to face elections. Such steps toward what the International Monetary Fund (IMF) calls "fiscal responsibility" tend to be prerogatives of autocratic governments, which by eliminating many types of political rights are able to ignore public opinion.

Political repression in Latin America therefore can be viewed as a function of ruthless economic policies designed to combat inflation and balance-of-payments difficulties and to allow the country concerned to enter a new cycle of economic growth. These policies are subject to modification on two fronts.

First, the need for draconian stabilization measures may well be intermittent. For example, Brazil between 1964 and 1967 did manage to tame inflation, and in early 1974 when domestic growth was exuberant the Ernesto Geisel government did begin to experiment with various types of political freedoms. This particular liberalization drive was dampened by the 1974–75 oil-induced world recession, and subsequent attempts to open the political system have been compounded by new waves of domestic inflation and renewed balance-of-payments pressures. This example emphasizes a point made earlier. Capitalist growth is a cyclical phenomenon and it is at least conceivable that various Latin American nations will enter periods where their growth strategies are less prone to inflationary and balance-of-payments distortions. In short, the constraints of the 1960s and 1970s will be replaced at least temporarily by more balmy days, which may be more compatible with political freedoms.

Second, the political costs of economic crises in the Third World can be modified by external forces. The IMF, for example, often has designed stabilization programs for Latin American nations and made financial assistance contingent upon carrying out these programs. While various forms of austerity are essential ingredients in any inflation-control package, it is increasingly felt that the IMF cracks down too hard and too quickly for the political health of Latin American nations.[29] In other words, if stabilization programs were more gradualistic and if international lenders were willing to coexist with slightly higher rates of inflation for longer periods of time, regimes in Latin America would not be called upon to enact such extreme policies and might be able to retain a wider spectrum of political rights and civil liberties.

It also is possible to trace a direct connection between U.S. foreign policy and the political costs of economic crises in Latin America. For instance, the United States is capable of ameliorating the balance-of-payments problems of these countries. In the recent past, an easing of U.S. import restrictions on manufactured exports of Third World nations would have compensated in part for the huge increases in the import bills of these countries' in the wake of the oil crisis; this in turn might have precluded some of the harsher policy stances of the last few years. But this leads once more to the crucial issue of vested interests. The United States has had its own economic problems as a result of the oil crisis, including a trade deficit, and these problems have prompted an actual tightening of trade restrictions as external account problems have made the U.S. Congress more than usually sympathetic to appeals from industry for greater protection. In short, policy once again has been guided by national self-interest rather than high-minded notions of the importance of political rights in Latin America or any other part of the Third World.

In conclusion, it should be stressed that social justice and political freedom are separate phenomena. Not only do they interact somewhat differently with the growth dynamics of Latin American nations and affect different groups within their populations but they have quite different implications for foreign policy. The U.S. attitude is capable of affecting the issues of civil liberty and political freedom, and constructive action is a feasible—if not likely—policy outcome. But on the social welfare front, the problems are too fundamental to be addressed by marginal foreign policy changes. To put this distinction in concrete terms, a milder stabilization program (promoted by U.S. policy) would reduce the need for wage suppression and would lessen the need to clamp down on unions and labor leaders, but it would do nothing to alleviate the massive poverty afflicting 75 percent of the population in most Latin American countries. This latter condition is a function of political priorities and national development strategies over which the U.S. government can exercise no beneficial influence for the simple reason that such action would involve prohibitive costs and risks.

Understanding these points helps explain what is perhaps the most contradictory element in recent policy initiatives in the sphere of human rights. In the fall of 1977 President Carter signed the UN Covenant on

Economic and Social Rights—after it had been rejected by three previous administrations—finally acknowledging that social justice and the "right to the fulfillment of such vital needs as food, shelter, health care, and education" were legitimate items on the human rights agenda.[30] As Carter has put it: "More than 100 years ago Abraham Lincoln said that our nation could not exist half slave and half free. We know that a peaceful world cannot long exist one-third rich and two-thirds poor."[31]

However, the Carter Administration "has not been forthcoming with plans to restructure the international economy so as to give poor countries a favorable prospect for solving problems of domestic poverty."[32] It should be clear from the arguments spelled out here that massive poverty and increasing inequality are deeply rooted phenomena and doing anything about them would involve the U.S. government in serious economic costs and political risks. No wonder "the expansion of the conception of human rights to include economic rights has been mostly verbal up to this point and hardly evident in policy settings."[33]

NOTES

1. I. ADELMAN and C. TAFT MORRIS, ECONOMIC GROWTH AND SOCIAL EQUITY IN DEVELOPING COUNTRIES 192-94 (1973).
2. *See, for example,* H. CHENERY *et. al.*, REDISTRIBUTION WITH GROWTH (1974).
3. *See* A. FISHLOW, *Brazilian Size Distribution of Income,* 62 AM. ECON. REV. 391-402 (May 1972); A. BERRY and M. UNRUTIA, INCOME DISTRIBUTION IN COLOMBIA (1976).
4. T. CARLYLE, PAST AND PRESENT 5 (1967).
5. S. Kuznets, *Economic Growth and Income Inequality,* 45 AM. ECON REV. 18 (March 1955).
6. *See* A. B. ATKINSON, THE ECONOMICS OF INEQUALITY (1975), for the British data; and L. C. THUROW, GENERATING INEQUALITY (1975), for the U.S. data.
7. KUZNETS, *Supra* note 5, at 25.
8. H. G. JOHNSON, MONEY, TRADE AND ECONOMIC GROWTH 153 (1962).
9. In this study I restrict the use of the phrase "late development" to countries of the Third World that began industrialization in the 1930s and 1940s. In some rigorous sense, they perhaps should be called late, late developers (southern Europe and the Soviet Union being the original late developers). This distinction is irrelevant to my argument.
10. H. ARENDT, ON REVOLUTION 55 (1963).
11. *Id.*, at 58.
12. A similar proposal has been put forward in T. H. MARSHALL, CITIZENSHIP AND SOCIAL CLASS (1950).
13. These figures are taken from M. LIPTON, WHY PEOPLE STAY POOR 39-41 (1977).
14. KUZNETS, *Supra* note 5, at 25.
15. E. J. HOBSBAWM, LABORING MEN: STUDIES IN THE HISTORY OF LABOR 272 (1964).
16. P. Streeten, *Social Science Research on Development: Some Problems in the Use and Transfer of an Intellectual Technology,* J. OF ECON. LIT., 1290 (Dec. 1974).
17. A. GERSCHENKRON, ECONOMIC BACKWARDNESS IN HISTORICAL PERSPECTIVE 6 (1965).
18. S. Schwartzman, *Back to Weber: Corporatism and Patrimonialism in the Seventies,* AUTHORITARIANISM AND CORPORATISM IN LATIN AMERICA 89 (J. Malloy ed. 1977).
19. This has been recognized in some recent writings; *see, for example,* A. O. HIRSCHMAN, THE TURN TO AUTHORITARIANISM IN LATIN AMERICA AND THE SEARCH FOR ITS

ECONOMIC DETERMINANTS (Feb. 1977) (mimeo of the Institute for Advanced Study, Princeton).

20. ARENDT, *supra* note 10, at 54.

21. The consensus in the developed world seems to be that material deprivation is an entirely relative phenomenon. A classic article on this subject is Townsend, *The Meaning of Poverty,* 13 BRIT. J. OF SOCIOLOGY 210-27 (1962). Townsend argues that "both 'poverty' and 'subsistence' are relative concepts and that they can only be defined in relation to the material and emotional resources available at a particular time to the members of either a particular society or different societies." (*Id.,* at 210.) In the developing world, the consensus is that both absolute and relative criteria are relevant to understanding the meaning of poverty. For example, the universal declaration refers to the minimum requirements for sustaining physical life—health, food, housing, clothing, work, and literacy—as absolute human rights.

22. For convenient texts of the universal declaration and covenants, *see* BASIC DOCUMENTS IN INTERNATIONAL LAW 144-86 (2d ed. I. Brownlie ed. 1972).

23. A good example of this school of thought is R. J. BARNET and R. E. MULLER, GLOBAL REACH (1974).

24. A comprehensive list of countries that went through severe stabilization programs in order to combat inflation and balance of payments difficulties in the 1960s and 1970s is contained in R. N. Bee, *Lessons from Debt Reschedulings in the Past,* EUROMONEY (April 1977).

25. Brazil is such a "success" story. After a three-year stabilization period (1964-67), the economy moved forward into an extended period of extremely rapid growth based on export-orientated policies. So successful was the 1968-74 period that it often is called the "economic miracle."

26. F. Stewart, *Technology and Employment in LDC's,* in EMPLOYMENT IN DEVELOPING NATIONS 117 (E. O. Edwards ed. 1974).

27. *See* ADELMAN AND MORRIS, *supra* note 1.

28. *See* C. GERALDO LANGONI, DISTRIBUICÃO DA RENDA E DESENVOLVIMENTO ECONOMICO DO BRASIL 13 (1973).

29. A recent article, *Price is High for IMF Loans,* N.Y. Times, Dec. 4, 1977, § 4, at 3, stresses the fact that recent austerity measures insisted on by the IMF tend to "strain already weak democratic structures."

30. Cyrus R. Vance, *Human Rights Policy,* speech delivered on Law Day at the University of Georgia Law School (April 30, 1977, Athens, Georgia; Department of State: Bureau of Public Affairs).

31. J. Carter, speech at Notre Dame (May 22, 1977), *quoted in* 76 DEP'T STATE BULL. 624 (1977).

32. R. Falk, "Ideological Patterns in the United States Human Rights Debate: 1945-1978," at 22 (1978; mimeo, Departmetn of Politics, Princeton University.

33. *Id.*

Chapter 8

POLICY IMPLICATIONS OF THE POSSIBLE CONFLICT BETWEEN CAPITALIST DEVELOPMENT AND HUMAN RIGHTS IN DEVELOPING COUNTRIES

Tom J. Farer

Estimates of the longevity and salience of human rights objectives must rest on an understanding of their place within the framework of foreign policy, of the national interests they serve or express, and of their domestic constituencies. Stanley Hoffman notes that human rights fit neatly into neither of the great, organizing categories of contemporary international relations: on the one hand, "the politics of conflict between the chief rivals . . . the traditional state-of-war aspects of international relations" and on the other, "world order concerns [whose] ultimate objective is accommodation" rather than enhancing our own options and constraining those of potential opponents.[1]

Although Hoffman seems to believe that the human rights issue comes closer to the cooperative rather than the competitive aspects of foreign policy, it is nevertheless incongruent with the former because it "breeds confrontation. Raising the issue touches on the very foundations of a regime, on its sources and exercise of power, on its links to its citizens or subjects."[2]

That is precisely the thrust that so infatuates cold warriors of the Daniel Patrick Moynihan school. For them, human rights are a political instrument, a means of "ideological resistance" to communism.

As an available weapon in the presumably apocalyptic struggle against "totalitarian communism," human rights certainly have a future in a country where the executive branch still gets its greatest support from Congress when tensions with Moscow are highest. Of course, it also has a long if not altogether distinguished past. The OAS resolution excluding "the present government of Cuba from participation in the Inter-American System"—in support of which the United States was joined by several of the most repugnant dictatorships in Latin America—referred in its preamble to "respect for the freedom of man and preservation of his rights and the full exercise of representative democracy" as objectives and principles of the system. By implication, Cuba was a unique apostate from these high ends.

Like other great powers, the United States has invoked widely shared moral ideals to justify the pursuit of crasser interests. Perhaps more than others, it has confused the two. The lofty tone of Theodore Roosevelt's corollary is one among a legion of examples. Moynihan's conception of human rights as an ideological shillelagh seems to have roots in this grand tradition of mixing moral enthusiasm and conventional Great Power interests. The alternative conception of human rights—jeeringly indicted by Moynihan as "a humanitarian aid program, a special kind of international social work"—has a decidedly more problematic connection with conventional conceptions of what constitutes an advantage in the game of nations.

These two views of human rights must coexist uneasily. Those who agree with the Moynihan faction—that U.S. fear of communism has never been and cannot be inordinate, that the East-West competition overshadows every other international issue, that U.S. relations with Third World states must vary with their support in that struggle, and that rightwing regimes are in principle less obnoxious than leftwing authoritarians inevitably will oppose serious sanctions against anticommunist regimes. For one does not beat "allies" about the head. Conversely, those who, reversing Moynihan's deprecatory idiom, believe the main aim should be "to be of help to individuals," will conclude that, regardless of a government's stance in the ideological cold war, the United States should enjoy comparatively good relations with it as long as it does not torture, murder, or arbitrarily imprison masses of its people.

Slavering anticommunism expresses fractures in the U.S. body politic—conflicts of race, ethnicity, region, culture, and class that by their nature will not heal. Conventionally, they are cited in terms of left and right. The symbolism of human rights is profoundly important to both sides. Their endless conflict assures a permanent set of antagonistic domestic constituencies who will keep the issue alive. Occasionally, because of the need to appeal to the political middle and because there always will be Cambodias to pair off against South Africas, they apparently will even lend joint support to human rights initiatives.

Paradoxically, a humanitarian approach to human rights may be a more effective way of defending capitalism than the discriminatory, polemical manipulation of the issue seemingly urged by Moynihan. Equating capitalism with political freedom strengthens capitalism's moral legitimacy. When self-styled Marxist governments stifle elementary freedoms, they confirm the proposed equation. It is threatened, conversely, by the delinquencies of rightwing governments marching

---

*Those who believe all that, of course, would believe anything.

under the capitalist banner, even extolling the libertarian virtues of "free enterprise." In exemplifying the possible coexistence, if not the enthusiastic collaboration, of a capitalist economic system and a brutish political order, such governments inflict more ideological injury on the capitalist cause than the venomous polemics of its avowed Marxist enemies. So an evenhanded, humanitarian approach may be attractive to conservatives as a means of strengthening both domestic capitalism (in its struggle against the sort of democratic socialism covertly espoused by populists and left-liberals) and the United States in its competitive relations with the Soviet Union.

But the attractions of this approach to enlightened conservatives could prove evanescent, resting as they do on the hope that democracy and the capitalist growth model will not prove incompatible in most of the Third World. Once a widespread and enduring incompatibility were generally recognized, human rights would be seen to threaten both the ideological and material interests of international capitalism. For any campaign on their behalf then would focus attention on the incompatibility and, to the extent it was successful in opening up political systems, would release forces propelling governments toward socialist development models.

The degree and incidence of injury to capitalist interests in the United States resulting from a change in growth models is unclear. At a minimum, the change would hurt corporations supplying luxury consumer goods to Third World elites, since socialist regimes would reduce the income disparities that enable the upper classes to maintain living standards comparable to those enjoyed by the vast middle classes in affluent countries. Moreover, by decommercializing the communications media—that is, by barring their use to predetermine consumer preference—socialist regimes would reduce the profit margins of companies that rely heavily on the creation of consumer preference for brand names in order to reduce effective competition among essentially similar goods. This would adversely affect a number of U.S.-based multinational corporations. Furthermore, by favoring agricultural production for local consumption over export-oriented agriculture, a socialist regime would reduce foreign exchange earnings and thereby possibly jeopardize the country's capacity to service loans from the U.S. private sector and to permit the repatriation of income earned by subsidiaries of U.S. corporations. But this change in orientation would not necessarily injure U.S. agricultural exports because demand for food products, released by the redistribution of income to the hungry classes, might far outstrip the growth of local production.

In any event, the assumption that a socialist model is undesirable for the national interest shapes U.S. foreign policy. That assumption has deep and, at least in the short run, seemingly unshakable roots. And so the odds against the continued prominence of human rights in U.S. foreign policy will lessen if there is a slump in confidence about the compatibility of human rights and Third World capitalism.

Although Sylvia Hewlett presents a strong case for pessimism in the preceding chapter, at this point it is possible to remain agnostic. The case possibly exaggerates certain differences between the European and the Third World setting and does not take entirely convincing account of such new factors as the egalitarian ideology that seems to have displaced the nineteenth century's reigning emphasis on individual autonomy. Another new factor is the capacity of the state apparatus, particularly in the more advanced developing countries, to accumulate and invest capital; growth is no longer at the mercy of the marginal propensity of the affluent to save. Yet another novel factor rich in unpredictable implications is the emergence of the military as an independent social group with passions, interests, and ambitions that are not invariably congruent with those of the moneyed classes.

On the other hand, the fact that a handful of Third World capitalist states—Taiwan, Singapore, perhaps South Korea—have managed to incorporate most of the population into the modern industrial sector and to place a floor under extreme poverty should not weigh heavily against the pessimists. The fact that all are within the Chinese cultural zone, that two are comparatively small, that two were beneficiaries of extraordinarily large amounts of foreign aid, that all possess relatively sophisticated, well-organized, and homogeneous populations, that the two larger ones were at a critical time extremely susceptible to the reforming advice of their U.S. advisers—these facts make them seem if not sui generis then at least very far removed from the situation in most of Latin America.

Nevertheless, given our natural and tremendous collective urge to believe in the compatibility of human rights and Third World capitalism, we are bound to flatten compromising distinctions and hence to magnify the promise of these success stories. Economic failure and political atrocities in self-proclaimed Marxist states among the developing countries reinforce our national faith in the virtues of the capitalist model wherever it may be employed. The high degree of state intervention even in regimes purportedly capitalist, such as Brazil, provides additional protection against the demoralizing conclusion that the free market may not always maximize the potential for human freedom and dignity.

If it is correct that the U.S. public generally will remain unimpressed by theories of conflict between Third World capitalism and human rights, the prospects for holding together a liberal-conservative coalition on human rights are favorable. And this in turn makes it likely that human rights will not soon be driven off the list of foreign policy objectives.

NOTES

1. S. Hoffman, *The Hell of Good Intentions*, 29 FOREIGN POLICY 7–8 (Winter 1977–78).
2. *Id.*

Chapter 9

HUMAN RIGHTS AND THE INTER-AMERICAN SYSTEM

Bryce Wood

INTRODUCTION

A Controversial Agency

The Inter-American Commission on Human Rights (IACHR) since 1973 has become the most controversial institution within the Organization of American States (OAS). Controversy over policies and jurisdiction occurs, of course, in other OAS agencies, but nowhere does it equal the bitterness of the attack upon the fundamental attributes of the IACHR.

The formal objective of the commission is bland enough: "to promote respect for human rights." The tension has arisen from two main developments: first, the establishment of military governments in major South American countries since 1963 and the unprecedented number and severity of their violations of human rights; second, the vigor and courage demonstrated by the commission in interpreting its mandate "to promote."

The confrontation might have been avoided had the Latin American governments been able to maintain their refusal, until 1976, to permit discussion of the annual IACHR reports in the OAS General Assembly, or had the IACHR limited itself to undifferentiated remonstrances and pious exhortations. However, the worldwide publicity given the inhumane treatment of thousands of political opponents by the military regime in Chile after September 1973 made it impossible for the OAS to ignore the commission's report in 1976, and the commission itself has issued reports on the situation in Chile and other countries that are strongly accusatory of the regimes, buttressed by specifics on means of torture and names of persons who have been arrested or have "disappeared." Denunciations of the commission by the Chilean government have not silenced its members, and in 1978 reports on human rights in Paraguay and Uruguay accused each government of "serious violations" of the rights of their citizens as set forth in the American Declaration of the Rights and Duties of Man, to which the governments are signatories. The governments have replied—denying some accusations, defending themselves against others, and questioning the authority of the IACHR to pursue its course of action.

In establishing the commission, the OAS members accepted the risk of creating tensions. There is tension between the expression in the OAS Charter of the intent to promote human rights, and the evident failure of some governments to evince a modicum of respect for them. By the very nature of its mission, the commission's slightest initiatives may run counter to the vital interests of governments contributing to its support. Some of the issues have been starkly depicted by Ben Stephansky:

> Several countries in Latin America are governed by cruel and oppressive political regimes, which have virtually enshrined the erosion of human rights as a matter of ideological principle. Brazil considers the violation of human rights a necessary condition for economic development; Chile conceives it as a "state of war" to extirpate a socialist ideology; Bolivia regards it as a principle of political stability, as do other military regimes.[1]

Cuba also might have been included here as having violated human rights as part of the process of building a communist society.

Another source of tension is a product of changes in the orientation of governments over time. The social and political climate in Latin America in the late 1950s, when several notorious dictators were overthrown, was strongly supportive of the establishment of the IACHR in 1960. More recently, the new challenge from the extreme left, with spreading use of terrorism by right and left, has caused violent reactions from governments in some countries where there is little or no observance of human rights. A study of the deterioration of the older, more tolerant ambiente from 1960 to the present would be of great interest, not only with respect to human rights. Eight of the ten South American states are now controlled by military regimes.

Finally, there is tension because the IACHR is an institutional anomaly. The OAS is an organization of sovereign states, intended to foster the economic, political, and social concerns of governments, that is, of those in control of governmental machinery at any given time. The IACHR is an agency comprising seven persons, named in their independent capacities and not as representatives of governments. The essential function of the commission requires it to conduct inquiries, ask questions of, and make recommendations to governments on behalf of individuals who may be political enemies. Small wonder then that it may come to be viewed as a source of harassment, annoyance, exposure, and interference by some of the very governments voting in the Permanent Council for its statute and providing funds for its operation. The commission is a self-induced, benign boil upon the body politic of the OAS, no less resented because of the legitimacy and impartiality of its prickling.

In the Americas, where politics in some countries are a bitter competition among nominally democratic parties where the winner takes all or nearly all; or a ferocious struggle among rival military groups; or determined efforts by an entrenched family or authoritarian regime to maintain its privileged position against any challenge, issues of human rights become matters of the survival of ruling groups, or exile, or loss of property. When political moderation cannot be anticipated from a change of regime, a deep concern for the protection of the human rights of opponents is rare among those in control of supreme power. Happily, some OAS members fall outside the above categories, and it is due to this group's support for international efforts to defend human rights that the IACHR was created in the first place and has been able, surprisingly, to survive for nearly two decades.

But the commission's future is highly uncertain, due to the coming into force of the American Convention on Human Rights on July 18, 1978, with the deposit of the ratification of Grenada, which was preceded by ratifications by Colombia, Costa Rica, Ecuador, El Salvador, Guatemala, Haiti, Honduras, Panama, Dominican Republic, and Venezuela. The commission now is endowed with a treaty, as distinct from its past statutory legitimacy—but only among the ratifiers of the convention. The question will then be raised of whether the commission will retain its current authority to investigate and issue reports on the situation with respect to human rights in nonratifiers of the convention, which include Argentina, Brazil, Chile, Mexico, Uruguay, Paraguay, and the United States.

In a fairly narrow sense as dealt with by the IACHR, human rights are claims by individual persons for areas of freedom from control or domination by governments. They represent assertions by individuals that governments cannot do some things to them. Governments may tax, but they must not torture. Governments may detain, but they must justify imprisonment fairly, grant amparo or habeas corpus, afford equitable circumstances of trial before members of an impartial judiciary.

The ultimate demands of people—the consent of the governed—have been enshrined in bills of rights, declarations of rights, and constitutions of modern states since 1776 in the United States, 1789 in France, and 1824 in Latin American countries; they find their origins as far back as Grecian views of democracy or liberties hard-wrung from British sovereigns in the thirteenth century.

In a much broader sense, therefore, the very persistence of these claims for freedom means that their minimal observance is essential to the operation of any society that is responsive to the needs of all its sectors and allows their free expression.

But these traditional libertarian, civil, and political rights are not the only human rights for which claims have been made. There is a whole range of economic, social, and cultural rights that have been given attention in various international instruments completed in the past half-century. These include the right of association, promoted by the International Labor Organization, and those rights included in the Inter-American Charter on Social Guarantees. The civic and political rights are primarily negative defenses against governmental oppression; the economic and social rights are primarily positive demands upon governmental assistance for a more equitable distribution of benefits. Of the former, several are usually described as "basic," and for the OAS, the IACHR has been directed to devote special attention to those provided for in Articles 1 (life), 2 (equality before the law), 3 (religion), 4 (speech), 18 (right to a fair trial), 25 (right of freedom from arbitrary arrest), and 26 (right to due process of law) of the American Declaration of the Rights and Duties of Man. The protection of these rights has been especially although not exclusively entrusted by the OAS to the IACHR. The fostering of other rights is the concern of the Economic and Social Council and other agencies within the OAS system.

Enshrinement in a nation's fundamental documents does not necessarily ensure observance of human rights, even in countries professing to follow the Western liberal tradition. The constitutional guarantee does not always stay the truncheon. In every society the tree of liberty may need to be watered by the blood, not only of patriots but also of local defenders of civil liberties. Foreign or "mother country" oppression is not alone to be dreaded and resisted; the enemy may be in the homeland.

Until fairly recent times, the treatment a sovereign government accorded its citizens, however deplorable, was not regarded as a legitimate concern of other governments. But World War II atrocities, brought about a change, and the charters of the United Nations and OAS, and the Genocide Convention, express a concern by governments for the universal protection of human rights. These treaties were followed by declarations of human rights, and then by conventions establishing institutions and procedures having as their main objective the provision of assistance to individuals to defend their basic rights against encroachment by their own officialdom.

Nearly all governments were willing to sign the idealistic, nonobligatory statements of intent to observe the rights of persons mentioned in the new charters and in the several declarations of the rights and duties of man. But signing conventions creating institutions was another matter, and action was markedly different in the several regions. Western European countries have created a highly sophisticated, formal system for international protection of human rights; it has little to do because the member states, except for Greece, have been accustomed to give such sympathetic application of the rule of law that the Court of Human Rights, thus far the only international institution of its kind, has had to deal with very few cases in its first decade. In other words, in Western Europe the international protection of human rights has been nearly unnecessary because the governments and the national systems of law and police administration are so well attuned to responding to popular demands that appeals for justice to any supranational authority have been relatively rare. Elements of cost of litigation and scope of jurisdiction enter here, but the basic factor seems to be the existence of substantial justice and humane practice at the national level. But it should be noted that the European court recently required the government of the United Kingdom to discontinue certain "deprivations" and other practices employed by its police in endeavoring to secure information from terrorists in Northern Ireland.

The situation is rather different elsewhere. Not in Africa nor Asia nor Eastern Europe is there a regional international system aimed at the defense of individuals against arbitrary action by their governments. On the other hand, in the Americas there are provisions of the Charter of Bogotá; there is an American Declaration of the Rights and Duties of Man; there is an American Convention on Human Rights that is now in force among 11 states; and there is an institution, a "principal organ" of the OAS, the Inter-American Commission on Human Rights.

There also is a United Nations Commission on Human Rights (UNCHR) that, after an initial period of ineffectiveness, has since the mid-1960s given its principal attention to problems of racial discrimination in Rhodesia and South Africa. However, in 1974 and 1975 the UNCHR also passed resolutions condemning Chile's record of violating human rights. The UNCHR, however, is composed of governmental delegates and, as a political body, it is to be distinguished from the largely nonpolitical group of individuals forming the IACHR.

SOME ASPECTS OF THE IACHR RECORD

The creation of the IACHR may be traced to motivations productive of the Universal Declaration of Human Rights and the Genocide Convention. As early as 1902 the American states signed a Convention Relative to the Rights of Aliens; several conventions on rights of women were signed at subsequent conferences; and the Lima conference of 1938 approved a resolution on the defense of human rights. In consequence of World War II, the notion became widely held that governments most observant of human rights were least likely to attack their neighbors.

More specifically, in the late 1950s several American countries threw off the yokes of dictatorship—Peru and Venezuela, for example—and some of the new regimes included statesmen who sought to encourage internatonal efforts to promote the observance of human rights in the Western Hemisphere. The urge was not new, since it can be traced to the Rodríguez Larreta Doctrine of 1946, the OAS Charter, and the American Declaration of the Rights and Duties of Man of May 2, 1948, which was signed some seven months before the Universal Declaration of Human Rights.

The new support for protection of human rights by means of international agreements and institutions attained such proportions by the summer of 1959 that the Fifth Meeting of Consultation of Ministers of Foreign Affairs of the American Republics adopted the Declaration of Santiago for the promotion of human rights. It also passed resolutions calling for the drafting of a convention on human rights and for the creation of a commission whose precise character and functions would be defined by the OAS Council until the convention came into effect. The statute defining the commission's role was approved by the Permanent Council in June 1960 and the IACHR held its first meeting later that year. As a result of a combination of factors including the energetic but prudent activity of the commission and its own liberal interpretation of its original mandate, its capabilities were broadened significantly at the Second Special Inter-American Conference at Rio de Janeiro in November 1965. The new powers were contained in Article 9(bis) of the statute.[2] Instead of listing these powers in formal fashion, there follows an informal analysis of commission capabilities that is derived less from the statute and regulations than from an examination of what it actually has done.

In a formal sense, OAS arrangements for protection of human rights have been far less structured than those of the European commission. For example, the European commission can make recommendations to the Committee of Ministers of the Council of Europe or to the Court of Human Rights, which may make decisions ranging from ordering a state to pay compensation to an individual whose rights have been infringed to suspending the country from participation in the council, as in the case of Greece. Further, the European Convention on Human Rights is in force among nearly all members of the council. By contrast, the convention among the American states is just entering into force, less than half the OAS members have approved it, there is yet no court, and it is doubtful that the OAS Permanent Council has power to coerce a member state over violations of human rights. Nor has it ever shown the slightest desire even to condemn a member in such a case.

Informally, however, the IACHR has developed a set of capabilities that give it a unique position as compared with the commissions of the United Nations or European Community. The following account of the powers of the IACHR is based remotely on its statutory functions and capacities but immediately on a review of some of its specific actions over the past 18 years. This review is illustrative rather than exhaustive, and it only occasionally points to comparisons with the other two international commissions. The powers of the IACHR have rested not only upon its statute as approved by the Permanent Council but also upon its having been made a "principal organ" of the OAS in the revision of the charter in 1965, and the argument has been made that the IACHR cannot be abolished or divested of its existing powers without an amendment to the charter.[3] However, now that the convention has come into force for 11 states, the issue of the commission's competence with respect to the remainder is certain to be raised in the near future as an important issue in the Permanent Council.

The commission meets for a maximum of eight weeks a year. Its members, who are lawyers and diplomats, some retired, take their responsibilities seriously, but membership is only a part-time occupation. The flow of business is not inconsiderable. In the first seven years, 1,525 communications were "received"—that is, accepted by the commission, and on 498 of these the commission requested information from individual governments. The total number of communications that arrived in the mail was about three times that number.[4] For the whole period through 1975, just over 2,000 communications were accepted and given case numbers, thus becoming the subject of various types of action.

The commission staff is small, although of high quality, with ten professional and eight clerical members. Its $303,100 budget for 1975 was less than 1 percent (0.0089) of the total OAS budget of $34,047,300. The commission's allotment of funds was about three-quarters of that designated for development of tourism. Since 1975, however, the IACHR budget has been increased by some 160 percent, so that its relative standing among OAS agencies has been enhanced in fiscal terms as well as prestige. The U.S. government, since 1976, has been a prime mover in these developments. In mid-1978 the members of the commission were Andrés Aguilar, chairman (Venezuela), Carlos A. Dunshee de Abranches, vice chairman (Brazil), Tom J. Farer, (United States), Gabino Fraga, (Mexico), Carlos García Bauer, (Guatemala), Marco G. Monroy Cabra, (Colombia), and Fernando Volio Jiménez (Costa Rica).

The country of citizenship is given only for information; the members are not governmental delegates. The executive secretary of the commission in 1978 was Edmundo Vargas Carreño.

The IACHR will "receive" and "take cognizance of" complaints of violations of human rights or other relevant information made available by individuals, national and international private associations such as Amnesty International, and governments belonging to the OAS.

In terms of its scope of action on complaints,

1. The IACHR staff or the commission itself may reject a complaint as insubstantial or scurrilous, or for other reasons such as the fact that local remedies have not been exhausted.

2. A complaint may be used as the basis for requesting information from a government and, in conjunction with other information and actions by the commission, a complaint may become grounds for suggestions or recommendations by the commission to a specific government.
3. A complaint may be used to support a request to a government for an on-site visit to investigate the situation.
4. Complaints may provide information utilized in an annual commission report or in a special report on the situation in a single country.

Three key words in the above outline of commission action should be elucidated for an understanding of commission workings: visits, report, and publicity.

Visits

There are two types of visits in the commission's repertoire. Visits may be made, with the consent of the government in question, by some or all commission members or by the executive secretary to investigate a situation that has given rise to complaints, especially when complaints are numerous and serious and when they are of such a nature—for instance, inhumane treatment in prisons—that inadequate redress would be afforded by the slow procedure of awaiting exhaustion of local remedies. The outstanding examples of this type of visit are the two to Chile in 1974—one by then executive secretary, Luís Reque, and the other by five commission members.

Another kind of visit, lasting a full year, was made to the Dominican Republic in 1965-66, to aid in the protection of human rights in a civil war. At least one commission member was present at all times, and commission services were welcomed by both sides. The commission members heard oral complaints from individuals throughout the country; they were sometimes accompanied on their trips by members of the press; they went to prisons, protested conditions directly to the responsible authorities, and secured changes in treatment of inmates; they appealed to officials at the ministerial level without regard to the niceties of recognition; they arranged asylum and supervised safe-conducts by accompanying fleeing politicians to airplane flights. The circumstances may have been unique, but in this instance the visit demonstrated that the commission could be an "action body."[5] The commission here demonstrated its usefulness so effectively that the extension of its powers in 1965 was readily approved. Similarly, Honduras and El Salvador both invited the commission to send members to observe and report on matters affecting missing persons and treatment of prisoners during their armed conflict in 1969, and commission members remained in each country for about four months.

The actions that commission members may take on visits are far from codified. In the case of Chile, they included the following:

1. Interviews were held with cabinet ministers and judges.
2. Members went to prisons and places of detention such as the National Stadium.
3. Prisoners were interviewed, and the interviews frequently were tape-recorded.
4. Inquiries, suggestions, and recommendations were sent to the foreign office while the commission was in Chile.
5. The commission "held court" in the Hotel Crillon in Santiago; more than 400 persons made oral representations and were given special forms for registering complaints.
6. Members of the commission went to detention camps as far as 525 kilometers from Santiago.
7. Interviews were held with wives of prisoners and detainees.
8. Interviews were held with members of international agencies represented in Chile, including the UN High Commission for Refugees.
9. Riverbanks were examined to check reports that detainees had been killed there.
10. Members of the commission attended hearings in military courts to observe trial procedures.[6]

Several governments have refused formal requests by the IACHR to permit visits either by the commission or by one of its members; these include Brazil, Cuba, Paraguay, and Uruguay. The ability of the commission to make visits to member states is one of its most important attributes, even though necessarily limited by the consent of the states concerned.

In 1977 and 1978 the number of actual and prospective visits to member states increased. The IACHR now informs a government that it plans to write a report on the human rights situation and suggests that the government issue an invitation for a visit. Invitations recently have been forthcoming from Panama, El Salvador, Haiti, and Nicaragua, and negotiations are under way for a visit to Argentina. Visits ordinarily are made by a commission subcommittee, and their increased number is made possible by the larger staff funded by the increased budget voted at the General Assembly meeting at Grenada in June 1977.

Reports

The IACHR makes five types of reports:

1. A report on work accomplished at each session. Through 1977, a total of 42 sessions were held, each lasting from ten days to three or more weeks. The reports vary from 25 to 100 pages.

2. Annual reports have been made since 1970 to the ad hoc Working Group of the Permanent Council to Study Reports of OAS Agencies, for transmission to the General Assembly. These are substantial mimeographed documents of up to 143 pages (1974).
3. Special reports on the situation concerning human rights in individual countries. Such reports have been made on the following states: Chile, three; Cuba, four; Dominican Republic, four; Haiti, four; Guatemala, one; Paraguay, one; Uruguay, one. These vary in length but may be as long as 177 pages (1974) on Chile.
4. Studies such as that by Durward V. Sandifer, "The Relationship between the Respect for Human Rights and the Effective Exercise of Representative Democracy" (1962). These take the form of articles or essays by members of the commission.
5. Inter-American Yearbooks on Human Rights (1960–67; 1968; 1969–70).

The first three types of reports are specific with regard to acts charged as violations of human rights. They give names of individuals against whose persons the alleged acts were committed; they contain explanations and denials by governments in individual cases; and they include denunciations of governmental actions by the commission. The IACHR is no pussyfooting or whitewashing organization. If it makes a request during a visit—for example, to go to "a section of military hospital, in which tortures are reportedly controlled with medical supervision"—it so reports and records the fact of the Chilean government's denial of access on the ground that this was one of several "'military areas' where visits were not permitted."[7]

Similarly, the commission does not hesitate to list as one of several detainees interviewed in the National Stadium in Santiago: "Margarita Echeverría, a Chilean who had been arrested the preceding night. Her face showed visible effects of having received hard blows. She said her husband had also been beaten and that she did not know the reason for her arrest."[8]

At the same time, the commission states that, in response to one of its recommendations, the government of Chile released a prisoner, Hugo Anselmo Chacaltana Silva, who was a minor.[9]

The description of additional case studies is unnecessary here. Suffice it to say that in the report on Chile and other special reports, there is more than ample personal and eyewitness testimony for the preparation of a guide to the brutality of police and other armed forces of American governments; to their techniques of torture and other means of intimidation; and to the physical and mental suffering of their victims. It is not necessary to gain access to confidential files of the IACHR; the public record is crystal clear.

In some cases, notably Brazil, special reports have not been issued, but the reason is to be found in the small size of the commission's staff rather than deference to any distinctive position that country may occupy in the Inter-American family of nations. The best evidence is provided by the commission's treatment of two notable cases, Nos. 1,683 and 1,684, in which the Brazilian government was charged with permitting torture and murder and failing to punish responsible officials. The cases are set forth at length, in precise and grisly detail, in the commission's annual report for 1973, and the kinds of information provided are comparable to those given in the special report on Chile, mentioned above.

Some features of the Brazilian cases are of interest. In 1970 the commission had appointed as rapporteur one of its members, Durward V. Sandifer, who was not permitted to enter Brazil to investigate the circumstances of either case. Charges made by several persons were sent by the IACHR to the Brazilian government, which replied that the individual in one case, Olavo Hansen, a leader of textile workers in São Paulo, had neither been tortured nor murdered while in custody but had committed suicide by drinking Parathion, a potent insecticide. The commission sent copies of the government's explanation to the individuals who signed the original complaint; they responded with additional information and asserted that they could not accept the suggestion that this was a case of suicide. In his fifth report on the case, the rapporteur pointed out that, while the doctor who first had examined Hansen's body had "not found signs of violence," a later autopsy at the Institute of Legal Medicine in São Paulo had found marks of violence.

The commission's judgment was that the Brazilian government's answer to the charges was inadequate and, having permitted the proper time to elapse, the commission placed an extensive, detailed report of the case into its annual report for 1973 and rendered as its formal judgment that the Brazilian government had been responsible for "exceedingly grave violations of the right to life."[10]

It is typical of the exemplary completeness of the commission's reporting that the negative vote by one of the members, Dr. Carlos A. Dunshee de Abranches, is recorded on each occasion in the consideration of the Brazilian cases. In general, IACHR reports are models of their kind: References to previous documents are complete so case histories may be traced; translations from the Spanish are satisfactorily idiomatic; and the standard of typographical excellence is remarkably high.

Copies of the IACHR annual reports are sent to the above-mentioned working group of the Permanent Council, whose practice is simply to transmit the reports to the General Assembly. But on one occasion in 1963 it is reported that a sharp interchange took place in the council between the Nicaraguan representative, Guillermo Sevilla-Sacasa, and the Ecuadoren, Gonzalo Escudero, who stoutly defended the commission's position against Sevilla's complaint that the council had never intended that the commission interpret its statute so liberally in making public its reports, especially those leveling charges against member states.[11] Special reports are first sent to the country concerned, and then to the Permanent Council and General Assembly. Reports of IACHR proceedings are sent to individuals and organizations on its mailing list. The studies written by commission members appear in the yearbooks.

Until 1976, the uniform practice of the OAS General Assembly was to pass a unanimous resolution in which it might "take note, with appreciation" of the IACHR reports. Before 1976 there had never been a General Assembly debate on a report from the commission.

Reasons for this curious practice are difficult to gauge from the barren records of the General Assembly, but they are open to conjecture. One surmise is that the delegations generally were reluctant to raise objections to the report and thereby call attention to it—either to attack the commission for doing less than its duty or to censure it for exceeding its authority. When all states are more or less vulnerable, each is inclined to keep quiet when another is charged with violations. The second surmise is that delegations were reluctant to positively approve a report that might include detailed information and serious charges that a member state was responsible for violating human rights on its own territory—the accused state might try to defend itself in a debate that would be embarrassing for all concerned. These considerations may be summarized as follows: No approval, no debate; no disapproval, no debate; no debate, no attention; no attention, no publicity; no publicity, inaction and obscurity.

In the case of Chile, the General Assembly at its 1975 meeting varied only slightly from its routine and suggested that the commission's special report on Chile, of October 25, 1974, might be out of date; it asked the commission to report at the following meeting, held in June 1976 in Santiago, Chile.[12] This vote was taken at a moment when, erroneously as it turned out, it was anticipated that the Chilean government would allow a visit by a delegation from the UN Commission on Human Rights.

The General Assembly's effective technique of giving no attention to the work of the IACHR became sufficiently notorious that in 1974 the Committee on Foreign Affairs of the U.S. House of Representatives formally recommended that the Department of State "should propose that the OAS strengthen the role of the Inter-American Commission on Human Rights through adoption of the following measures: (a) a public discussion by the OAS General Assembly of the substantive issues contained in the Commission's report, including allegations of human rights violations in particular countries."[13]

In 1975 the Department of State did not act as if it were giving any heed to this recommendation, but in 1976 its position was reversed, as indicated below.[14]

Until very recently, the commission has been isolated within the OAS General Secretariat, as well as nearly ignored by the Permanent Council and General Assembly. Further, for 15 years the commission chairman was not invited to take a place on the rostrum when its annual report was scheduled on the General Assembly agenda; he was not invited to comment on the commission's reports; and in 1975 he was prevented from speaking by a vote of the delegations. And this happened despite the listing of the IACHR in OAS publications as a "principal" or "major" OAS organ.[15]

It is apparently with these considerations in mind that the U.S. Congress recommended that the Department of State "strengthen the role" of the IACHR by proposing to the OAS "the creation within the OAS Secretariat of a Human Rights Division comparable to the Directorate of Human Rights of the Council of Europe."[16]

A consequence of the commission's administrative and substantive isolation in the OAS political system is that it has operated independently, without supervision, without formal appreciation, and also until lately without formal criticism. The IACHR executive secretary has reported only nominally and rarely to the OAS secretary general and the latter, until very recently, showed little interest in the work of the commission. In other words, the General Assembly practice of ignoring the reports of the commission during its first 15 years of work was duplicated within the General Secretariat. But in 1976, largely because of protests by the Chilean government, the IACHR, along with certain other agencies, was specifically placed under the supervision of the OAS assistant secretary general, and the administrative effects of this innovation may become significant in time.

Publicity

Oddly enough, the IACHR statute does not deal with the important issue of publicity about the commission's deliberations, communications, and reports. One directive to the commission, in carrying out its broad responsibility "to promote respect for human rights" (Statute, Article 1) is "to prepare such studies or reports as it considers advisable in the performance of its duties" (Statute, Article 9c).

Regulations drawn up by the IACHR authorize the commission's secretariat, following commission approval of a report, to "publish the report as an official document" of the IACHR "for internal or general circulation as the Commission so decides" (Regulations, Article 33). The reports contemplated by Article 33 apparently are mainly the "studies," although reports on the situation in individual countries also may be included here (Article 52).

It appears to have been assumed that the commission's annual reports to the General Assembly would be public documents, although there has been vagueness as to when they may be made public by the commission. In practice, the documents have been placed in the public domain following formal action upon them by the General Assembly.

Reports of actions taken by the commission at its approximately semiannual sessions are issued automatically, as soon as compiled by the secretariat.

Publicity given commission reports on alleged violations of human rights by specific governments involves more delicate and complicated considerations. If the commission requests information from a government and the information is not supplied within 180 days, the commission may presume that "the occurrence of the events" in question has been "confirmed" (Regulations, Article 51). In such cases the commission may make recommendations to a particular state "without prejudice to the preparation and publication of the reports that the Commission may consider proper, in accordance with Article 9c or 9(bis)c of its Statute" (Regulations, Article 52).

Thus, by not answering at all, a government may defer action by the commission for six months, and the Commission is authorized, at its discretion to extend that period by an additional 180 days. If, a government does not reply within such period to a request for information the commission may make appropriate recommendations to that state. If the commission's recommendations are not adopted by the government within a reasonable time, the commission may comment in its annual report, and may give its report publicity if the OAS General Assembly does not make observations on the recommendations and the government continues its noncompliance.

If a government provides the information requested or otherwise responds to the commission's inquiries but the commission still finds for the plaintiff and the government still does not "within a reasonable time adopt the measures recommended by the Commission," the government may be "named" in the commission's annual report as rejecting the recommendations. Then the commission "may publish its report," if the General Assembly has made no observations on it and the government does not change its position. The phrase "its report" might refer either investigation of a specific complaint or to a special report like that on Chile. This bit of vague drafting unfortunately gave rise to a serious dispute within the OAS about the scope, nature, and timing for publicity about IACHR reports.

In its resolution of May 19, 1975, the General Assembly noted that the first IACHR report on human rights in Chile had been "sent to the United Nations and was considered at the Thirty-first Session of the United Nations Commission on Human Rights," which voted to authorize a working group to visit Chile to study the situation.[17] The resolution noted and approved the Chilean government's acceptance of the visit, and perhaps for that reason the resolution contains no suggestion that the report should not have been "sent" to the United Nations by the IACHR. It was determined later that the report was delivered to the United Nations at the request of the UN secretary general by IACHR Executive Secretary,

Luís Reque, with the previous authorization of OAS Secretary General Gala Plaza Lasso.

Subsequently, however, the Chilean government reversed its position, refused to permit the visit by the UN group, and attempted to secure Reque's dismissal for "improperly" sending a copy of the IACHR report to the UN commission before the OAS General Assembly had received it from the Permanent Council. But the OAS General Secretariat rejected the Chilean demand, and Reque's resignation in June 1976 does not appear to be connected with this incident.

The views of the Chilean government may be inferred from a statement by President Augusto Pinochet in commenting upon a condemnatory resolution approved in November 1975 by the UN commission. He charged that the resolution did not give due consideration to Chile's defense of its actions and that it demonstrated the extent to which "international organizations" had become infiltrated by a "Marxist-Leninist campaign." He also charged that the IACHR executive secretary had "divulged charges in violation of the Regulations."[18]

Since publicity—in combination with requests for information, recommendations, and condemnations—is one of the most important commission capabilities in promoting the observance of human rights, the form of the publicity is not without interest.

In general, the IACHR definition of publicity seems to be a passive one: to make available, to persons who request them, single-spaced, mimeographed reports of up to 200 pages, with no guided tours in the form of summaries or selected highlights. These are the formal, detailed, technical reports as made to the OAS and sent to member governments—and there publicity stops. The IACHR does not hold press conferences. The question may be raised as to whether the commission should consider lifting its sights to a wider public. There are obvious issues of staffing and funding here, as well as policy. Better publicity might result in new limitations on the powers of the IACHR, which is both financed and tolerated by the governments it is authorized to pillory. The commission's reports, however forbidding in format, contain adequate information to fuel campaigns by activist groups, but so far these groups seem lax in making full use of the reports. At present the commission may be commended for solidity and seriousness, but it hardly can be accused of flamboyance in its promotion of human rights.

Government Responses to Accusations

The commission, as producer of a single good, is purveyor of a single message: Human rights must be respected by governments. In carrying out its assignment, the commission is required "to bear in mind" that "the rights of each man are limited by the rights of others, by the security of all, and by the just demands of the general welfare and the advancement of democracy."[19] The "security of all" is a diffuse expression, but it offers an entry into a review of the types of responses made by governments to charges of human rights violations.

A major justification for governmental acts is the delcaration of a "state of siege," sometimes referred to, as in the title of Article 27 of the American Convention on Human Rights, as "suspension of Guarantees." The article begins:

> In time of war, public danger, or other emergency that threatens the independence or security of a State Party, it may take measures derogating from its obligations under the present Convention to the extent and for the period of time strictly required by the exigencies of the situation.[20]

However, this provision does not authorize suspension of articles of the convention dealing with the right to life, right to humane treatment, and other specified rights.

In the twilight world of the operative statute of the commission, no exception is made for a state of siege but neither are there any limits on a state of siege. The commission is free to condemn, but the states are free to "derogate," and for as long as it pleases them—and the effective line has been drawn by the inaction of a mute General Assembly. This means that governments determine the nature of their actions in and for the duration of a state of siege, unimpeded within the OAS save by the protests of the IACHR.

This is not to say there is no justification for the declaration of a state of siege. With respect to Chile, the commission admitted that governments that "reach power through a revolutionary movement, are forced in such convulsive periods to suspend certain guarantees." However, the commission based its position on "American international law" and the assertion that "in the absence of conventional standards . . . 'the most accepted doctrine'" is that set forth in the American Convention on Human Rights "whose ratification has already begun."[21] It therefore maintained that exceptional situations of "war, public danger, or other emergency" did not authorize "deprivation of life, torture, retroactive application of the more severe penal law . . . disregard of the right of minors to special protection and treatment.[22]

This position was challenged sharply by the Chilean government in its reply to the commission report. It was asserted that the commission, which was in Chile for only 11 days, had not adopted a "suitable method of work" in studying the situation and was "not in a position to give proper assurance as to the degree of danger that threatened the nation." The government justified its actions between the coup of September 11, 1973, and the time the commission met in Chile (July 22–August 2, 1974) on the existence of a "state of internal war" existing since September 11, and asserted that "with much more knowledge and properness it believes that the state of war was 'imminent' during the 11 days the Commission remained in Chile." Further, on September 11, 1974, the Chilean government terminated the state of internal war and replaced it by a different state of siege "in the degree of internal defense." Thus the government indicated that it would gradually reestablish the temporarily suspended freedoms, "bearing in mind that its essential duty is the peace and tranquility of all its inhabitants."[23]

Carrying this argument to its logical conclusion, the government of Chile asserted:

> If the Government, in an irresponsible way, did not carry out the measures that the law, enacted much before, gives it to protect its inhabitants, it would be making itself responsible for the eventual consequences that could bring about, which, given the support it has from the citizenry, would constitute an attack against the country and the basic rights of those who have the privilege of living in it.[24]

This deplorable official translation barely allows one to interpret the essential element of the Chilean government's position to be that, if it were not able by means of at least a state of siege to defend the Chilean people against the enemies of the regime, the "basic rights" of the people would be endangered. In other words, the human rights the commission asserts are endangered by the state of siege are the very rights the government insists would be endangered if the state of siege were not in effect. If the alternative to one authoritarian regime is another, equally authoritarian, the Chilean government thus claims it has a case.

The IACHR operates in this regard on two assumptions: (1) that an authoritarian regime, even in an emergency situation, should not commit murder or torture and (2) that an alternative regime is not necessarily authoritarian. The IACHR is concerned with individual human beings, not regimes, and it continues under its monolithic mandate to press for the primacy of the right to life and humane treatment. In their extreme terms, the claims here between governments and commission are nearly irreconcilable. In recognition of this the OAS Permanent Council and General Assembly have buried their heads in the sand. Is there a non-ostrich alternative?

The principal issue for the OAS in the field of human rights is to seek ways to open a discussion of accommodation between its objective of fostering the protection of human rights and demands by member governments for unhampered freedom to violate those rights when they deem such violations to be essential to security, stability, or economic or social policies.

In one sense, the discussion was opened at the 1977 General Assembly session in Grenada with the introduction of an Argentine resolution that sought approval for the proposition that governments are justified in infringing on human rights when they are engaged in the suppression of terrorism. The resolution was defeated after a debate in which the delegates of Mexico and Venezuela put forward the broad view that the appropriate solution for terrorism was political freedom and the narrower view that, in effect, the IACHR was correct in its position that the state was not justified in adopting the methods of terrorists. The resolution passed on terrorism merely asked the Permanent Council to continue studies it already had been asked to make on aspects of terrorism; it also denounced kidnapping, extortion, and other terrorist activities.

The IACHR stated clearly its current position in a report on Uruguay:

> Overall, the Commission has repeatedly condemned practices used by groups which, in an attempt to impose their political and ideological opinions, resort to all forms of criminal activity such as murder, kidnapping, assault, maintenance of private jails, and cruel treatment. On the other hand, on other occasions the Commission has generally maintained that the authorities cannot deprive subversives of the minimal treatment to which enemy combatants and prisoners are entitled both during international wars and during armed conflicts that are not international in nature.[25]

To this position, the Uruguayan government made two responses: (1) that "while the IACHR is an organ of the OAS . . . Uruguay is a sovereign state with member status in the OAS" and (2) Uruguay "agrees that for the IACHR 'it is more than ever necessary to take immediate steps to clarify, beyond any doubt and leaving no room for unfounded suspicions, both the existing situation as regards respect for or violation of those norms that guarantee human rights and the rectitude and legitimacy of the procedures the commission has used to date in order to establish those facts.'"

The statement in inner quotations had been used by IACHR Chairman Andrés Aguilar to justify a request for a commission visit to Uruguay. But the statement here is used by Foreign Minister Alejandro Rovira as a part of his justification for refusing the request, and the head-on collision is manifest. The government, in its formal response to the commission's 1977 report, provided what it regarded as a satisfactory denial or explanation of complaints. The commission did not find the response convincing and requested a visit, which was refused. The commission then issued a second report in 1978, with new detailed accounts of tortures, and concluded that "there have been serious violations" of human rights in Uruguay. Finally, the IACHR made several recommendations that went so far as to assume the accuracy of reports challenged by the Uruguayan government; for instance, the commission urged that "the Government of Uruguay . . . order a thorough and impartial investigation in order to determine those responsible for the deaths of those individuals who died as a result of torture while being held under detention or arrest, and that it duly inform the Commission of the results of such investigations."[26]

The sovereign states belonging to the OAS are unaccustomed to being addressed in so bold a manner by a mere OAS commission, especially one that does not, with respect to them, possess the authority of a treaty base; therefore, an assault on the competence of the IACHR with respect to nonratifiers of the American Convention on Human Rights is to be anticipated.

Of course, governments make other types of responses to requests for information and IACHR recommendations. These include making no reply whatever; bland assertions that the laws of the country offer adequate protection for human rights; and comforting assurances that those laws are being observed. In some cases the charges are challenged, as in Brazilian case No. 1,683 mentioned above; in others, governments offer the general defense that the "only basis of evidence for the majority of cases in which tortures are denounced is the testimony of the complainant himself, without there being produced any other effective means of proof."[27]

This is a topic that might be spun out at length. It raises an issue that may be baldly stated as follows: The IACHR has the single purpose of promoting observance of human rights. Member governments have multiple purposes; of these, the most important is national security, which many of them equate with regime stability. To these governments, observance of human rights has low priority or even negative priority if it means that regime opponents, however terroristic, should receive humane treatment. Therefore, in critical situations many governments will give little or no heed to the strongest measures the IACHR may take—the publication of its recommendations and of its characterizations of violations of human rights.

It is worthy of note that there is one specialized limitation on the state of siege, in the existence of agreements on diplomatic asylum. Diplomatic asylum is deeply cherished and well observed in Latin America. It is, of course, a specialized derogation from the rigors of a state of siege, and in general although not always, it is a refuge for political elites due to their advance information about hostile changes in regimes. The number of people who can gain asylum is limited by the living quarters of hospitable foreign embassies, so in a social revolution, as distinct from a military shuffle, only a small fraction of a new regime's potential victims can gain shelter.

Nevertheless, it is remarkable that in Chile after September 11, 1973, diplomatic asylum was respected almost completely for some 2,000 persons; further, safe-conducts for leaving the country were granted in nearly all cases. There were some difficulties about reservation of the right subsequently to extradite individuals given safe-conducts on grounds that they had committed common criminal as distinct from political acts, but on the whole the institution of asylum survived nearly unscathed.

POLICY ISSUES

Certain policy differences both within the OAS and between it and the U.S. government, are beginning to emerge. An attempt to sketch them will be made here, and questions will be noted with the intent of arousing awareness rather than proposing solutions.

PUBLICITY

The European commission makes far less use of publicity than the IACHR, and this difference indicates some fundamental distinctions. Because the level of respect for human rights already is relatively high in Europe, the aim of most of the European commission's actions is to deal with isolated, usually aberrant cases of minor violations. Its role is that of a conciliator, and publicity for its activities would be counterproductive. Referral to the Committee of Ministers or the Court of Human Rights is a last resort and decisions, except in the special case of Greece, usually are orders to administrative officials rather than condemnations of national government policies.

In America, by contrast, where the level of respect for human rights is deplorably low in many countries, the IACHR—first trying conciliatory methods through inquiry and other means, and then allowing six months for a reply—has found itself in a position of confrontation with unheeding governments. Lacking any higher authority to which to appeal, the commission goes to publicity as a last resort. The publicity has become increasingly specific—naming individuals mistreated; identifying addresses of "places of interrogation"; reproducing tape-recorded interviews; and describing methods of torture. In America, as distinct from Europe, publicity is presently the ultimate sanction and its use requires delicate judgment. The UN commission also relies heavily on publicity as a form of pressure.

In broad terms, the issue is the extent to which various types of publicity may be employed by the commission "in exercise of its irrevocable mandate to watch over observance of human rights," to use its own words.[28]

In still broader terms, the question is whether the commission, acting with commendable boldness in a situation where its mandate is largely undefined, may have reached or even overstepped the limits of toleration by member states.

Implementation of Sanctions

Beyond the restricted range of publicity, are there other methods by which the IACHR might promote the observance of human rights? This is an important and complex question that can be given only a sketchy response at this time.

In the United Nations, the sanction of an economic boycott was approved by the Security Council against Rhodesia on the ground that violations of human rights through racial discrimination were so serious as to create a "threat to peace." The observance of the boycott by a number of countries may have placed some small limitations on Rhodesia's economic growth, but these appear to have been only minor annoyances.[29] In the OAS, collective intervention or sanctions of any kind are probably illegal and certainly impracticable if their intent is to cause member governments to change their policies toward the protection of human rights. Collective action in wartime may be feasible, but the American states are notoriously reluctant to undertake collective measures to preserve democratic rights or civil liberties among themselves.

Under the terms of the convention, the Inter-American Court of Human Rights is given authority to "rule": (1) that "the injured party be ensured the enjoyment of his right or freedom that was violated"; (2) that "the consequences of the measure or situation that constituted the breach of such right or freedom be remedied"; and (3) that "fair compensation be paid to the injured party" (Article 63). The states that signed the convention "undertake to comply with the judgment of the Court" (Article 68). The efficacy of these provisions remains to be tested in practice.

However, beyond publicity there is another possible way to exert pressure on American governments that violate human rights. This is the termination of military and/or economic aid to such countries by the government of the United States.

Since 1973, at the urging of Rep. Donald M. Fraser, chairman, of the subcommittee on International Organizations of the House Committee on International Relations, and of Sen. Edward M. Kennedy, chairman of the Subcommittee to Investigate Problems Connected with Refugees and Escapees of the Senate Committee on the Judiciary, the U.S. Congress has amended legislation to attempt to make military and some economic aid dependent on a recipient country's observance of human rights.[30]

First, the International Development and Food Assistance Act of 1975, continued in 1976, prohibits development aid to "the government of any country engaging in a consistent pattern of gross violations of internationally recognized human rights" unless "the aid will benefit needy people." The Agency for International Development (AID) may be required by either appropriate committee of Congress to submit a report demonstrating that certain aid will benefit "needy people." If either committee disagrees with the AID presentation,

> it may initiate action to terminate aid under section 617 of the Foreign Assistance Act. In deciding if any government falls within such provisions, consideration must be given to the extent of its cooperation with investigations by international agencies. The President is to report annually on steps taken to carry out this section.[31]

Earlier, in 1974, the Congress prohibited any military assistance to Chile. In November 1975, upper limits were placed on economic assistance to Chile—$90 million for 1976 and $50 million the next year.[32] The prohibition was maintained in 1976, and for the period July 1, 1976—September 30, 1977, total economic assistance to Chile could not exceed $27 million. This amount could be doubled if the president certified: (1) that Chile "does not engage in a consistent pattern of gross violations of internationally recognized human rights"; (2) has permitted "unimpeded investigation" by international commissions of alleged violations of human rights; and (3) "has taken steps to inform the families of prisoners of the condition of any charges against such prisoners."[33]

This linkage is novel with respect to fellow members of the OAS. It offers the unprecedented possibility of the application of a unilateral and significant sanction to implement some decisions of the IACHR. The implications are complex, tinged with politically delicate overtones, and subsequent discussions have not hardened into firm policies.

The issue emerged in September 1973 when Kennedy inquired at a congressional hearing: "Now, as I understand it, we have been a member since 1960 to the Inter-American Commission on Human Rights. Are we using that as a mechanism now to try and protect human rights?"[34] The reply, by Assistant Secretary of State Jack B. Kubisch, was thought unresponsive, and Kennedy requested a note from the department "about whether the Department thinks it worthwhile to try to utilize the Inter-American Commission on Human Rights, what went into its decision not to use it, or if they think it can be used now or should be used, now, what the policy considerations are?"[35]

The department provided a brief note stating what the IACHR had done with respect to Chile but offering no answers to the senator's queries.[36] Kennedy then stated, "The point I am concerned about is whether we are using all the machinery which is available to us within the OAS."[37] Kubisch responded, "We are using all avenues available to us—including the Inter-American Commission, but particularly the United Nations Commissioner for Refugees and the International Red

Cross, the two organizations represented in Chile and working with the Chilean authorities on this question, and also bilateral contacts with the Government."[38]

A related but distinct position on this issue was observable in Fraser's contention, later supported by Kennedy, that "the United States should establish a clear-cut policy that with respect to all countries, human rights is an important component in determining U.S. bilateral relations. . . . I would say that individual liberties rank higher than our efforts at economic investment."[39]

The Department of State country director for Brazil, Stephen Low, agreed that "there is a basic minimum of treatment that would be possible to agree upon," but then the "real problem" arises of determining whether the basic minimum has been observed. This is difficult, especially for an individual nation, he said, because most governments regard their treatment of their own citizens as a matter of domestic jurisdiction. It is particularly difficult for the United States because "we are working out new relationships on this continent . . . and we have to take a position in which we do take a lower profile, in which we permit very much more equal give and take." Therefore, "governments have preferred to work through international organizations in this area. If what you do is going to be resented and going to make it more difficult, you don't want to do it."[40]

In response, Fraser said that while he agreed with the change in U.S. policy toward a lower profile, he hoped "in the process we don't abandon our values." But he added, "our concern should be limited to those rights which are internationally recognized. Consequently, we would not be imposing our value system on them."[41]

The logical next step in the discussion was taken by William Buffum, assistant secretary for international organization affairs, in the Department of State. With respect to the 1974 resolution of the UN Economic and Social Council (ECOSOC) on "Protection of Human Rights in Chile," he said: "In fact it is very helpful to have this matter pending before the Human Rights Commission because it gives us a natural point of departure in raising and initiating discussions with some of the countries concerned."[42]

Seizing on this, and admitting that his question might be "too far down the road now to be realistic," Fraser inquired: "Could it be that ultimately the judgments of the [UN] Commission, the Council or the General Assembly might in turn become a guide for bilateral relations with governments" and for the World Bank or regional banks?

This was a "very complex problem," Buffum commented, adding that it is

> much easier for us to attach special weight to an adverse finding of an international body and performance in the human rights field when that

finding relates to a country with whom we do not have particularly close relations . . . it is a fact of international life that one gives special considerations to one's closest allies even when we are not completely satisfied with their performance in a given situation. . . . [But] the action of any international body in the human rights field vis-a-vis a given country should be taken into account in determining the rest of our bilateral relationships to that country.[43]

On a worldwide scale, in 1976, Congress made it "the policy of the United States . . . to promote and encourage increased respect for human rights and fundamental freedoms for all . . . by all countries."[44]

This might be dismissed as congressional rhetoric were it not for provisions in the legislation directing the president to conduct security assistance programs so as to avoid identification of the United States "with governments which deny to their people internationally recognized human rights and fundamental freedoms" and ordering the secretary of state to make annual reports on "the observance of and respect for internationally recognized human rights in each country proposed as a recipient of security assistance."

The linkage of U.S. policy to international organizations is provided by the requirement that such annual reports give consideration to "the relevant findings of appropriate international organizations" and to the extent of a government's cooperation with such organizations by "permitting an unimpeded investigation" by them, or one of them.[45] This is a far more demanding and sophisticated provision than the permissive section of the 1973 act, and it apparently was drafted as a result of congressional dissatisfaction with the Department of State report in early 1975 entitled "Report to the Congress on the Human Rights Situation in countries Receiving U.S. Security Assistance." That report was a general review of the problems of expressing U.S. concern about human rights, and it mentioned no cases of possible violations in any specific country. The committee had asked for a country-by-country report, and the department refused to provide it.[46]

The new legislation opens up many intriguing policy potentials, only a few of which may be touched upon here. For example, if a country refused to allow a visit requested by the IACHR, would that be regarded by Congress as grounds for disapproving a "certification" by the president that U.S. national security interests required the provision of security assistance? For certain countries, the administration might be pleased to apply the "objective test" of the rejection of such a visit as a justification for refusing security assistance; for others, the test might be embarrassing.

Further, in this largely unexplored region of national (U.S.) sanctions in support of IACHR strictures, what kinds of pressures might be brought upon the commission? In the Chilean case, the U.S. government did not accept Kennedy's suggestion that it request an investigation by the

IACHR. Might it take such an initiative in the future, with respect to an American government it was less concerned to shield than Chile from the commission's inquiry? How might the character of the commission's decisions be affected if it knew that, should a country refuse a visit, U.S. aid to that country (except that to "needy people") might well be terminated? It is one thing to denounce, however firmly, and be ignored; it is quite another to denounce and thereby become responsible for serious economic consequences to one of the American republics.

Kennedy's suggestion that the IACHR be "utilized" by the U.S. government reflects a misapprehension of the commission's essential nature. It is not a body that can be manipulated by governments. With regard to what may become the critical issue of visits, the commission has explained that, with respect to Chile:

> While the regime that was overthrown on September 11, 1973 was in power, neither the number nor the seriousness of the complaints or denunciations received by the Commission were considered as grounds making it necessary to request the consent of the government of that country to conduct an "on-the-spot" examination of the situation.[47]

Efforts to bring influence to bear upon the commission, whose members are rightly jealous of its independence, could hardly be effective. The U.S. and other governments, of course, may "utilize" a decision by the commission once it is made, but that is very different from "utilizing" the commission as an institution and, for example, instructing it to investigate or condemn a given government.

With this new legislation in the U.S. Congress, it may be said that the IACHR has been catapulted into a position where it might become, in fact as well as name, a principal organ of the OAS.

The issue has arisen for the OAS as to how to deal with this unanticipated development. Will the Permanent Council review the IACHR statute and try to eliminate the commission's existing capability to request and make visits? Will the commission negotiate quietly for visits and make no request it knows would be rejected? These and other interesting questions arise out of the unique feature of the OAS among comparable international organizations, namely, that one of its member states is so relatively powerful that it alone can, even in limited ways, partially "utilize" the organization by allocating its own resources to apply effective sanctions that would not be voted by the responsible bodies of the OAS itself.

Extending IACHR Capabilities

In view of the developments outlined above, it is "no surprise," as Assistant Secretary Rogers has stated, that "the issue of human rights has become, in very recent times, a major interest and a vexing dilemma for our relations with the other nations of this Hemisphere."[48] The United States desires to "help enhance respect for human rights," but it cannot impose its own standards on others. Therefore, the standards must be those "which derive their authority, not from our experience and tradition, but from international conventions." There then arises the question of "measuring the observance" of the standards, and this process also must, "in the first instance, be international." Hence, "it is essential that we lend our assistance to strengthening the authority and the self-confidence of the international instruments of human rights observance," including the inter-American and the UN commissions on human rights.[49]

Rogers noted that there are dangers here; for example, "member states may cripple them [the commissions] out of fear that they will prove dangerous." However, it was U.S. "obligation" to "insure that the Commissions are blessed with effective and courageous members, that they are adequately staffed, that their budgets allow for the full range of essential activities and that finally their efforts are encouraged and supported in the member states."

This was not just rhetoric, even when Henry Kissinger was secretary of state, for the department made significant organizational changes to bring human rights considerations more directly into foreign policy decisions. Further, on November 3, 1975, Rogers, in a letter to Kennedy, gave the department's vigorous support to the senator's amendment to the International Development and Food Assistance Act of 1975 that provided, for 1976 and 1977, a total of $714,000 "to be used only for budgetary support for the Inter-American Commission on Human Rights."[50] This amount was over and above the regular U.S. contribution to the OAS, and it allowed the IACHR to operate on a total two-year budget of $922,000 or about 50 percent more than the figure allocated to the commission in the OAS budget. Kennedy made it clear, in deploring proposed cuts by the OAS in allocations to the IACHR, that those cuts would have forced the commission "to cancel its planned seminars, special studies, and certain pending investigations of the situation of human rights in the Americas."[51]

The authorization of these funds raised a serious issue for the OAS, and the matter immediately became controversial. In the meeting of the OAS Permanent Council on November 19, 1975, the Chilean representative, Manuel Trucco, denounced the Kennedy amendment as an unprecedented attack on OAS autonomy and warned of dangerous consequences that might result from a fiscal intervention violative of the princples of the OAS Charter and affecting matters that are exclusive OAS prerogatives. There were precedents for the receipt by the OAS of additional funds for special activities in other fields so long as they, as in this case, did not interfere with allocations made by the OAS in its formal budget presentation. However, in this situation a substantial increase in IACHR resources on the initiative of the U.S. government, without a previous request by the OAS for such funds, gave rise to strong criticism.

On the one side, Kennedy said, "I can conceive of no more important organ within the OAS than the Commission. . . . In our relations with other (*sic*) Latin American nations it is invaluable to have an inter-American agency with the prestige of the Commission available to investigate, report, and make recommendations with regard to the condition of human rights within the hemisphere."[52] And Rogers asserted, "Its success—the extent to which the Commission can indeed nurture, protect and enhance respect for human rights in the Hemisphere—could come to be considered the most significant accomplishment of the Inter-American System in the years to come."[53]

On the other side, to judge from the tone of Trucco's scathing remarks, bitter opposition may be expected in the OAS to any U.S. efforts to foster the "success" of the commission.[54]

THE BREAKTHROUGH AT SANTIAGO IN JUNE 1976

The issue of human rights as one of high policy for the OAS was brought into the full light of day for the first time at the sixth session of the General Assembly, held Santiago, Chile, in June 1976. A meeting held in Chile at that time could not ignore issues of human rights. The silence on the Commission's work was broken, and a significant debate ensued.[55]

The second IACHR report on Chile was given serious attention by the General Assembly. Further, the Chilean government published the text of the report, completely and accurately in *El Mercurio* on June 9, 1976, together with its own reply. Aware for a year that its status was under attack by Chile, the IACHR did not back down but expressed its conclusion in no uncertain terms: "While decrees are being issued [by the Chilean government] for the purpose of tranquilizing or confusing world opinion, the practice of arbitrary jailings and persecution and tortures continues up to the present."[56]

In the debate, Secretary of State Henry Kissinger said that "the condition of human rights as assessed by the Inter-American Commission on Human Rights has impaired our relationship with Chile and will continue to do so."[57] He further stated that the commission's record demonstrated that "it deserves the support of the Assembly in strengthening further its independence, evenhandedness, and constructive potential." Therefore, the General Assembly should "broaden the Commission's mandate so that instead of waiting for complaints, it can report regularly on the status of human rights throughout the hemisphere"; toward this end, the United States proposed "that the budget and staff of the Commission be enlarged."[58] For itself, the United States offered a voluntary contribution of $102,000 specifically to enable the IACHR to engage in new activities, and it proposed to other OAS members that they also make voluntary contributions for the same purpose. This speech appeared to mark a significant milestone in the secretary's inter-American policy, for he had not previously expressed overt concern about either the activities of the IACHR or the importance of the observance of human rights in his calculations of interstate relationships.

After debate, in which the IACHR chairman for the first time was allowed to participate, the General Assembly voted three resolutions. The first "named" Chile and appealed to its government to "continue adopting and implementing procedures for ensuring respect for human rights"; it also asked Chile to "provide appropriate guarantees to persons or institutions that may provide information, testimony or other types of evidence." The second reaffirmed that the safeguarding of human rights is one of the high purposes of the OAS and thanked the commission for its reports. The third resolution referred two Chilean proposals on IACHR procedures and powers to the Permanent Council for a report at the next General Assembly session.

In the course of the debate, it became evident that the work of the commission had its supporters and its opponents. Support came from such countries as Colombia, Jamaica, the United States, and Venezuela; opposition from such countries as Argentina, Brazil, Chile, Grenada, Paraguay, and Uruguay. Other governments lay in a vague, undeclared middle range.

The succeeding 12 months saw two significant developments in the career of the IACHR: the adoption of a positive policy toward the promotion of human rights abroad by the Carter administration and the commission's successful defense of its policies in response to the two Chilean resolutions calling for a review of its findings accepted in Santiago, whose intent was to weaken the IACHR. The status of the commission in the OAS system was given extensive and serious attention at the General Assembly meeting in Grenada in June 1977 in a debate that occupied well over three-quarters of the time available for the scheduled sessions. The resultant resolution was a victory for IACHR supporters, although they numbered barely enough to provide the minimum absolute majority of 14: Barbados, Costa Rica, Dominican Republic, Ecuador, Grenada, Haiti, Jamaica, Mexico, Panama, Peru, Surinam, Trinidad and Tobago, United States, and Venezuela.[59] Three delegations were absent: Bolivia, Honduras, and Nicaragua. The remaining eight—Argentina, Brazil, Chile, Colombia, El Salvador, Guatemala, Paraguay, Uruguay—abstained, which in the circumstances amounted to voting in the negative. The resolution expressed approval of the commission's work; adopted a 1978–79 budget that more than doubled the resources available in 1976–77; and recommended cooperation with the commission by OAS members.

However, 18 states voted for another resolution stating that, in early stages of economic development, the political and social climate did not foster "necessary respect for, and protection of human rights" and requesting the IACHR to prepare a report on how the principle of equality of states might be harmonized with the commission's investigation of human rights violations.

As of early 1978 the commission had not prepared this study, but it had been active. Visits were made to El Salvador and Panama, with reports to be issued before the end of 1978. The commission's reports on Paraguay and Uruguay were denounced by the two countries concerned, but there was no broad attack on the commission's competence or procedures at the eighth annual session of the OAS General Assembly, held in Washington, D.C., in June-July, 1978. It was agreed that the new Inter-American Court of Human Rights should be located in Costa Rica. The question of the future status of the IACHR with respect to states that have not ratified the convention was referred to the OAS Permanent Council. It was clear only that this was a time of transition for the IACHR as it sought an appropriate role within the unexplored terms of its newly ratified basic instrument. The commission functions as set forth in Article 41 of the convention are essentially the same as those of its statute, but it is probable that experience and practice may bring out significant differences.

As indicated, the Ford administration began to lend important support to the IACHR in 1976, and the Carter administration enhanced this support, both directly as an OAS member and indirectly through what President Carter calls "our open and enthusiastic policy of promoting human rights." In three important ways, the Carter administration went beyond its predecessor. First, it was in accord with Congress in its desire "to demonstrate that there are costs to the flagrant disregard of international standards."[60] This reference was made more specific by Deputy Assistant Secretary of State for Human Rights Mark L. Schneider, who pointed out that as the result of reducing or terminating security assistance programs and in other actions "we are beginning to see governments weigh the costs of repression for the first time" in their relations with the United States and the world community.[61]

Second, the Carter administration is not limiting itself to rhetorical flourishes from Washington. Deputy Secretary of State Warren Christopher described this sharp contrast with previous practice as follows:

> The primary ingredient of human rights diplomacy has a seeming simplicity: We frankly discuss human rights in our consultations with foreign diplomats and leaders. . . . and very often these very frank discussions have led to beneficial results. Sovereign governments have reexamined conditions in their capitals and provinces, and releases of prisoners and other positive actions have followed.[62]

Third, President Carter signed the American Convention on Human Rights on June 1, 1972 and the Department of State placed the convention before the Senate on February 23, 1978; however it has not yet been ratified.[63]

It seems probable that these policies have been influential in the ratification of the convention by nine states in the space of two years, since ratification only by Costa Rica (1970) and Colombia (1973) had been announced previously.

In one sector, however, little movement has been visible. The U.S. government has shown no signs of linking its penalities against violators of human rights to IACHR findings or recommendations, a possibility suggested above. It may be that the IACHR findings actually have been influential in official circles and that it has been thought advisable to refrain from saying so publicly, out of concern that the IACHR then might be assailed as an arm of U.S. foreign policy.

If so, it is curious that Deputy Secretary Christopher, in the speech cited above, asked the American Bar Association for advice on how to create an international clearinghouse that would provide "an objective, authenticated data base on human rights conditions in all countries." Such an institution, he thought, would be able to meet the issue created when challenges are made to the validity of information collected by the U.S. Foreign Service on human rights conditions. It is curious that he did not mention the IACHR in this connection; it is international and objective and provides as authentic a data base as is likely to be obtained short of voluntary confessions by torturers.

The IACHR is an ombudsman in a primitive international society, and it creates dilemmas for all types of statesmen. As Christopher observed, "Human rights, while a fundamental factor in our foreign policy, cannot always be the decisive factor." Therefore, the Department of State cannot be expected to say that it would halt all aid to a regime found by the IACHR to have committed "serious violations" of human rights, although that would seem to be a simple solution. It may be assumed, equally, that if the absolutely ideal clearinghouse could be established, the Department of State would find ways of evading, in critical circumstances, the manifest implications of its authentic data on human rights. Very different types of statesmen may, by refraining from ratifying the convention, limit or even escape IACHR jurisdiction. For its part, the commission may find it more congenial and less frustrating to deal with the more civilized countries that accept the convention, and over the long run its efforts may contribute to widening the realm of man's humanity to man.

NOTES

1. Latin America International Affairs Series: B. Stephansky, *"New Dialogue" on Latin America,* LATIN AMERICA: THE SEARCH FOR A NEW INTERNATIONAL ROLE 166 (R. Hellman and H. Rosenbaum eds. 1975).

2. The documents, with historical background, are contained in INTER-AMERICAN COMMISSION ON HUMAN RIGHTS (IACHR), HANDBOOK OF EXISTING RULES PERTAINING TO HUMAN RIGHTS (1978).

3. T. Buergenthal, *The Revised O.A.S. Charter and the Protection of Human Rights,* 69 AM. J. INT'L L. 835 (Oct. 1965).

4. OAS, ACTIVIDADES DE LA COMISIÓN INTERAMERICANA DE DERECHOS HUMANOS, 1960–1967 25.

5. A. SCHREIBER, THE INTER-AMERICAN COMMISSION ON HUMAN RIGHTS 119 (1970); IACHR, REPORT ON THE STATUS OF HUMAN RIGHTS IN CHILE (1974).

6. COMISIÓN INTERAMERICANA DE DERECHOS HUMANOS, INFORME SOBRE LA SITUACIÓN DE LOS DERECHOS HUMANOS EN CHILE (1974). This report is also published in English.

7. IACHR, REPORT ON THE WORK ACCOMPLISHED BY THE INTER-AMERICAN COMMISSION ON HUMAN RIGHTS AT ITS THIRTY-THIRD SESSION (Special) (July 22–Aug. 2, 1974). This session was held in Santiago, Chile.

8. IACHR, REPORT ON CHILE, at 14.

9. IACHR, REPORT, *supra* n. 7, at 17. The text of the Chilean reply is printed in the REPORT.

10. IACHR, ANNUAL REPORT 32–45, 45–74 (1973). The quotation is at 39; the Spanish is: "un caso gravísimo de violación de derecho a la vida." It is just possible that Brazilian officials may have learned something from IACHR's action in this case. In the more recent case of Vladimir Herzog, a journalist who also died after a short time in custody, army officers refused a second autopsy and police guarded the closed coffin at the funeral. Again, the official verdict was suicide. *See* A. Ternes, *At Least I'm Alive: Turmoil, Terror and Death in Sao Paolo,* Wash. Star, Jan. 18, 1976. Less cynically, it also is possible that the IACHR's action may have helped bring about a change in the "linha dura." It is reported that in early January 1976 President Ernesto Geisel transferred Colonel José Barros Paes, "chief of the Segunda Secão in Sao Paolo and directly responsible for Herzog's death, to Mato Grosso." 10 LATIN AMERICA 15 (Jan. 9, 1976).

11. SCHREIBER, *supra* note 5, at 72. Escudero was at the time a member of the IACHR, as well as Ecuador's representative on the council. The commission, apparently reflecting a widely observed pattern of multijobholding in Latin America, has accepted the practice that commission members may hold simultaneous appointments as officials of their governments. The U.S. practice has been to nominate persons who have retired from the Foreign Service or other public office, although its third nominee is a professor of law. In this instance, Nicaraguan President Anastasio Somoza was reported to have asserted that some members of the IACHR had been communists for many years. *Id.*

12. Text of resolution in DEP'T STATE BULL. 881 (June 23, 1975). At this same session, the General Assembly "having seen" the Commission's Annual Report for 1974, resolved "To Take Note" of it and to "thank the Commission for the important work it has been doing." *Id.*

13. HOUSE COMM. ON FOR AFF., REPORT OF THE SUBCOMM. ON INTL ORG. AND MOVEMENTS, HUMAN RIGHTS IN THE WORLD COMMUNITY: A CALL FOR U.S. LEADERSHIP, 93rd Cong., 2nd Sess. 8 (1974).

14. See the noncontroversial comments during the 1975 General Assembly session by Assistant Secretary of State William D. Rogers, DEP'T STATE BULL. *supra* n. 12, at 879.

15. For example, OAS DEP'T OF INFORMATION AND PUBLIC AFFAIRS, THE OAS AT YOUR FINGERTIPS (1972).

16. HOUSE COMM. ON FOR. AFF., HUMAN RIGHTS IN THE WORLD COMMUNITY, *supra* n. 13, at 48.

17. See DEP'T STATE BULL. *supra* note 12, at 881.

18. Dispatch from Tocopilla, Chile (LATIN) (Nov. 17, 1975), *reproduced in* OAS, Servicio Informativo 13 (Nov. 18, 1975).

19. Statute of the Inter-American Commission on Human Rights, Art. 10, OAS Doc. OEA/Ser. L/V/II. 26, Doc. 10 (Nov. 2, 1977); American Declaration of the Rights and Duties of Man, Art. 28.

20. IACHR, HANDBOOK, *supra* note 3, at 52.

21. IACHR, REPORT ON THE STATUS OF HUMAN RIGHTS IN CHILE, *supra* note 6, at 2–3.

22. *Id.*, at 3.

23. OAS General Assembly, Observations by the Government of Chile on the REPORT ON THE STATUS OF HUMAN RIGHTS IN CHILE prepared by the Inter-American Commission on Human Rights 6–8 (Apr. 6, 1975).

24. *Id.*, at 7.

25. IACHR, REPORT ON THE SITUATION OF HUMAN RIGHTS in URUGUAY 8 (1978).

26. *Id.*, at 6, 69.

27. The Chilean government in its Observations, *supra* n. 23, at 25. In this connection, the government also observed: "The Report [of the IACHR] is written in a deliberately dramatic tone, whose sole objective is to predispose the reader against the Government of Chile." Id., at 25.

28. Telegram from the IACHR to Patricio Carvajal, acting minister of foreign affairs of Chile (May 16, 1974), *quoted in* REPORT ON THE STATUS OF HUMAN RIGHTS IN CHILE, *supra* note 6, at 56. This cable was the response to one from Chile saying that the commission's request to make a visit on June 1 was "somewhat premature." The commission went on to state that it "holds to its firm intention to visit Chile as soon as possible to study *in loco* denunciations which allege violations of human rights." Carvajal, in reply to this strong message, which he evidently regarded as presumptuous, said: "I cannot fail to express to you my surprise" at the commission's statement since it seemed to forget that "the prior consent of the Government of Chile is required." However, he approved the visit, which began in late July. Cable of May 23, 1974, *id.* at 58. These cables were quoted in a press release issued by the OAS.

29. N.Y. Times, Jan. 12, 1976.

30. There is an extensive congressional bibliography on this subject. *See, e.g., Hearings on International Protection of Human Rights: The Work of International Organizations and the Role of U.S. Foreign Policy, Before the Subcomm. on Int'l Org. and Movements of the House Comm. on For Aff.*, 93rd Cong., 1st Sess. (Dec. 7, 1973); *Hearings on Human Rights in Chile, Before the Subcomm. on Int'l Org. and Movements of the House Comm. on For. Aff.*, 93rd Cong., 1st and 2nd Sess. (Dec. 7, 1973; June 18, 1974; Nov. 19, 1974); *Hearings on Torture and Oppression in Brazil, Before the Subcomm. on Int'l Org. and Movements of the House Comm. on For Aff.*, 93rd Cong., 2nd Sess. (Dec. 11, 1974); *Hearings on Review of the U.N. Commission on Human Rights, Before the Subcomm. on Int'l Org. and Movements of the House Comm. on For. Aff.*, 93rd Cong., 2nd Sess. (June 18, 20, 1974).

Also, HOUSE SUBCOMM. ON INT'L ORG. AND MOVEMENTS, COMM. ON FOR. AFF., REPORT ON HUMAN RIGHTS IN THE WORLD COMMUNITY: A CALL FOR U.S. LEADERSHIP, 93rd Cong., 2nd Sess. (Mar. 27, 1974); *Hearings on Human Rights in Chile, Before the Subcomm. on Int'l Org. of the House Comm. on Int'l Relations,* 94th Cong., 1st Sess. (Dec. 9, 1975); *Hearings on Chile: The Status of Human Rights and Its Relationship to U.S. Economic Assistance Programs, Before the Subcomm. on Int'l Org. of the House Comm. on Int'l Relations,* 94th Cong., 2nd Sess. (Apr. 29; May 5, 1976); SUBCOMM. ON INT'L ORG. OF THE COMM. ON INT'L RELATIONS, FOREIGN ASSISTANCE LEGISLATION FOR FISCAL YEAR 1979 (Part 4) (Feb. 15, 16, 28; Mar. 7, 8, 1978), HOUSE CONF. REPORT ON THE INTERNATIONAL SECURITY ASSISTANCE AND ARMS EXPORT CONTROL ACT OF 1976, H.R. 13680, *Hearings on Refugee and Humanitarian Problems in Chile, Before the Sen. Subcomm. to Investigate Problems Connected with Refugees and Escapees of the Sen. Comm. on the Judiciary,* 93rd Cong., 2nd Sess. (Sept. 28, 1973; Jul. 23, 1974); SUBCOMM. ON FOREIGN ASSISTANCE OF THE COMM. ON FOR. RELATIONS, HUMAN RIGHTS REPORTS PREPARED BY THE DEPARTMENT OF STATE (Mar. 1977).

31. HOUSE CONF. REPORT ON INTERNATIONAL DEVELOPMENT AND FOOD ASSISTANCE ACT OF 1975, H.R. 9005, 94th Cong., 1st Sess. (Dec. 4, 1975).

32. CONG. REC. S19096 (Nov. 3, 1975).

33. HOUSE CONF. REPORT ON INTERNATIONAL SECURITY ASSISTANCE, *supra* n. 30, at 34.

34. *Hearings on Refugee and Humanitarian Problems in Chile, supra* n. 30, at Part I, 30. The senator was inaccurate in referring to the United States as "a member" of the IACHR. U.S. citizens who serve on the commission are appointed by the OAS Permanent Council and are not representatives of the U.S. government.

35. *Id.*

36. *Id.*, at 30–31.

37. *Id.*

38. *Id.*, at 24–25. The department's note mentioned above, *supra* n. 36, did not indicate any instance of "use" of the IACHR by the U.S. government.

39. *Hearings on the International Protection of Human Rights, supra* n. 30, at 214. The Kennedy statement, including the view that "we must work for a forthright national policy of compassion for people—a humanitarian policy which is fully integrated into the overall conduct of our foreign relations," is cited in *id.*, at 221ff.

40. *Id.*, at 216, 212. It may be noted that, more recently, Assistant Secretary of State William D. Rogers stated flatly, "We do not regard human rights as an exclusively domestic concern." Remarks at an informal meeting of heads of delegations to the OAS, Washington (May 16, 1975), *quoted in* DEP'T STATE BULL. 879 (June 23, 1975).

41. *Hearings on the International Protection of Human Rights, supra* n. 30, at 216–17.

42. *Hearings on Review of the U.N. Commission on Human Rights, supra* n. 30, at 19.

43. *Id.*, at 22.

44. International Security Assistance and Arms Export Control Act of 1976, Sec. 301, *quoted in* CONFERENCE REPORT ON INTERNATIONAL SECURITY ASSISTANCE, *supra* n. 30, at 22ff.

45. *Id.*, at 23.

46. Text of report, mimeographed, undated, furnished by the office of the House Committee on International Relations.

47. REPORT ON THE STATUS OF HUMAN RIGHTS IN CHILE, *supra* n. 8, at 1.

48. Address by Assistant Secretary of State William D. Rogers, Pan American Society, Boston (Nov. 4, 1975; mimeo., at 1).

49. *Id.*, at 10, 11.

50. Letter from William D. Rogers to Edward Kennedy, CONG. REC. S19100 (Nov. 3, 1975).

51. *Id.*

52. *Id.*

53. Rogers, Address to Pan American Society in Boston, *supra* n. 48, at 13.

54. The ambassador referred (the translation is not official) "to a serious act which could infringe upon the powers and attributes which belong to the Permanent Council and which constitutes an assault upon high officials of this organization." The Kennedy amendment to provide additional financial support for the IACHR constitutes "flagrant violations of the constitutional norms which govern this Council. . . . What we cannot accept, as much for its insolent form, as much as for the disgraceful political purpose which lies behind it, is the result which violates the principles and intents of the Charter and which at the same time furthers intervention in matters which are the exclusive prerogative of the OAS." Smoke and flame were added to this remarkable speech by references to "dedicated professional demagogues who seek to raise the banner of human rights and who on occasion have submerged themselves in murky waters" and to "the arrogant young Senator from Massachusetts." Speech by Ambassador Trucco in the Permanent Council of the OAS (Nov. 19, 1975).

55. Ambassador William S. Mailliard stated at the hearing conducted by the subcommittee on International Organizations of the House Committee on International Relations, Aug. 10, 1976, that "an important breakthrough in OAS treatment of this sensitive and vital matter" consituted "a precedent which can ensure that the status of human rights in the hemisphere receives a full and frank airing at the annual OAS General Assembly." Mimeo text of statement, distributed at the hearing.

56. SECOND REPORT ON THE SITUATION OF HUMAN RIGHTS IN CHILE, approved by the IACHR, March 12, 1976. OAS/Ser. L/V/II. 37; doc. 19, corr. 1 119 (June 28, 1976).

57. Text of speech in Dep't State Publication 8866, SIXTH GENERAL ASSEMBLY OF THE ORGANIZATION OF AMERICAN STATES 3 (June 1976).

58. *Id.*, at 4.

59. For vote counting, Cuba is regarded as one of the 26 members.

60. These quotations are from President Jimmy Carter's address to the General Assembly's inaugural session (June 21, 1978). On the contrast between the attitudes of the two administrations on human rights, *see* Drew, *Human Rights,* THE NEW YORKER (July 18, 1977).

61. Remarks by M. Schneider before the Subcommittee on International Organizations of the House Committee on International Relations, *quoted in* Dep't State Statement (Oct. 25, 1977).

62. Address by Warren Christopher to the American Bar Association, The Diplomacy of Human Rights: The First Year (Feb. 13, 1978) *reprinted in* 78 DEP'T STATE BULL. 30 (Mar. 1978).

63. In his address at the General Assembly, Carter referred to the IACHR as "one of our region's most important instruments," and he devoted more than one-quarter of his address to the subject of human rights. In contrast, Secretary General Alejandro Orfila, in his speech on the same occasion, referred to the work of five OAS agencies, none of which was the IACHR, and gave less than one-tenth of his space to the subject of human rights. The text of Orfila's address was issued by the Public Information Department of the OAS.

Section
C
SECURITY, PEACEKEEPING, AND ARMS CONTROL

Chapter 10

THE INTER-AMERICAN MILITARY SYSTEM: HISTORICAL DEVELOPMENT, CURRENT STATUS, AND IMPLICATIONS FOR U.S. POLICY

John Child

INTRODUCTION: CONCEPTUAL TOOLS AND THEORETICAL FRAMEWORK

This study examines the historical development, current status, and implications for U.S. policy of the Inter-American Military System (IAMS) in terms of contemporary analytical tools suggested by the systems approach to the study of international relations.

The study is organized as follows: First, the conceptual tools and theoretical framework are presented. Then the historical development of the IAMS is examined over five periods: prior to World War II, World War II (1942-45), early cold war years (1945-61), late cold war years (1961-67) and contemporary period (1967-present).

Each period is studied in terms of strategic assumptions, geopolitical perceptions, threat scenarios, rationale and purpose of the IAMS, changes in the IAMS and its components from the previous period, achievements and beneficiaries of the IAMS, systemic functions performed by the IAMS, dominant strategic concept, and dominant system model.

Next the IAMS is analyzed at its apogee (1961-67) in terms of the linkages between its various components. The final section assesses the future of the IAMS in light of current trends in the Inter-American System, draws conclusions from the preceding analysis, and suggests possible actions relating to U.S. policy initiatives in the current move to reform the Inter-American System.

It is evident from even a cursory examination of the Inter-American System and U.S.-Latin American relations that there exists a number of multilateral and bilateral military entities with a wide range of activities and goals. What is not so clear is whether these entities justifiably can be called elements of a military system in the sense of being a part of an organized, integrated, and goal-oriented larger whole.

It is quite possible that an IAMS, defined in fairly rigorous terms, does not in fact exist. But the concept merits consideration merely by virtue of the fact that politically significant individuals and institutions within the Americas have acknowledged its existence and have expressed concern over its purposes and strength. For example, the eighth and ninth conferences of the chiefs of American armies (meeting in 1968 and 1969) passed resolutions calling on each American army to study the IAMS and means for improving it.[1] Similarly, the staff of the Inter-American Defense Board (IADB) in 1971 prepared a study entitled "The Inter-American Military System," but differences of opinion within the IADB Council of Delegates prevented approval of this document.

Further evidence of the concept came at the tenth conference of American armies (1973), when the Peruvian delegation called for abolishing the IAMS while the Argentine delegation, speaking in support of the Peruvians, demanded a revision of IAMS goals and organization.[2]

In yet another instance, elaborating on this theme in a book, a recent prime minister (and army commander) of Peru presented the argument that the IAMS was created by the United States to serve its anachronistic security interests, and therefore must be reorganized to fit current realities.[3]

These examples serve to underscore the need to study the IAMS and project its future, within a contemporary conceptual framework.

This study uses the tools of systemic functions, linkages, and system models to argue that:

1. No IAMS existed prior to World War II.
2. During World War II the foundations for an IAMS were created in the face of a strongly perceived external threat.
3. The IAMS declined as a functional system in the early cold war years (1945-61) due to divergent U.S. and Latin threat perception.
4. The IAMS reached its structural and functional apogee in the 1961-67 period in reaction to the strongly perceived threat of Castro-inspired guerrilla warfare.
5. Since 1967, the IAMS has entered a period of fragmentation and dysfunctional decline.
6. The present moment, and the current moves to reform the OAS, offer an opportunity to halt this decline under a new strategic concept stressing a mature military relationship between the United States and Latin America.

This study employs Talcott Parson's system functions criteria to assess the performance of the IAMS as a system.[4] These are:

1. Pattern maintenance: Are recurring and identifiable patterns of interaction maintained within the System?

2. Goal attainment: Do the System and its components have clear goals and is visible progress being made to achieve those goals?

3. Adaptation: Do the System and its components show a capacity to cope with changes in the environment?

4. Integration: Is the System progressing toward greater integration, defined as a closer interdependence of its components and a greater sense of shared values?

James N. Rosenau's linkage concepts are employed to analyze the relative significance of individual system components.[5]

For each of the 24 different hypothesized components of the IAMS, there are potential linkages to each of the other components. Thus: 24 × 23 = 552 possible linkages within the IAMS. Each of these linkages (as defined below) will be classified as: P = penetrative, R = response, E = emulative, I = indirect, or N = none. A matrix showing these 552 possible linkages is included in Appendix A.

Borrowing heavily from Kaplan's possible models of the international political system, we can hypothesize six possible models for the Inter-American Military System.[6] It should be noted that we are not suggesting that any of these models would have an existence independent of the political milieu of U.S.-Latin relations. On the contrary, they almost certainly would be merely the military facet of the broader body of hemispheric international relations.

The six models suggested, in decreasing order of integration, are:

1. The universal-regional model, in which military transnationalism is the major force. The model would require almost total submergence of nationalism and could exist only in a political environment of complete regional integration and effective government by an OAS more powerful than any state or group of states in the hemisphere. Needless to say, this model is highly utopian and extremely improbable.

2. The alliance model, in which nations maintain their identity and sovereignty (this model thus differs from the universal-regional model) but no nation exercises hegemony. Such an IAMS would require almost unanimous political and military consensus or a clear and present armed threat to make the alliance cohesive. A further condition is that there must be at least two alliance partners with roughly equal power to avoid the emergence of a hegemonic power in the alliance.

3. The hegemonic model, in which one major power in the hemisphere outclasses the remaining nations and uses the IAMS for its own strategic-security purposes. While these purposes are not necessarily detrimental to the interests of the lesser states, they clearly must give up a measure of their independence and sovereignty in order to participate in

the system (in fact, they may have no choice about participating if the hegemonic power so decides).

4. The bipolar model envisions a polarization of the hemisphere nations around two axes of approximately equal power. There would be, in effect, two competing IAMS at the service of the two poles.

5. The multipolar model with a series of subregional "military systems" that would replace the hemisphere-wide IAMS.

6. The fragmented model, which would imply a complete breakup of the IAMS into narrow national military-strategic interests. The United States, if involved at all in this model, would enter by means of bilateral military arrangements with key countries.

HISTORICAL DEVELOPMENT OF THE IAMS

Prior to World War II

As indicated, there was no IAMS prior to World War II. From the time of independence until the mid-1930s the U.S. strategic approach to Latin America was basically unilateral, with little concern for creation of a multilateral or bilateral IAMS. This unilateral approach was the major factor in preventing the emergence of an IAMS.

The basic strategic assumption was that there was no military threat to the hemisphere and thus no need for an Inter-American Military System.

The principal U.S. geopolitical perception of the hemisphere at the time stemmed from the maritime world views of Admiral Alfred Thayer Mahan and U.S. naval strategists, who saw the hemisphere in terms of two geopolitical areas: (1) the "U.S. lake" (Caribbean, Central America, and the north coast of South America) where U.S. economic, diplomatic, and military attention was focused and (2) the rest of the hemisphere outside the "U.S. lake," which had a much lower priority.

On the part of Latin nations within the "U.S. lake," there was no real geopolitical consciousness or belief that anything could be done about U.S. intervention. Latin nations outside the "U.S. lake," since they were not significantly affected by U.S. actions, had little reaction to the U.S. geopolitical approach to the "lake."

Other Latin geopolitical concerns of the time included: Chile's attempts to maintain its territorial gains of the War of the Pacific (1879–83) and to keep the Southern Pacific the "Chilean lake" it had been in the late nineteenth century; Colombian and Ecuadorean concern over Peruvian expansion into the upper Amazon basin; continuing Argentine-Brazilian rivalry for paramountcy in the River Plate Basin, centering on Brazil's concern with keeping open its riverine lines of communications (Plate, Parana, and Uruguay rivers) to interior southern Brazil.

No threat scenarios existed, except for the threat of U.S. intervention in the countries of the "U.S. lake." In a negative sense, the United States benefited from the lack of an IAMS in that an IAMS might have restrained unilateral U.S. action in the "lake." The dominant strategic concept was the unilateral concept of the "U.S. lake," but there was no dominant system model.

World War II

With the Good Neighbor policy initiative of 1933, the United States abandoned the "U.S. lake" strategic concept, thus creating a strategic void (strategic benign neglect) that was not filled until World War II. The World War II period saw the creation of the IAMS in the face of the strongly perceived threat of the Axis.

In terms of strategic assumptions, it was generally assumed: (1) that the war posed a real threat to the hemisphere in 1941–42, a fear that diminished after the Allies went on the offensive, and (2) that if the hemisphere were to have political, diplomatic, and economic unity in the face of this threat, there had to be a multilateral military structure and a strategic concept consistent with this political, diplomatic, and economic unity. The unilateral "U.S. lake" strategic concept clearly was not suitable.

In terms of U.S. geopolitical perceptions, the military departments (Navy and War) saw World War II hemisphere geopolitics in terms of special bilateral relationships with the key countries (Brazil, Mexico, Ecuador, Panama) in the so-called "quarter-sphere,"[7] which was the area enclosed in the optimum U.S. defensive perimeter running from Alaska to the Galapagos to the Brazilian bulge to Newfoundland.

Such a strategy can be seen as a limited expansion of the "U.S. lake" concept, with the following attractions: It was the optimum military perimeter for defending the continental United States; it included the soft underbelly of the United States (the Gulf Coast); it protected the Pacific approaches to the Panama Canal; it denied the Axis the strategic area of northeast Brazil, the closest point to potential German bases in West Africa; it committed the least amount of U.S. troops and arms; and it made minimal use of the Latin American military, which was not regarded by the U.S. military as operationally ready for intensive combat.

But the U.S. Department of State saw a need for a geopolitical and strategic concept ("hemisphere defense") that would be compatible and supportive of the multilateral thrust of the Good Neighbor Policy. The Department, and specifically Sumner Welles, argued that, if the United States was going to achieve hemisphere unity in political, diplomatic, and economic terms, there had to be a military strategy that would give each Latin nation a sense of participation in the defense of the hemisphere. This strategy was the hemisphere defense concept, and its drew its roots from Bolivarian precepts, the original presentation of the Monroe Doctrine, and the ideals of unity of the hemisphere.[8] But this concept was not particularly realistic from a military viewpoint since it overextended U.S. resources and included allies that had been strongly influenced by Germany and Italy, such as Argentina.

These divergent U.S. geopolitical perceptions were reconciled at the 1942 Third Meeting of Consultation of Foreign Ministers, where the Department of State got its multilateral symbol of hemisphere military cooperation (the Inter-American Defense Board) while the U.S. Military Departments kept the IADB impotent and pursued their preferred strategy of special bilateral relations with the principal countries of the "quarter-sphere."

While geopolitical perceptions and consciousness were not generally high in most of Latin America, there was an emotional and diplomatic commitment (at least in economic, political, and psychological terms) in the war on the side of the Allies.

Brazil, in addition to the above factors, saw an opportunity to tip the strategic balance with Argentina in its favor through a quid pro quo arrangement under which the United States would obtain access to the strategic northeast bulge in exchange for substantial military and economic aid.

Argentina, for its part, had initial doubt that the Allies would win the war, followed by growing concern over the impact of U.S. military and economic aid to Brazil and its implications for the Argentine-Brazilian rivalry for the geopolitically key area of the River Plate Basin.

Meanwhile, although U.S. concern over a direct Axis military threat to the hemisphere diminished after the Allies went on the offensive, in 1941–42 the following threat scenarios caused grave concern:

1. Use of the North Africa-Dakar-Natal-Caribbean "corridor" as a possible German invasion route. It should be noted that in 1944–45 this route was employed in reverse as a major Allies supply line.
2. German submarine warfare in the western Atlantic, especially the Atlantic Narrows between Dakar and Natal.
3. Japanese attacks on the Panama Canal and the southwestern part of the United States.
4. Axis Fifth Column activities in the hemisphere nations.

The basic rationale and purpose of the IAMS was to provide a multilateral military device for enhancing hemisphere cooperation in diplomatic and economic spheres while permitting the U.S. military to follow special bilateral relations in the quarter-sphere for substantive strategic matters.

Changes in the IAMS from the preceding period were major and significant, since there had been no IAMS until World War II. This period saw the creation of many important IAMS institutions that continue to this day. (For additional data on these institutions, see Appendix B.)

In multilateral terms, World War II gave birth to the Inter-American Defense Board (IADB) as the principal organ of the multilateral IAMS, although opposition by the U.S. military departments limited the IADB's role to recommending and advising. Other multilateral elements included: an increase in the attaché system, both in numbers and activity; the foundations of a collective security arrangement later to be formalized in the 1947 Rio Treaty; and a primitive but growing sense of military transnationalism.

Bilateral elements of the IAMS (favored by the U.S. military) included: lend-lease as a precursor to the Military Assistance Program; military missions; bilateral commissions with Brazil and Mexico to coordinate the combat support provided by those nations in the war; and training of the Latin American military in the continental United States and the Panama Canal Zone.

Unilateral elements of the IAMS also were created or enhanced, especially: the regional military headquarters for Latin America (U.S. Army Caribbean Command, later to become the triservice U.S. Southern Command); and U.S. military Latinists.

The major achievements of the IAMS in this period were to create a framework of linked institutions that permitted a feeling of hemispheric military cooperation at the multilateral level (principally the Inter-American Defense Board), along with a series of special bilateral military arrangements that solved for the United States the two basic hemispheric strategic problems of World War II (control of the Brazilian bulge and protection of the western approaches to the Panama Canal).

The principal beneficiaries of the IAMS in World War II were the United States in terms of hemisphere solidarity and the solution to the strategic problems mentioned above; Brazil in terms of substantial amounts of lend-lease and economic aid; Mexico, for the same reasons but to a lesser degree; and the remaining Latin nations, which were provided with a channel for psychological participation in the military phase of the war effort.

A notable exception to the beneficiaries of the IAMS was Argentina which, because of its reluctance to break relations or declare war on the Axis, received no lend-lease or economic aid during World War II.

In general, the IAMS fulfilled the system functions well in the World War II period. Patterns of World War II cooperation measures were maintained. The IAMS attained the goals of anti-Axis alliance and adapted itself well to the Allies' wartime goals. There was a good sense of shared values, but integration of military establishments was minor (except, in a limited sense, for Brazil and Mexico) because of the overwhelming U.S. power and the U.S. military's lack of interest in operational ties to the Latin military.

The dominant strategic concept of the time involved an interplay of a token multilateral symbolic concept ("hemisphere defense") that served as a cover for the true operating strategy: the special bilateral relationship with the key nations in the quarter-sphere.

The dominant IAMS model in World War II was a combination of the alliance and hegemonic models. Elements of the alliance model were present in that there was a collective security understanding against the Axis threat. However, the dominant model was basically hegemonic because of the overwhelming U.S. superiority in all aspects of national power.

The Early Cold War Years, 1945–61

In the early cold war, the IAMS declined as a functional system from its World War II performance under the pressure of divergent U.S.-Latin perceptions of the threat and priorities.

In terms of strategic assumptions, the United States assumed that Latin America was a very secondary arena of the cold war; that if a nuclear war broke out, Latin America would have only a minimal role to play; and that Latin America's major contribution would be as a supplier of strategic raw materials.

These assumptions gave rise to the early U.S. strategic approach to Latin America in the cold war as an area of "secondary space" that could be benignly neglected in the face of higher priorities.[9]

Some thought was given to linking the Rio Treaty to NATO in an "Atlantic triangle" strategic concept, but this idea, proposed by Secretary of State John Foster Dulles in the mid 1950s, was abandoned when the Latins received it with little enthusiasm.

For their part, the Latin nations assumed that there was no real strategic role for them to play and that the U.S. "benign neglect" was not only strategic but also economic and political.

Meanwhile, the U.S. global geopolitical outlook had shifted to an aerospace view (propounded by Alexander de Seversky and others) under which the monolithic communist enemy could best be contained by the strategies of atomic deterrence and massive retaliation.

On the part of Latin America in general there was grudging acknowledgment of the geopolitical perceptions held by the United States, but also resentment over U.S. neglect of Latin America.

Certain Latin American nations were developing significant geopolitical perceptions of their own. Brazil was digesting the implications of the geopolitical "Travassos Doctrine," which stressed the national integration of its interior in a march westward. Of increasing importance were the geopolitical ideas of General Golbery do Couto e Silva, which went beyond the Travassos Doctrine in a search for the continental projection of Brazil as an ally of the United States.

Argentina continued its traditional geopolitical rivalry with Brazil, but with greater impetus under Perón's concept of a Greater Argentina exercising influence in the Southern Cone.

There was no credible threat scenario involving Latin America in this period, except as a very secondary theater in a cold war or nuclear conflict. It was very difficult to postulate any circumstances in which the World War II hemisphere defense concept would become operational—the specter of Russian or Chinese divisions invading Latin America was not particularly believable. With the exception of the Colombian battalion and destroyer provided to UN Forces in the Korean War, the Latin nations did not respond to U.S. expressions of concern over the Sino-Soviet threat in that conflict.

With no credible threat scenarios, the rationale and purpose of the IAMS suffered accordingly. U.S. strategists envisioned the Inter-American System primarily in terms of the collective security arrangements (the Rio Treaty), but the 1955 attempt to tie Latin America more closely into the network of anticommunist containment alliances (NATO, SEATO, CENTO) failed in the face of Latin reluctance to militarize the OAS.

A secondary (and unwritten) purpose of the IAMS in this period from the U.S. perspective was that the U.S. domination of the IAMS was a useful mechanism for denying European arms sellers an entry into the Latin American market. This U.S. concern was operationalized in terms of standardization efforts under which Latin American military establishments would be equipped mainly with U.S. arms and encouraged to accept U.S. training, organization, and doctrine.

The significant change in the IAMS from the preceding period was that it languished due to the lack of a credible threat scenario or a strategic concept in which the IAMS could have a meaningful role.

IAMS institutions continued, but with a diminished sense of purpose. The IADB was hard pressed to plan meaningfully for hemisphere defense. The collective security arrangement was formalized in the 1947 Rio Treaty, but it clearly was much weaker than NATO and soon was employed more as a politico-diplomatic instrument than as a military alliance.

Meanwhile, the OAS Charter (1948) included a hypothetical military organ (the Advisory Defense Committee or ADC) but specifically excluded the IADB from the formal OAS structure, a situation that can be interpreted as a reflection of Latin concern over a militarized OAS.

At the same time, the Joint Mexican-U.S. Defense Commission declined in activity as Mexico showed a clear reluctance to maintain a tight security relationship with the United States.

In the early 1950s the United States began establishing a series of military assistance groups in Latin America by means of bilateral mutual security treaties with 17 Latin nations. While these treaties were justified as implementing multilateral IADB plans for hemisphere defense, in retrospect they clearly were bilateral in nature and served primarily to operationalize U.S. standardization objectives.

Because of the lack of a credible threat, IAMS achievements were very limited in the early cold war period. To the extent that Latin America was quiescent the United States benefited in that strategic resources could be committed to higher priority cold war concerns. The United States also benefited from the standardization aspects of the mutual security treaties. Further, it can be argued that Latin American military establishments benefited from the arms and training supplied under the Military Assistance Program, although by the late 1950s there was mounting criticism that these weapons and training were not being used for hemisphere defense as much as for the suppression of internal political dissent.

In general, systemic functions were severely weakened by the U.S.-Latin divergence on threats and priorities. Limited and erratic patterns of an anticommunist alliance were maintained. U.S. goals of forging an alliance were imperfectly attained. But adaptation was poor as the Latins resisted U.S. efforts to involve them more deeply in the cold war. Integration, meanwhile, was weakened by divergent goals. The security assistance programs and U.S. efforts at achieving weapons standardization produced limited integration.

No single strategic concept dominated the IAMS in this period. Officially, hemisphere defense continued as the basic strategic concept for the IAMS, but in a cold war context there seemed little likelihood of a direct Soviet or Chinese invasion of the Western Hemisphere, even in the case of a nuclear Armaggedon.

U.S. global cold war strategy tended to divide the world into a "power belt" of "primary space" from latitude 10° North to 40° North in which the bulwark of Western civilization (NATO) was locked in a bitter struggle against a tight Sino-Soviet bloc. The rest of the world (including most of Latin America) was in "secondary space" with a supporting role in terms of providing raw materials.

In the mid 1950s the United States attempted to involve Latin America in an "Atlantic triangle" strategic concept by which the Rio Treaty (Latin America and the United States) would be tied to NATO (Western Europe, Canada, and the United States) in a triangular strategic relationship. However, as indicated above, the Latins resisted this concept and it never became operational.

During this time, the dominant system model of World War II—the alliance-hegemonic model—shifted toward a more purely U.S. hegemonic model in the face of Latin reluctance to become too closely tied to the U.S. anticommunist alliance network.

The Late Cold War Years, 1961–67

These late cold war years saw the IAMS reach its greatest structural, organizational, and functional expansion as a reaction to Fidel Castro's attempts to export guerrilla warfare in Latin America.

In the wake of Castro's 1956–59 triumph over Fulgencio Batista and his subsequent attempt to export revolution, key strategic assumptions were that Castro-inspired and supported guerrilla warfare under the "foco" strategic concept was a very real threat to Latin America and U.S. interests in the hemisphere; that the "antifoco" strategic concept that applied internal defense and development (IDAD) techniques to the Latin environment was a viable counter to the "focos"; and that the old concept of hemisphere defense in World War II or cold war terms was losing credibility as the basis for the U.S.-Latin military relationship.

In terms of geopolitical perceptions, there was general agreement that Latin America was a suitable theater of operations for guerrilla warfare. This perception involved a shift away from classical spatial geopolitical frameworks (maritime, continental, and aerospace geopolitical analyses) to the "revolutionary" geopolitical concept in which guerrilla warfare would be fought mainly in the interior space of the hearts and minds of the rural (and later urban) masses of Latin America.

The predominant threat scenario was the Castro-Che Guevara-Régis Debray vision of "One, two, three, many Vietnams in Latin America" under the foco concept in which the Andes would become the Sierra Maestra of America.

The first expression of the foco theory is contained in Che Guevara's 1961 book *Guerra de Guerrillas,* in which he argued, contrary to traditional Marxist-Leninist theory, that it is not always necessary to wait for all the objective conditions for a revolution since the guerrilla foco can create them.

Castro's attempts to export the Cuban Revolution in the early 1960s operationalized this theory and caused major concern among U.S. military strategists. The concern was linked to a growing belief in the quasi invincibility of the guerrilla in a nuclear stalemate among the major powers. First Mao in China, then Giap in Vietnam, then Algeria and Cuba—all seemed to indicate that conventional strategic concepts were now obsolete.

Mao had preached that the guerrilla had to survive among the people as a fish among water; popular support was the sine qua non for guerrilla movements. For Mao, popular support was guaranteed by the objective conditions of harsh repressive governments and the guerrilla's programs of reform.

Obsessed by the victory of Castro, Guevara and Debray agreed that the objective conditions were not as important as the example set by the mystical guerrillas fighting heroically in the mountains.[10]

Despite its immediacy, the threat was not evenly perceived. Several key Latin nations (Mexico, Chile, Uruguay, Brazil in 1962–64) saw the threat as much less severe than did the United States or the countries directly affected by the foco theory.

The basic purpose of the revitalized IAMS in this period was to forge an effective counter to the threat of the focos. For the Latin nations directly threatened by guerrilla warfare, the antifoco strategy was an exercise in self-preservation.

For the United States, the rationale for the antifoco contained several elements. It was seen as the militarily most realistic answer to the threat of guerrilla warfare, and it was considered compatible with the Alliance for Progress in that it gave the Latin American military a role in creating the stable conditions required for the orderly development of the alliance's programs.

There was also the hope that, by giving the Latin military forces a realistic role in counterinsurgency and nation building, their energies would be absorbed in productive endeavors that might make them less likely to intervene in the political milieu.

The antifoco concept also produced a rare convergence of U.S. congressional, Departments of State and Defense views on the Latin American military, a fact that did much to assure speedy legislative approval of implementing programs.[11]

The IAMS in this period saw very significant growth, with the revitalizing of existing institutions and the creation of new ones. Clearly the apogee of the IAMS was reached in the mid 1960s as U.S. and Latin resources were mobilized to face what was seen as a very real threat.

Initially the framework for this revised U.S. military interest in Latin America through the antifoco concept was handled in the context of the old Military Assistance Program system. However, the MAP system was basically a series of bilateral U.S.-Latin nation agreements and had the disadvantage of not lending itself to the multilateral thrust of the Alliance for Progress. Accordingly, a conscious effort was made in the early and mid-1960s to expand greatly the multilateral aspects of the Inter-American System under U.S. aegis.

In functional terms, the changes in the IAMS involved a rapid shift from the rather mythical hemisphere defense role in a nuclear war to a much more realistic role as the instrument for a cooperative U.S.-Latin military effort to prevent the outbreak or contain the spread of the guerrilla warfare focos.

In structure, the IAMS saw significant growth. There was a shift in the Military Assistance Program away from conventional warfare arms and training to the tools of the antifoco: internal defense and development, counterinsurgency, and civic action. The Inter-American Defense Board was revitalized and the Inter-American Defense College was created (1962). Subregional military cooperation agreements were created, most notably the Central American Defense Council (CONDECA), and there was an increase in the size and significance of the U.S. military regional headquarters for Latin America, the U.S. Southern Command (USSOUTHCOM).

Periodic conferences of the chiefs of each service were held, along with frequent maneuvers and tactical exercises, which were naval (the highly successful UNITAS series) as well as ground, air, and combined. Inter-American military radio nets were set up, and there was an increase in the size and scope of U.S. training programs for the Latin military in both the Panama Canal Zone and the United States. In addition, a U.S. Army Special Forces Group was created in the Canal Zone, with Latin America as its primary operational area. There also were attempts to create a permanent standby inter-American peace force.

Proponents of the IAMS point to the failure of the focos as a major achievement of the IAMS. A more objective assessment also would have to consider that the focos failed basically because the Cuban Revolution was not an exportable commodity where specific favorable conditions did not exist. In retrospect, it seems fair to conclude that the IAMS in this period accelerated and made more likely the failure of the focos, but that they eventually would have failed regardless.

The beneficiaries in this process were both the United States and each of the Latin nations threatened by guerrilla warfare. In addition, there seemed to be a bonus effect for the United States in the existence of a vastly expanded IAMS in the mid-1960s, especially when the degree of U.S. influence in the IAMS in the period is analyzed. However, as will be examined below, the unity and sense of purpose of the IAMS that existed in the mid-1960s quickly evaporated in the late 1960s and early 1970s.

In general, systemic functions performed by the IAMS in this period were effective but somewhat uneven due to the lack of unanimity of the perception of the Castro foco threat. Strong patterns of reacting to the foco theory were maintained, and the goal of defeating the focos was achieved. But two observations should be made in passing.

First, in retrospect it appears the antifoco concept may have had only marginal impact on the focos. Guerrilla warfare in general, and the Cuban Revolution in particular, no longer seem to be the easily exportable commodity that Castro, Guevara, and Debray once believed them to be. The absence of internal objective conditions probably did more to defeat the export of revolution than any U.S. efforts through the IAMS.

Second, the linking of the concept of development to that of defense may have been a significant factor in the raising of the political, social, and economic consciousness of the Latin military and the resulting military reformist movements in the 1967–76 contemporary period.

In terms of other systemic functions, there was good adaptation to the internal defense and development IDAD concept by nations that accepted the concept; however, the adaptation was not unanimous nor was it permanent. Integration was substantial in terms of the greatly expanded IAMS. However, integration, like adaptation, was neither unanimous nor irreversible.

The dominant strategic concept in the IAMS was the antifoco, which in operational terms meant the application of IDAD techniques to the specific environment of Latin America.

The IDAD concept has two operating parts: (1) internal defense, which is the use of military counterinsurgency techniques to trap and eliminate the guerrillas (small unit actions, aggressive patrolling, high mobility, fast communications) and (2) internal development, which is the employment of civic action by which military resources (educational skills, construction equipment, communications and transportation assets) are used to improve the economic and social conditions of the lower classes so the government, and not the guerrillas, retains the people's loyalty and support.

Overwhelming U.S. power and influence in the expanded IAMS make it clear that the dominant system model in this period was hegemonic, although with elements (not unanimous) of an anti-Castro alliance model.

From 1967 to the Present

Background

The most recent period has been one of considerable disarray and dysfunctional tendencies in the IAMS. Because of the significance that this trend has for the future of the IAMS, it will be explored in some detail here before turning to the analysis.

General factors causing dysfunction of the IAMS include diminished perceptions of the danger of guerrilla warfare in Latin America. With the death of Che Guevara, the threat of severe and victorious rural guerrilla warfare spent itself; the shift to urban guerrilla warfare and terrorism was seen as a real threat in most countries for only a brief period until it degenerated into random violence and political assassination, although it remains a significant threat in a few areas.

Meanwhile, the Alliance for Progress declined as it became clear that the optimism of the early 1960s was unjustified. Latin America was relegated to a low priority as the U.S. military, and the United States in general, focused attention on Southeast Asia.

Other factors in IAMS dysfunction include U.S. abandonment of the 1961–66 attempt to create a tightly integrated IAMS; the use of dependency analysis as a theoretical framework from which past and present U.S. actions are seen in imperialistic terms; new currents among the Latin American military, especially populist reformism; deliberate attempts by the Latin American military to break dependency on the United States; a decline in importance of the IDAD concept as other military approaches (national defense, classic preparation for conventional war) gained; and the increased possibility of open conflict in Latin America (Chile-Peru, Honduras-El Salvador, Guatemala-Belize).

A key feature of this period was the emergence of a totally new and profoundly significant political factor: military reformism. While there always had been isolated cases of military reform movements in the past, these usually had proved to be either opportunistic or incapable of generating coherent plans for action.

Two separate currents of military reformism can be identified in this period. One is the Peruvian, with emphasis on social reforms. While economic factors were not ignored, they clearly had a lower priority than the attempt to restructure Peruvian society along the models developed by the CAEM (Centro de Altos Estudios Militares). What emerged from the Peruvian Revolution was a military reform movement that was radical, populist, and intensely nationalistic. While the Peruvian Revolution recently appears to have entered a more moderate phase, its military populism remains a new and powerful model.

The other model was the Brazilian, with emphasis on economic growth of the industrial and commercial sectors at the expense of social and political reforms. What emerged was a technocratic and authoritarian reform movement that, for the time being at least, is closely tied to the United States.

There is no general agreement on the causes of the emergence of the so-called "new military" in Latin America, but many observers note the following factors: a higher percentage of officers from the middle class than in the past; better education (including heavy doses of the social sciences) than their predecessors; and more exposure to the realities of underdevelopment in Latin America, especially as seen in the framework of dependency theory.[12]

The following specific rationale also is suggested: The emergence of a reformist and nationalistic "new military" can be linked to the heavy emphasis on IDAD and the IAMS by the United States. In this context, it is argued that the civic action component of the IDAD concept raised the social consciousness of many Latin American military officers by sensitizing them to the plight of the lower classes in their nations, while the counterinsurgency component of IDAD convinced them that guerrilla wars cannot be won by military means alone. Politically, this raising of military social consciousness caused many military officers to evaluate the effectiveness of reforms proposed by civilian governments and find them unsatisfactory. The result was an increase in coups as the military reformists felt they could do a better job than the civilians. In addition, the strong U.S. push to create an IAMS was discredited severely by the

1965 Dominican Republic intervention, causing a strong nationalistic backlash among the military and a profound mistrust of any moves to integrate the military of the hemisphere.

This period also saw a very significant decline in the size, nature, and importance of the U.S. Security Assistance Program (SAP) in Latin America.

Apart from the fact that Vietnam requirements left very few U.S. military resources available for Latin America, a series of congressional restrictions and ceilings made it increasingly difficult to grant or sell weapons to Latin America and caused strong Latin American military reaction to what was viewed as paternalism and interference.

In operational terms the SAP grant program was reduced sharply and the sales component fell off as more and more of the congressional restrictions made their impact felt.

One result was a dramatic increase in arms purchases from Europe, especially France and Great Britain. In 1967–72, the six largest South American countries spent $1.2 billion on major arms purchases (mainly jet aircraft) in Europe and only $216 million in the United States.[13]

With the ending of U.S. commitments in Southeast Asia, U.S. arms manufacturers made efforts to reverse this ratio. However, the purchase of a major weapons system such as high performance jet aircraft is a long-range proposition that includes maintenance, training, and supply support for many years. Thus, these purchases have tended to lock in significant elements of the Latin American military to European suppliers in a technological dependency relationship that the United States will have difficulty breaking in the immediate future. Of special contemporary concern is the Peruvian-Soviet arms link, with the Soviet Union supplying major quantities of armor, artillery, and aircraft. There is considerable Chilean concern that these weapons are being obtained in order to refight the War of the Pacific (1879–83) before its centennial arrives.

This period also saw several deliberate Latin attempts to break military dependency on the United States. Some were technological, others strategic or tactical.

Technological examples include Argentina's Plan Europa to enter into licensing agreements with major European arms producers as a means of stimulating Argentina's own arms industry while reducing dependency on the United States. Another example is the emergence of Brazil as a supplier of arms, aircraft, and military vehicles to the smaller South American nations. In 1975 alone Brazil sold or granted more than 35 aircraft and numerous vehicles to Chile, Paraguay, and Ecuador.[14] These arms transfers represent both obsolete weapons systems of U.S. origin and the more significant products of Brazil's own weapons industry.

The move to break Latin strategic military dependency on the United States has been led by Peru, and to a lesser degree Argentina. Specific instances include a call for changes in the Rio Treaty to make it serve Latin America's concerns and not merely U.S. strategic interests,[15] as well as the identification of economic security, plurality of ideologies, and defense against (U.S.) economic aggression as major security problems.

Another example is the concept of integral security as the cornerstone of Western Hemisphere defense. While no one is quite sure what "integral security" will mean, the Peruvians have defined it in terms of an anti-U.S. umbrella concept that will include economic security and the acceptance of a plurality of ideologies.

Other points include reform of the remnants of the IAMS to make them more responsive to Latin needs and less under U.S. domination[16]; the return of Cuba to the Inter-American System and possibly the OAS and related organs; and the holding of exclusively Latin military conferences, with U.S. participation excluded.

Meanwhile, there has been a noticeable shift in this period away from the IDAD-counterinsurgency tactical precepts and back to more conventional concepts of a nationalistic defense against a foreign invader.

Analysis

The most striking characteristic of the present period is the absence of any strategic assumptions accepted by a majority of hemisphere nations. In part, this is a natural result of the decline in the threat of guerrilla warfare from the 1961–67 peak. But as noted above, other and deeper ills beset the IAMS and the Inter-American System as a whole.

A key concern is the effect of the U.S. obsession with Vietnam and its own internal problems, which relegated Latin America once again to low-priority status. Related issues are Latin attempts to break the perceived bonds of dependency (including military dependency) on the United States and the distrust over U.S. goals and methods stemming from the 1965 Dominican Republic intervention.

Furthermore, several Latin nations (especially in the Southern Cone) consider that the United States is now an unreliable ally and therefore they must be prepared to go it alone, either individually or in a subregional alliance, against what they perceive as a renewed wave of guerrilla warfare.

Contemporary geopolitical perceptions are diverse and sometimes incompatible. The United States seems to lack any coherent geopolitical vision of Latin America's role in terms of the IAMS. From the Latin perspective, the United States seems to be looking inward, with strong indications that Latin America is once more being strategically benignly neglected.

In the apparent absence of a U.S. strategic or geopolitical vision, geopolitical thinking in Latin America itself is becoming more significant, especially in the Southern Cone nations where the military is in power. In several countries, geopolitical frameworks seem to be guiding both international relations and internal development programs.

In Brazil, for instance, the geopolitical ideas of Mario Travassos, Golbery do Couto e Silva, and Carlos Meira Mattos and the Escola Superior de Guerra are the guiding force in the linking of the concepts of national security and development as Brazil moves from national integration to continental projection to its self-perceived destiny as a world power.

In Argentina, geopoliticians (Juan E. Guglialmelli, Jorge E. Atencio, Carlos P. Mastrorilli) express concern over Brazil's movements and view with particular alarm Brazil's geopolitical conception of the "living frontier" as it pertains to influence in the traditional buffer states of South America and to Brazilian control of the hydroelectric resources of the River Plate Basin.

On the west coast of South America, geopolitical concerns focus on the centennial of the War of the Pacific and the impact of Chile's military inferiority in the face of Soviet arms to Peru.

Like current geopolitical perceptions, threat scenarios are varied and inconsistent.

The 1961–67 specter of successful Cuban-style guerrilla warfare remains alive, in its rural as well as urban manifestations.

For the military governments of the Southern Cone, the threat is not merely Cuban-inspired guerrilla warfare but also the perceived close coordination and mutual support between the various indigenous guerrilla movements (Tupumaros of Uruguay, Revolutionary Left Movement (MIR) of Chile, Peoples Revolutionary Army (ERP) of Argentina).

In Central America, the border problems between El Salvador and Honduras led to one armed conflict (1969) and rising tensions in mid-1976.

Conventional conflict also exists as a possible scenario in terms of Guatemala-Belize tensions and, more significantly, in the possibility of a Peruvian-Chilean clash.

Also, the Cuban military involvement in Africa has given rise to a new threat scenario, that of "intervention by consent" under which a revolutionary faction, rump government, or party in a border or internal conflict would request Cuban intervention.

For the more nationalistic and radical Latin regimes, the major threat scenarios are framed in the context of dependency theory analysis in which an imperialistic United States is the major threat.

The United States itself appears to perceive the strategic threat in terms of a combination of several of the above elements, with emphasis on Cuban military adventurism (guerrilla warfare or intervention by consent), with the added element of concern for a confrontation with a Latin America united by economic or political issues.

In light of the present divergences over threats, it is not surprising that there is little consensus on the rationale or purposes of the IAMS. Concern over Cuba's African involvements appeared to provide some common ground, but that now seems to have substantially dissipated.

The U.S. government has a considerable vested interest in the institutions of the 1961–67 IAMS and sees value (admittedly diminished) in supporting the IAMS as the framework for military cooperation under U.S. aegis.

U.S. arms suppliers also have a vested economic interest in the IAMS, and in particular the SAP as the principal conduit for arms sales to Latin America. Decline in the IAMS and SAP, coupled with aggressive Soviet and European arms exports, are a threat to these interests.

The more reactionary regimes in Latin America tend to view the IAMS as a useful forum that offers them a more friendly audience than the OAS. Chile in particular has been active in attempts to use the IAMS in this manner and to increase its significance in relation to the rest of the Inter-American System. Two recent examples illustrate this approach. At the July 1975 meeting of consultation, Chile floated the idea that the IADB should be consulted to determine if Cuba still represented a threat to the hemisphere. Subsequently, at the October 1975 conference of chiefs of American armies, the Chilean delegation argued that the IADB should be "institutionalized" (incorporated into the OAS Charter) to strengthen the military organs of the hemisphere. But given the current nature of the Chilean regime and the political realities of the OAS, neither of these initiatives is likely to succeed.

Meanwhile, the more radical governments in Latin America also view the IAMS as a useful forum but argue that it should be reoriented to the new threats of "economic and political aggression." The most noteworthy example of this trend is an analysis by General Mercado Jarrin of Peru.[17]

In terms of changes from the preceding period, the IAMS has seen a strong decline in both functional and structural terms from its mid-1960s apogee. Most of the institutions of the IAMS remain, but they reflect this decline.

For instance, the Military Assistance Program/Security Assistance Program has diminished greatly in impact due to a series of congressional restrictions (Hickenlooper, Conte, Pelley, Fulbright amendments), and in particular the 1976 congressionally mandated linkages to human rights actions and the required reduction in size and numbers of military assistance groups. Simultaneously, European, Israeli, and Soviet arms sales to Latin America have increased dramatically over their mid-1960s levels.

In addition, a strong reaction to the U.S.-dominated 1965 Inter-American Peace Force made the permanent institutionalization of that entity highly improbable; the collective security arrangement (Rio Treaty) came under pressure to include provisions against economic aggression; U.S. training for the Latin military has declined as a result of the general drop in the MAP/SAP program and may decline further in light of developments with Panama implementing the 1977 treaties with regards to the status of U.S. training facilities in the Canal Zone; and the Special Consultative Committee on Security (an OAS organ created to monitor Cuban subversion) was disestablished in late 1975.

The IAMS can point to few, if any, achievements in this period except for the simple survival of most of its institutions in the face of a general disintegration of consensus, goals, and rationale.

An overall assessment of systemic functions for this period must conclude that they were dysfunctional. The momentum of patterns maintained in the 1961-67 period continues, but with greatly declining support. No clear IAMS goals are defined, and the IAMS has adapted poorly to the new system-changing challenges. In terms of integration, the IAMS is seen as disintegrating from its apogee of 1961-67.

Nor is there a single dominant strategic concept in the IAMS at present. The antifoco remains but has lost credibility. The Cuban Angolan episode and Soviet arms supplies to Peru have brought a renewed interest in the hemisphere defense concept by the more conservative governments.

U.S. hegemony remains in the institutions of the IAMS but provides fewer dividends to the United States due to increasing criticism, and the dominant model appears to be one of fragmentation in the face of strong divergences on threat, rationale, and strategic concept.

More disturbingly, elements of bipolar or multipolar models can be discerned. The bipolar model might appear in one of two variants. One would be a "United States versus Latin America" bipolar arrangement as an offshoot of further deterioration of U.S.-Latin relations. The hypothetical Latin American military system would not necessarily be hostile to the U.S. military system but clearly would be independent of it. The other bipolar model would involve an ideological bipolarity between a "revolutionary" pole (Cuba, Peru) and a "status quo" pole (Brazil, Chile). In this model, hostilities between the two poles could break out, possibly in attempts to export revolution via guerrilla warfare.

The multipolar model suggests poles coalescing around three or more of the following: a U.S.-oriented bloc, CONDECA, a Southern Cone, a Brazil bloc, a revolutionary bloc, a reactionary bloc, or a Venezuelan-Caribbean-Central American bloc.

LINKAGE ANALYSIS

As noted above, this section analyzes the linkages existing within the IAMS in its 1961-67 apogee.

Adapting Rosenau's typology to our needs, we define five types of linkages:

1. A penetrative linkage exists from IAMS component A to component B when A participates significantly and authoritatively in the decision-making process of B.

2. A response linkage exists from IAMS component C to component D when C tends to make decisions primarily in response to D's influence.

3. An emulative linkage exists from IAMS component E to component F when E tends to make decisions based on imitation of F's decision patterns.

4. An indirect linkage exists from IAMS component G to component H when G and H share significant numbers of personnel or have linkages through a third component.

5. No linkage exists when none of the above patterns is found.

The 24 identified components of the IAMS can be arranged in a matrix to generate 24 × 23 = 552 possible linkages, with the nature of the linkage shown as: P = penetrative, R = response, E = emulative, F = indirect, and – = none. Such a matrix for the IAMS is contained in Table 10.3.

Of the total of 552 possible linkages, our chart shows 164 actual linkages, distributed as follows:

Penetrative linkages	54
Response linkages	54
Indirect linkages	55
Emulative linkages	1
Total	164

The components with the largest number of linkages (thus indicating the largest number of integrating ties in the IAMS) are:

IADB	16
U.S. military Latinists	16
Military transnationalism	16
Security Assistance Program (SAP)	15
Attaché network	9
CONDECA	7
Service chiefs conferences	7
Tactical exercises	7

The components having the smallest number of linkages (thus indicating little or no role in the IAMS) are:

Latin unilateral arrangements	2
SCCS (OAS Special Consultative Committee on Security)	2
Inter-Latin arrangements	3

The components having the most powerful influence in the IAMS can be determined by noting which components have the greatest number of penetrating linkages:

SAP	15
Attaché network	4
Rio Treaty	4
Service chiefs conferences	4
US SOUTHCOM	4
IADB	3

Our linkage analysis leads us to the following conclusion: While the IADB, military transnationalism, and U.S. military Latinists have the greatest number of linkages to other components of the IAMS, it is the Security Assistance Program that has by far the greatest quantity of penetrative linkages, thus indicating where influence in the IAMS really lies.

Our linkage analysis, plus the observations made earlier, now allow us to classify the IAMS components according to the following taxonomy:

1. Components essential to the IAMS (as presently constituted) are the SAP (by far the most important); the IADB; U.S. military Latinists; military transnationalism; the attaché network; the Rio Treaty; the service chiefs conferences; US SOUTHCOM; the Inter-American Defense College.

2. Components of some value to the IAMS are CONDECA; tactical exercises; communications networks; the Inter-American Peace Force; military observation forces; Joint Brazil-U.S. Defense Commission/Joint Brazil-U.S. Military Commission; training in the United States and Panama; U.S. mobile training teams; Latin commissions in the United States; and the Special Forces Group.

3. Components of marginal value to the IAMS: are the OAS Advisory Defense Commission and Special Consultative Committee on Security; Joint Mexican-U.S. Defense Commission; inter-Latin bilateral arrangements; and Latin unilateral arrangements.

THE FUTURE OF THE IAMS

The IAMS clearly is in a period of decline that has paralleled the declining and confrontational nature of U.S.-Latin relations since 1967.

This section of the study lists the major IAMS dysfunctional trends identified in the analysis, analyzes possible future rationales for the IAMS, assesses general U.S. policy options, offers a conclusion, and suggests possible actions for implementing this conclusion.

Dysfunctional Trends

Dysfunctional trends on the part of Latin America include the fear that a strong IAMS would come under U.S. influence and be used for U.S. strategic purposes; Latin reluctance to militarize or "NATO-ize" the essentially civilian focus of the OAS; increasing Latin American nationalism and the concomitant desire to break any U.S.-Latin military links perceived to be of dependency; Latin reluctance to accept the U.S. military concept of standardization of arms, training, and doctrine; the possible emergence of subregional military groupings other than CONDECA; and an increase in confrontation tactics in multilateral military forums.

On the part of the United States, meanwhile, there is a preference for using unilateral and bilateral channels and techniques in its military dealings with Latin America, as well as a reluctance to give U.S.-Latin multilateral military organs greater control of the Security Assistance Program.

Other contributing factors are excessive domination of the multilateral military organs (IADB, Inter-American Defense College) and declining U.S. influence and interest in Latin America.

Dysfunctional trends in the OAS include a tendency to create ad hoc military organs (observer and peacekeeping forces) rather than enhance the status of the existing multilateral organ (the IADB) or convoke the Advisory Defense Committee. Also, the OAS has a tendency to use the collective security treaty of Rio as an instrument for peaceful settlement, which is a function more properly carried out by the defunct Bogotá Pact.

Possible Future Rationales for the IAMS

Future rationales will depend on the specific threat scenarios actually experienced in the late 1970s.

Increased levels of guerrilla warfare may lead to a revival of the 1961–67 antifoco rationale for the IAMS. However, the focos of the late 1970s probably will be highly selective and much more geared to favorable local conditions than the focos of the 1960s. Thus, hemispheric consensus on a renewed antifoco rationale for the IAMS does not seem as likely as the subregional cooperation against guerrilla warfare that seems to be emerging in the Southern Cone.

Cuban intervention by consent could lead to an invocation of Article 8 (the last clause) of the Rio Treaty and the creation of an inter-American force. However, there will have to be a high level of consensus on the threat before such action could take place.

Or intrahemispheric clashes could give the IAMS a meaningful role as OAS peacekeeper or observer, but it should be noted that historically the OAS has resisted any institutionalization of a peacekeeping role for the IAMS or any of its elements.

Another possibility is that a Latin American arms race (to include the possibility of nuclear weapons development by Brazil or Argentina) could be moderated if the nations involved felt that an effective IAMS would make such an arms race less necessary.

Other rationales and purposes for the IAMS may emerge, such as a coordinating role in disaster relief or standardized search and rescue procedures.

Should the IAMS Be Preserved?

The above examination of the current status and rationale for the IAMS legitimately gives rise to a fundamental question: Should the IAMS be preserved? This section briefly explores the arguments for and against an IAMS and offers a conclusion. Many of the arguments have their origin in the narrower debate on the Military Assistance Program but have applicability here to the broader question of the IAMS itself.

Arguments for preserving the IAMS start with the military-strategic argument, which holds that the IAMS did in fact make a significant contribution to military cooperation in World War II, in the antifoco struggle (both in terms of counterinsurgency as well as nation-building civic action), and has the potential to do the same for a new threat, namely that of Cuban "intervention by consent."

Beyond meeting specific threats, the IAMS is presented in this argument as contributing to the achievement of U.S. strategic and security goals in the hemisphere. And in a negative sense, the IAMS serves a useful military purpose in terms of "military Monroism" by blocking outside military influences in Latin America.

The political influence argument, rarely voiced officially, maintains that the IAMS is a major vehicle for U.S. influence on a fundamental political actor in Latin America: the military. Beyond any manipulative implications, this political influence serves to strengthen the stability necessary for orderly growth.

The forum/channel of communication argument presents the IAMS as a valuable forum and channel of communication and understanding between important hemispheric military actors. Using the logic of functionalism, it posits the idea that greater communication will make internal conflict less likely and resistance to outside threats more credible.

Yet another approach, the arms control argument, presents the IAMS as a moderating element in the arms race. The United States is presented as a benevolent if somewhat paternalistic influence motivated by a desire to keep a lid on excessive arms purchases by the Latin Americans, for reasons that are both military (to reduce conflict potential) as well as economic (to limit resource diversion). By standardization on U.S. equipment, training and doctrine, as well as preemptive sales where necessary, the IAMS can serve as a vehicle for effecting U.S. efforts to control Latin arms spending.

The "insurance" argument uses the contingency approach to hold that the IAMS represents inexpensive insurance against future security requirements that cannot be foreseen. Since it is very difficult to create quickly alliance infrastructures and the intricate network of linked institutions in the IAMS, the System should be kept available and functioning as a hedge against future needs. Thus, the rationales listed previously (peacekeeping, humanitarian, and so forth) are in a sense peaceful surrogates for the real threats (Axis, focos) for which the System is intended. The surrogates thus serve to keep the machinery functioning and the institutions alive between threats.

Arguments against preserving the IAMS begin with the irrelevancy argument, which maintains that the IAMS is irrelevant and ineffectual in its major aims: It has not made a military or strategic contribution, it has not influenced the Latin military, it has not had an impact on the arms race, and it serves no useful purpose. Thus, it should be disbanded in the interest of economy and efficiency.

But the political cost argument, taking precisely the opposite position, holds that the IAMS has been all too effective and has cost the United States a great political price by linking it too closely to the forces of repression, conservatism, and status quo in Latin America. Thus, the United States in effect has become a hostage to the IAMS, which therefore should be dismantled or reduced.

The neo-Marxist dependency approach presents the IAMS as one of several instruments that tie Latin America to the United States in a colonial-imperial structure.

But on balance the present author finds the arguments for preserving the IAMS more persuasive than those against.

Clearly, the IAMS is not an alliance in the sense of NATO, and it would be unreasonable to expect high levels of strictly military or strategic benefits where threats and resource levels are much lower than in NATO. The limited military benefits stemming from the IAMS must be evaluated in terms of the very modest cost of the System.

The evidence is somewhat unclear on the arms control/arms race argument, but it seems obvious that the hemisphere nations will make sovereign decisions on arms purchases whether the United States stimulates or inhibits interest in the subject.

The political influence/political cost debate does not present convincing evidence that the IAMS should be abolished in order to avoid excessive entanglement with the forces of repression and hardline status quo. Presumably, the United States has enough political sophistication to draw the line somewhere between support of legitimate order and illegitimate repression.

What appears to tip the balance in favor of maintaining the IAMS, then, is that fact that it does provide limited but appreciable military benefits at modest cost, while serving as a useful vehicle for communication and influence. The fact that its value has peaked when threats peak supports the "insurance" argument that it would be well to maintain it on the assumption that it could be of value in future and unforeseen crises.

U.S. Policy Options

The United States has the following broad options in regards to the future of the IAMS:

1. A holding action that would minimize damage to the IAMS in the hope that the current radical overtones of the reform movement are temporary and will go away in the near future.
2. Complete abandonment of the IAMS and a retreat to unilateral strategic concepts.
3. Partial abandonment of the IAMS, stressing the bilateral organs of greatest pragmatic value and letting the multilateral organs die a natural death.
4. A mature military relationship stressing mutual respect and a realistic recognition that the U.S.-Latin military relationship involves only a partial convergence of interests, threat perception, goals, and shared values.

It is concluded that the IAMS is worth preserving as a useful vehicle for U.S.-Latin military cooperation and that the mature military relationship concept offers the best possibility of preserving it.

The holding action option is seen as an unrealistic assessment of the depth and strength of the current moves to reform the Inter-American System.

The complete and partial abandonment options are considered to involve an unnecessary destruction of a complex, long-lived, and unique military cooperative arrangement that offers potential for enhancing US-Latin relationships.

The mature military relationship would be based on mutual respect, which implies abandonment of U.S. military policies (especially pertaining to weapons transfers) perceived as paternalistic. Other principles would be: realistic recognition of U.S.-Latin divergences in strategic and military areas; U.S. willingness to give up a hegemonic role in the IAMS; Latin willingness to avoid confrontational situations with the United States in IAMS forums; joint commitment to explore areas of meaningful military cooperation such as peacekeeping and observation forces, humanitarian assistance, search and rescue; and increasing emphasis on the multilateral organs of the IAMS.

Several actions might be suggested as possible initial steps in the implementation of the mature military relationship.

Key issues are actions related to the Security Assistance Program which, as shown by the linkage analysis, is the most important component of the present IAMS in terms of its powerful penetrating linkages. A meaningful mature military relationship implies drastic changes in the nature of the SAP. The following are suggested: seeking to eliminate paternalistic congressional restrictions on arms transfers to Latin America; gradually eliminating the Military Assistance Program's materiel grant program and subsidized credit sales of arms; and drastically reducing the administrative and bureaucratic requirements of the Security Assistance Program.

In addition, the military assistance groups should be replaced in each country with: (1) a small liaison office assigned to the U.S. embassy; (2) U.S. mobile training teams sent on a short-term ad hoc basis; (3) Latin purchasing commissions (similar to the Brazilian commission in Washington); (4) joint U.S.-Latin bilateral commissions for the larger nations, patterned after the U.S.-Brazilian commissions, to facilitate high-level planning and supervise the carrying out of the revised Security Assistance Program.

In other areas, the IADB, and the Inter-American Defense College (IADC) as its subordinate organ, are seen as the principal multilateral organ of the IAMS and therefore the key to implementing a meaningful mature military relationship. Possible actions here include decreasing the high U.S. profile by rotating the key positions in the IADB and IADC rather than keeping them under U.S. control, as well as indicating a willingness to consider moving the IADB or IADC to a Latin nation.

The IADB should be involved in the SAP by: (1) keeping the IADB informed of the content of the bilateral mutual security treaties; (2) requesting that the IADB consider these treaties when it prepares plans for the defense of the hemisphere; (3) permitting the IADB to make recommendations on priorities and allocations of SAP funds; and (4) encouraging an operational IADB role in the coordination of the military aspects of disaster relief. This last point would mean a standing IADB plan for disaster relief and a small core of IADB staff members who would be available to go to the scene of a disaster and coordinate requests, priorities, and allocations, and to provide advice and assistance, if requested by the country concerned.

A related step would be to advocate the creation of an Inter-American Defense University to supervise the operation of the existing IADC plus a new entity, the Inter-American Defense School,' which would assume control of present U.S. military schools in the Panama Canal Zone (see below).

In general, the future status of U.S. military installations in the Panama Canal Zone could be a powerful indicator of U.S. willingness to support the concept of the mature military relationship. Possible actions include: limiting the functions of U.S. Southern Command headquarters to a command solely for canal defense; limiting military installations to those legitimately required for joint U.S.-Panamanian defense of the canal; and proposing that the U.S. Army, Navy, and Air Force training schools in the present zone be "internationalized" by turning their control over to the IADB.

A mature military relationship also could be implemented by actions pertaining to the OAS. For instance, the revised charter should drop the Advisory Defense Committee as an anachronistic and hypothetical organ. Possible incorporation of the IADB into the revised OAS Charter also should be explored. Should this not be feasible, a separate OAS General Assembly resolution should reconfirm the IADB mandate and juridical credentials. In addition, the OAS should be encouraged to solicit and use IADB advice on security matters and to use the IADB operationally for military expertise in manning OAS observer elements in the case of inter-American conflicts.

Actions pertaining to other multilateral military organs of the IAMS also could be taken. Service chiefs' conferences could increase their linkages to each other and to the IADB, possibly through a permanent secretariat at the IADB. Also, multinational tactical exercises and communication nets could be encouraged and realistically employed, possibly in conjunction with disaster relief or search and resuce plans of the IADB. Finally, the emergence of subregional military bodies should be encouraged as long as they are not systematically dysfunctional (that is, as long as they support the IAMS and are not confrontational).

All the actions listed above imply a radical change in the nature of the IAMS. In particular, they involve a substantial decline in U.S. control of the IAMS. Their full implementation undoubtedly would make the IAMS less immediately responsive to U.S. interests and will decrease, at least from the U.S. perspective, the efficient operation of the IAMS.

However, one of the conclusions of this study is that the IAMS is in a significant and perhaps fatal decline, partly because of excessive U.S. control. Efficiency and responsiveness to U.S. interests have been obtained at the price of increasing Latin resentment and distrust of the IAMS.

As the linkage analysis developed in this study suggests, the IAMS can be likened to a many-spoked wheel in which the U.S. Military Assistance Program functions as the hub. This hub, for a variety of reasons, is rapidly shrinking in size and influence. For the system to endure, a new hub must be found.

If the IAMS is worth preserving as an instrument of hemispheric military cooperation, its meaningful survival can be assured only through a revised and mature military relationship such as that suggested here.

NOTES

1. 1969 CONFERENCE OF AMERICAN ARMIES FINAL REPORT unpaged.

2. *Latin America,* Foreign Broadcast Information Service, Sept. 6, 1973, at 0-3.

3. E. MERCADO JARRIN and GENERAL EDGARDO, SECURITY, POLICY AND STRATEGY 170 *passim* (Washington JPRS 1975).

4. J. CHARLESWORTH, CONTEMPORARY POLITICAL ANALYSIS 92-97 (1967).

5. Rosenau, *Theorizing across Systems: Linkage Politics Revisited,* in CONFLICT BEHAVIOR AND LINKAGE POLITICS 42-43 (J. Wilkenfeld ed. 1973).

6. M. KAPLAN, SYSTEM AND PROCESS IN INTERNATIONAL POLITICS (1957).

7. Krock, *The Quarter Sphere Theory of Our Security,* N.Y. Times, July 11, 1940, at 18, col. 5.

8. H. BALDWIN, UNITED WE STAND! DEFENSE OF THE WESTERN HEMISPHERE 92 (1941).

9. J. Kieffer, *Defending the Western Hemisphere,* 7 AMERICAS 5-6 (August 1955).

10. R. DEBRAY, REVOLUTION IN THE REVOLUTION? 119-20.

11. W. BARBER and C. RONNING, INTERNAL SECURITY AND MILITARY POWER 66-67 (1966).

12. E. WILLIAMS, LATIN AM. POL. THOUGHT 22 (1974).

13. Pacific News Service, 1975.

14. *Latin America,* Foreign Broadcast Information Service, Jan. 3, 1975, May 30, 1975.

15. *See* MERCADO JARRIN, *supra* note 3, at 171.

16. *Id.,* at 172-74.

17. *Id.*

TABLE 10.1

Strategic Concepts of Latin America

	1: The U.S. Lake	2: Strategic Benign Neglect	3: Quarter-Sphere Defense	4: Hemi-sphere Defense	5: Special Bilateral Relationships
Definition	U.S. strategic concerns focused almost exclusively on the Caribbean	strategic low priority for Latin America	strategic perimeter from Alaska to the Galapagos to the Brazilian bulge to Newfoundland	collective responsibility for defending the hemisphere	substantive strategic relations with a few selected countries with a key role in U.S. strategy
Proponents	U.S. naval strategists; Admiral Alfred Mahan Theodore Roosevelt	none (not officially acknowledged)	U.S. military planners in World War II	FDR, Welles, State Department; some U.S. and Latin strategists	U.S. military departments
Philosophical bases	Manifest Destiny; big stick; dollar diplomacy; military-strategic realism	Latin America is taken for granted in the face of higher priority threats	military-strategic realism; disregard for Latin military; anti-Pan-Americanism	Bolivarian and Pan-American ideals; original Monroe Doctrine	pragmatic military-strategic realism
Time periods	mid-nineteenth century to 1933	1933–39, 1945–60 1967–present	Early World War II: 1939–42	1939–present	1942–present

6: Secondary Space	7: The Atlantic Triangle	8: The Foco Theory	9: The Anti-foco	10: Intervention by Consent	11: Mature Military Relationship
cold war division of the world into an industrialized primary space and an underdeveloped secondary space	strategic partnership between the United States, Latin America, and Western Europe	a series of guerrilla outbreaks in Latin America that provoke "one, two, three, many Vietnams"	application of counterinsurgency theory to the focos	Cuban (or Soviet) military intervention at the invitation of one party in a local conflict	Limited U.S.-Latin military cooperation with emphasis on mature multilateralism
cold warriors	John Foster Dulles	Fidel Castro, Che Guevara, Régis Debray	New Frontiersmen John F. Kennedy; Many U.S. and Latin officers	Castro (with Soviet support)	none identified to date
Pragmatic military-strategic realism; "power belt" "primary/secondary space	the cultural, historic, economic, and strategic unity of the triangle	classical ideas on guerrilla war as modified by Castro, Guevara, and Debray	Counter-insurgency and civic action theories	Cuban support of Marxist faction in an armed local conflict	mutual respect; realistic recognition of strategic divergences and common ground
cold war years	Never active; proposed in 1955	1959–present; peak in 1960–67	1960–present; peak in 1961–67	1976–?	?

TABLE 10.2

The IAMS: A System Analysis

Element	Prior to World War II	World War II: 1942–45	Early Cold War: 1945–61	Late Cold War: 1961–67	1967–Present
Dominant IAMS model	none	alliance-hegemonic	hegemonic, with limits	alliance-hegemonic	fragmented
Systemic functions	none	strong	weak	strong, uneven	dysfunctional
Pattern maintenance		yes: World War II cooperation	limited anti-communism	anti-Castro, but not unanimous	confused, vestigial
Goal attainment		good; anti-Axis	imperfect	prevention of focos achieved	goals are undefined
Adaptation		good adaptation to U.S. war goals	poor adaptation	fair; lack of unanimity	poor
Integration		good shared values; little integration	limited by divergent goals	good for brief period	disintegrating
System elements					
Multilateral					
1. Attaché network	*	*+	*	*	*
2. Inter-American Defense Board		*	*–	*+	*
3. Rio Treaty		* (precursor)	*	*	*–
4. Advisory Defense Committee (ADC)			*	*	*–
5. Inter-American Defense College				*	*
6. CONDECA				*	*
7. Service chiefs conferences				*	*–

8. Tactical exercises				*	*–
9. Communications networks				*	*
10. Inter-American Peace Force				*(1965 only)	
11. Military observation forces				*(ad hoc only)	*(ad hoc only)
12. Military transnationalism		*	*	*	*
13. Special Consultative Committee				*	*–
Bilateral					
14. Joint Brazil-U.S. Defense and Military Commissions		*	*+	*	*
15. Joint Mexican-U.S. Defense Commission		*	*–	*–	*–
16. Security Assistance Program		*	*	*+	*–
17. Training in United States and Panama		*	*	*+	*–
18. Mobile training teams				*	*–
19. Inter-Latin arrangements				*	*
20. Latin commissions in the United States		*	*	*	*
Unilateral					
21. U.S. military Latinists		*	*	*+	*
22. Special Forces Group				*	*–
23. U.S. SOUTHCOM		* (precursor)	*	*+	*–
24. Latin unilateral arrangements					*
Dominant strategic concept	U.S. lake; benign neglect	hemisphere defense; special bilateral; quarter-sphere	benign neglect; secondary space	antifoco	no consensus; Latin geopolitics
Principal perceived threat	none	fascist axis	cold war	focos	no consensus

Key: *+ = significant increase; *– = significant decrease.

TABLE 10.3

IAMS: A Linkage Matrix

	System Elements																							
	1	2	3	4*	5	6	7	8	9	10	11	12*	13	14	15	16	17	18	19	20	21	22	23	24
1		I	—	—	—	—	—	—	—	—	—	I	P	P	P	—	—	—	I	P	R	—	—	I
2	I		R	R	P	I	R	P	R	I	I	I	P	I	I	R	—	—	—	—	I	—	—	—
3	—	P		P	—	—	—	—	—	P	P	—	—	—	—	—	—	—	—	—	—	—	—	—
4	—	P	R		—	—	—	—	—	P	P	—	—	—	—	—	—	—	—	—	—	—	—	—
5	—	R	—	—		I	—	—	—	—	—	—	P	—	—	R	—	—	—	—	I	—	—	—
6	—	E	—	—	I		I	P	—	—	—	—	P	—	—	R	—	—	—	—	—	—	R	—
7	—	P	—	—	—	I		P	P	—	—	—	P	—	—	R	—	—	—	—	I	—	—	—
8	—	R	—	—	—	R	R		P	—	—	—	P	—	—	R	—	—	—	—	I	—	—	—
9	—	P	—	—	—	—	R	R		—	—	—	P	—	—	R	—	—	—	—	—	—	—	—
10	—	I	R	R	—	—	—	—	—		—	—	P	—	—	R	—	—	—	—	I	—	—	—
11	—	I	R	R	—	—	—	—	—	—		—	P	—	—	R	—	—	—	—	I	—	—	—
12	I	I	—	—	—	—	—	—	—	—	—		—	—	—	—	—	—	—	—	—	—	—	—
13	R	R	—	—	R	R	R	R	R	R	R	—		R	R	R	R	—	R	R	R	—	—	—
14	R	I	—	—	—	—	—	—	—	—	—	—	P		—	R	—	—	—	P	I	—	—	—
15	R	I	—	—	—	—	—	—	—	—	—	—	P	—		—	—	—	—	—	I	—	—	—
16	—	P	—	—	P	P	P	P	P	P	P	—	P	P	—		P	P	—	P	P	—	P	—
17	—	—	—	—	—	—	—	—	—	—	—	—	P	—	—	R		—	—	—	I	I	R	—
18	—	—	—	—	—	—	—	—	—	—	—	—	—	—	—	R	—		—	—	I	I	R	—
19	I	—	—	—	—	—	—	—	—	—	—	—	P	—	—	—	—	—		—	—	—	—	I
20	R	—	—	—	—	—	—	—	—	—	—	—	P	R	—	R	—	—	—		I	—	—	—
21	P	I	—	—	I	—	I	I	—	I	I	—	P	I	I	R	I	I	—	I		I	I	—
22	—	—	—	—	—	—	—	—	—	—	—	—	—	—	—	—	I	I	—	—	I		R	—
23	—	—	—	—	—	P	—	—	—	—	—	—	—	—	—	R	P	P	—	—	I	P		—
24	I	—	—	—	—	—	—	—	—	—	—	—	—	—	—	—	—	—	I	—	—	—	—	

Key: Numbered system elements refer to Table 10.2. Analysis is as follows:

P = penetrative linkage	54
R = response linkage	54
E = emulative linkage	1
I = indirect linkage	55
— = no linkage found	388
	552 (23 × 24 = 552)

*Hypothetical since the ADC has never been convoked.

†Now hypothetical since the SCCS was disestablished Dec 1975.

TABLE 10.4

Status of Western Hemisphere Nations on Key Variables for IAMS

	OAS Member?[a]	Rio Treaty Signatory?	IADB Member?[b]	U.S. Military Assistance Group Present	U.S. Embassy Security Assistance Office Present	Resident Defense Attaché	Diplomatic Relations with Cuba?
Argentina	Y	Y	Y	Y	—	Y	Y, May 1973
Bahamas	N	—	—	N	—	N	Y, Nov. 1974
Barbados	Y	N	N	N	—	N	Y, Nov. 1972
Bolivia	Y	Y	Y	Y	—	Y	N
Brazil	Y	Y	Y	Y	—	Y	N
Canada	N[c]	—	—	N	—	Y	Y
Chile	Y	Y	Y	Y	—	Y	N
Colombia	Y	Y	Y	Y	—	Y	Y, March 1975
Costa Rica	Y	Y	N[d]	N	Y	N	N
Cuba	N[e]	N[e]	N[e]	N	—	N	—
Dominican Republic	Y	Y	Y	Y	—	Y	N
Ecuador	Y	Y	Y	Y	—	Y	N
El Salvador	Y	Y	Y	Y	—	Y	N

[a]OAS membership requires signing the OAS Charter. Signing the Rio Treaty is not a condition for OAS membership.

[b]IADB membership requirements are not specified. However, it is generally accepted that IADB membership requires OAS membership in good standing.

[c]Canada and Guyana have observer status at OAS.

[d]Costa Rica is technically an IADB member but has not had a representative at the IADB since December 1966. Its flag is present in the Council Room.

[e]Cuba ratified the OAS Charter in 1952 and the Rio Treaty in 1948 and never has formally denounced either ratification. By a resolution of the eighth Meeting of Foreign Ministers (Punta del Este, 1962) the present government of Cuba was excluded from participation in the OAS (to include the IADB).

(Table 10.4 Continued pg. 190)

TABLE 10.4 (*Continued*)

	OAS Member?[a]	Rio Treaty Signatory?	IADB Member?[b]	U.S. Military Assistance Group Present	U.S. Embassy Security Assistance Office Present	Resident Defense Attaché	Diplomatic Relations with Cuba?
Grenada	Y	N	N	N	—	N	Y
Guatemala	Y	Y	Y	Y	—	Y	N
Guyana	N[c]	—	—	N	—	N	Y, Dec. 1972
Haiti	Y	Y	Y	N	Y	Y	N
Honduras	Y	Y	Y	Y	—	Y	N
Jamaica	Y	N	N	N	—	N	Y, Nov. 1972
Mexico	Y	Y	Y	N	Y	Y	Y[f]
Nicaragua	Y	Y	Y	Y	—	Y	N
Panama	Y	Y	Y	Y	—	N	Y, Aug. 1974
Paraguay	Y	Y	Y	N	Y	Y	N
Peru	Y	Y	Y	Y	—	Y	Y, July 1972
Surinam	N	—	—	N	—	N	N
Trinidad & Tobago	Y	Y	N	N	—	N	Y, Dec. 1972
United States	Y	Y	Y	—	—	—	N
Uruguay	Y	Y	Y	N	Y	Y	N
Venezuela	Y	Y	Y	Y	—	Y	Y, Dec. 1974
	24	21	19	14	5	18	13[g]

[f] Mexico never broke relations with Cuba.
[g] Summary of nations with relations with Cuba: 7 of 21 Rio Treaty signatories; 10 of 24 OAS members; 13 of 29 hemisphere nations.

APPENDIX B: INSTITUTIONAL ASPECTS OF U.S.-LATIN AMERICAN MILITARY RELATIONSHIP

Multilateral institutions are:

1. The Inter-American Defense Board (IADB): created in 1942 by the third meeting of consultation; has met regularly since 1942 (the Council of Delegates normally has a session twice a month); has a permanent full-time chairman, staff, and secretariat; the United States as host country holds the key positions of chairman, director of the staff, and secretary, while Latin officers hold the second spot for each of these positions; 19 hemisphere nations participate; located in Washington, D.C., its stated mission is to plan for the collective defense of the hemisphere while its unstated mission is as a forum and channel of communications functions.

2. The Inter-American Defense College (IADC): founded by the IADB in 1962; runs one ten-month war college-level course each year for 35–50 students (military and civilian) of lieutenant colonel/colonel rank from 12–14 different member countries of the IADB; faculty is multinational located at Fort McNair, Washington, D.C.; the United States fills the key position of IADC director (major general/rear admiral).

3. The Advisory Defense Committee (ADC): included in the OAS Charter (Arts. 64–67) at the 1948 Bogotá Conference; is only a hypothetical organ since it has never been convoked; would be composed of the highest military authorities of the American states; if convoked, would be a short-term ad hoc organ assembled to give military advice to the OAS.

4. The attaché network: the United States maintains attachés in most U.S. embassies in Latin nations; the size of the U.S. attaché office varies from one to six officers; U.S. military attachés have frequent social and professional contacts with host country military and military attachés of other Latin nations in most capital cities of Latin America.

5. Central American Defense Council (CONDECA): a subregional military entity founded in 1963 and loosely tied to the Central American integration movement; six members; prepares plans for Central American defense, holds periodic meetings and infrequent tactical exercises; exchanges information with the IADB; has close ties with U.S. Southern Command in the Canal Zone; has headquarters and a small permanent staff in Guatemala.

6. Service chiefs Conferences: a series of annual or biannual conferences between the commanders of each of the three services (army, navy, air force) of most of the hemisphere nations; began in the early 1960s and to 1976 there had been 11 army, 9 navy, and 16 air force conferences; the early conferences were held in the United States, the Canal Zone, or Puerto Rico, but in recent years the venue has rotated among nations; the air force and naval conferences tend to be more technical and bland; the army ones are more political and controversial.

7. Exercises and maneuvers: began in the early 1960s under U.S. aegis; combined ground-sea-air totaled a series of four (1961–65) involving from four to six countries each, always including the United States; naval exercises are the annual UNITAS exercise from 1960 to date involving a U.S. Navy Task Force (two to four ships) that sails south along one coast and north along the other—As it passes each participating country, ships from that country join the task force for maneuvers; air exercises are coordinated transport exercise of six to eight nations, 1974 and 1975.

8. Military communications networks: each service (army, navy, air force) has a radio communications net in which the United States and most of the Latin nations have stations; net control stations are all in the Panama Canal Zone; the services hold frequent communications conferences.

9. Inter-American Peace Force: the basic concept of a standby military force was first proposed by Simon Bolivar at the 1826 Amphictyonic Congress; the only example of such a force was in 1965 in the Dominican Republic, in which the bulk of the troops (and almost all the logistic support) was provided by the United States although seven Latin nations did participate; several attempts to make the IAPF a permanent institution in the 1965–67 period failed.

10. Peace observer groups: the OAS has on several occasions created ad hoc military peace observer groups to investigate or monitor tense border crises (1955 Costa Rica-Nicaragua, 1957 Honduras-Nicaragua, 1969–70 and 1976 Honduras-El Salvador); the OAS has resisted all attempts to institutionalize these groups and has specifically rejected IADB offers to assume this role.

11. Special Consultative Committee on Security: created in 1962 by the eighth meeting of consultation to collect and disseminate information on Cuban-inspired subversion; while not technically a military organ, its focus was guerrilla warfare and its makeup was predominantly military; disestablished in December 1975.

Bilateral Institutions are:

1. Joint Brazil-U.S. Defense Commission (Washington) and Joint Brazil-U.S. Military Commission (Rio): created in 1942 as the vehicle for Brazil-U.S. military cooperation in World War II; handled the creation, training, and equipping of the 23,000-man Brazilian Expeditionary Force that fought in Italy in World War II; since World War II the commission in Washington has had only a minor role while the commission in Brazil in effect became the U.S. military assistance group in Brazil.

2. Joint Mexico-U.S. Defense Commission (Washington): created in 1942 as the coordinator for Mexican-U.S. military cooperation in World

War II, to include support for the 300-man Mexican Air Squadron 201, which fought in the Pacific Theater; since World War II has atrophied.

3. U.S. Lend-Lease/Military Assistance/Security Assistance Program: by far the most significant element of the U.S.-Latin military relationship; began with World War II lend-lease (approximately $400 million of which Brazil got 75 percent and Mexico 10 percent).

Military assistance programs are based on a series of bilateral mutual security treaties signed with 17 Latin nations in the early and mid-1950s. The program is now called Security Assistance Program and includes military assistance proper (the U.S. military assistance groups and grants of training and materiel) as well as foreign military sales (both cash and credit); straight commercial sales from U.S. arms manufacturers are not considered to be a part of the Security Assistance Program, although they are monitored and licensed.

Elements of the MAP/SAP include: U.S. military assistance groups in 13 Latin nations. From a mid-1960s high of 800 U.S. military personnel, the groups were down to 264 (1977); the military assistance groups have a command line to the regional unified command (U.S. Southern Command) in the Canal Zone and thence to the Joint Chiefs of Staff in Washington.

Other elements are grants of U.S. military equipment—this was a major element of the MAP in the 1950s but was down to $3 million for Latin America as a whole in 1977, most of which went to Bolivia. Also, foreign military sales credit to facilitate the purchase of U.S. arms and equipment—presently this is the major element of the SAP and stood at $195 million for Latin America in 1977.

Another element is training of Latin American military personnel in U.S. military schools in the United States and the Panama Canal Zone. Schools in the Canal Zone include the U.S. Army School of the Americas, the U.S. Air Force Inter-American Air Force Academy, and the U.S. Navy Small Craft Instruction and Technical Team. Instruction is in Spanish. In 1950–70, the United States trained almost 55,000 Latin military personnel (24,000 in the United States and 31,000 in the Canal Zone). The Military Education and Training Program (grant) for 1977 in Latin America was approximately $7 million.

Further MAP/SAP elements are tours of the United States by high-ranking individual Latin officers as well as complete war college and staff classes from some of the larger nations.

It should be noted that recent congressional actions have severely limited the scope and impact of the MAP/SAP. In addition to a series of paternalistic restrictions of the late 1950s and 1960s (Hickenlooper, Conte, Pelley, Fulbright), Congress has exercised increasing control over the MAP/SAP. In the 1976 International Security Assistance and Arms Export Control Act, Congress has stated that after September 30, 1977, no military assistance group may exist unless specifically authorized by Congress; after September 30, 1976, there may be no more than 34 military assistance groups worldwide—this provision resulted in the September 1976 termination of groups in Uruguay, Paraguay, and Costa Rica; no security assistance will be provided to any nation "which engages in a consistent pattern of gross violations of internationally recognized human rights."

Chapter 11

LIMITING INTRAREGIONAL VIOLENCE: THE COSTS OF REGIONAL PEACEKEEPING

Tom J. Farer

In this century, Latin America has been the scene of only one protracted war: the kamikaze struggle of Paraguay with all its neighbors, particularly Bolivia, which in the years between 1932 and 1935 consumed a quarter of Paraguay's adult male population. Since 1942, when a little struggle between Peru and Ecuador cost the latter a slice of territory, the peace of the Americas has been marred only by the harsh but brief "soccer war" between El Salvador and Honduras in 1969. Seen in 40-year retrospect, and ignoring the often murderous social conflicts within Latin American states, the hemisphere appears as a large island of peace in an ocean of war.

Peace has coincided with U.S. political and economic hegemony and active involvement in all facets of hemispheric life. It also has coincided with perspectives within the military establishments of most Latin states that emphasized extracontinental and internal threats largely to the exclusion of potential conflicts with neighboring states. This relative confidence in regional harmony stemmed from a variety of sources. One was the absence of salient conflicts of interest. A number of border disputes and unresolved territorial claims lingered on the back burner, but very few were seen to engage serious material interests. Most of the relevant territories were primitive, remote, thinly populated (where they were populated at all), and seemingly unendowed with commercially exploitable resources.

A second source of hemispheric tranquility was the paucity of interactions among the Latin states. Until the 1960s, for instance, intraregional trade was slight and investment negligible. Even today, intraregional trade accounts for less than 15 percent of the foreign trade of the Latin American states. Again until the last decade, the remote frontiers, an inwardly oriented road network, and the relative absence of gross asymmetries in the pace of development all restrained large-scale migration across national boundaries.

Ideological homogeneity contributed to peaceful relations. All states formally aspired to republican institutions; almost all fell short of the aspiration. Lounging in their glass houses, governments were not inclined to hurl stones from the windows. As soothed by the republican forms as it was satisfied by the often repressive reality, Washington did nothing to disturb this pool of ideological bonhomie except during the early days of the alliance when it cast a few pebbles before succumbing to dark visions of a guerrilla-enveloped hemisphere.

Washington's main contribution to peace and good fellowship was, however, more positive. It consisted of encouraging the assumption that the United States would not tolerate in others what it sometimes found desirable for itself, namely, a diplomacy of force. Intraregional conflict would threaten the lives and property of U.S. nationals, create opportunities for the Soviet Union to fish in the bloody waters, and weaken at least the losing state's capacity to control leftist dissidents. In conjunction with these obviously strong motives, actual demonstrations both within and outside the hemisphere of a will to intervene militarily periodically reinforced the assumption that the United States guaranteed the OAS Charter principle that "victory [in a war of aggression] does not give rights."

These various sources of tranquility are eroding rapidly and there are new factors in the equation. The risk of conflict, once remote, now begins to rise perceptibly.

One of the world's highest rates of population growth combines with vivid and growing intercountry differences in wealth, economic dynamism, and open land to propel people across national frontiers. A vastly expanded and more frontier-oriented transportation system often facilitates their passage. Leading examples are the hundreds of thousands of Colombians sucked into Venezuela's petrodollar boom, the impoverished El Salvadorean peasants who occupied empty Honduran land before their mass expulsion in 1969, and the Brazilians now flooding into Santa Cruz Province of Bolivia and especially into eastern Paraguay, where Portuguese threatens to become the dominant language.

Growing resource-based dependencies, particularly between Brazil and its smaller neighbors, are another form of interaction with a problematic balance of consequences for regional harmony. Inside Paraguay, the Brazilian government is developing the $500 million Itaipu hydroelectric project, which will make electricity Paraguay's most valuable export. Brazil hopes further to ease its energy requirements by developing Bolivian oil and gas reserves.

Resource hunger—everywhere sharpened by the retrieval capacity of new technologies and by the conjoint pressures of population growth, urbanization, and the balance-of-payments tensions accompanying accelerated industrialization—helps to revivify old border disputes such as those between Venezuela and Guyana, Venezuela and Colombia, Argentina and Chile, and ultimately perhaps to fuel new ones, particularly between Brazil and all its neighbors in the Amazonian heartland.

New and intensified national needs coincide in an uncertain linkage of cause and effect with new national capacities and strategies. In most states, the bureaucratic nerves of government run to distant borders where they brush against the effective authority of their neighbors. A growing number of armed forces are acquiring not only the raw instruments but also the technical competence for projecting national power across frontiers. The roads that carry migrants also will bear troops. As the empty spaces in countries fill up and crossborder links proliferate, military planners, less preoccupied with internal threats and incapable of conjuring a plausible extracontinental enemy, focus increasingly on the possibility of local conflicts. The spread of military-dominated regimes guarantees sensitivity at the apex of political power to military threat perceptions.

Prevalent military perceptions are encapsulated in a kind of ideology or world view that links economic development and national security. This orientation encourages the colonization of border areas and intensifies concern about nonmilitary developments in adjacent societies that could affect the country's progress toward the high technology, tightly integrated national lifestyle of a First-World State.

It is still unclear just how the rising influence and activism of Brazil on the one hand, and the declining influence and activism of the United States on the other, may affect the general trends. Brazil might choose to cooperate with the United States in restraining and brokering conflict. Or Brazil might precipitate and aggravate conflicts through coercive diplomacy. A third possibility is that, regardless of its actual intentions, Brazil's sheer capacity to coerce will galvanize competitive alliances among Hispanic states that will sharply limit any peacekeeping, honest brokering role for Brazil.

As the present occupant of that role, the United States still possesses two unmatchable qualities. One is economic and military power that no coalition of Latin states could approach even remotely. The other is a political ideology and a set of global interests that plainly inhibit exploitation of its hegemony in parochial matters of vital concern to Latin governments. U.S. elites do not, for instance, even contemplate seizure of Mexican and Venezuelan oil assets or extortion of oil from these countries at submarket prices as a means of mending the balance-of-payments hole in the dollar. Broader interests discouraged even the modest display of force that would have deterred Ecuadorean seizure of U.S. fishing boats. While condemning the 200-mile extension of coastal-state authority into the high seas, the United States preferred to compensate its fisherman rather than to confront Ecuador.

Incomparably powerful, relatively neutral in the sense that it prefers hemispheric peace to conflict regardless of the opponents and probable outcome, the United States remains peculiarly well placed to foster the pacific settlement of disputes. But the potential costs of this role may grow. Will there be commensurate benefits?

Costs may grow because there are more potential conflicts with more at stake for better-armed and more efficient combatants. And the United States will have fewer levers for exerting influence either to deter or to terminate those conflicts by means short of war. The loss of influence is a function of a reduced role as supplier of arms, capital, critical imports, and perhaps markets; this change is sometimes summarized as the rise of economic multipolarity. The loss is aggravated by enhanced vulnerability to economic countermeasures. For instance, while closure of U.S. markets to their products is a potentially tremendous sanction for most Latin states, the retaliatory exclusion of U.S. exports would hurt at a time when the United States has begun to run a persistent balance-of-trade deficit. Latin America is one of the few areas where the balance still tilts substantially in favor of the United States.

Under the terms of the Rio Treaty and the OAS Charter, an attack on one member state is an attack on all. In strictly legal terms, however, it does not follow that each state is obligated to help repel the aggression; each signatory in effect has reserved discretion to choose or reject armed involvement. Other forms of involvement such as economic sanctions can be made obligatory by a two-thirds vote of the member states acting through the organ of consultation. Whether, without such a vote, the signatory states have a formal obligation to do something to restrain the aggressor is unclear.

Whatever its formal obligations, legitimate concern for the credibility of its collective self-defense commitments in other parts of the world, particularly Europe and the Far East, would make it very difficult for the United States to stand aside. Yet apart from the problem of credibility and what is conventionally regarded as a long-term interest in discouraging violence, the United States often will have little to gain and much to lose. It will have little to gain because both belligerents will be Rio Treaty allies and they are unlikely to differ very much in their attitudes toward international issues that concern the United States. In other words, the conflict will not have the elements of a proxy test between the United States and the Soviet Union. Nor will it be a symbolic struggle between the representatives of communist and capitalist ideologies or the spokesmen for moderation and radicalism in north-south relations. Thus, the normal reasons for U.S. concern with the outcome of a local struggle will be absent.

The only likely gain is reinforced credibility as an ally. That gain, as intangible as it is uncertain, may seem immoderately small in relation to all too possible costs, starting with the loss of American lives. On top of that may come otherwise avoidable economic injuries. In most instances, the aggressor presumably will be the bigger, wealthier, more industrially advanced state. As such, it probably will be a larger market for U.S. exports, a larger debtor of U.S. banks, and host to more valuable U.S. investments than its victim. So in assisting the victim, the United States often may find itself acting against its own economic interests. Moreover, if the United States were not available to redress the local imbalance of power, the weaker state might yield to superior force without a fight and thus at no risk to U.S. economic ties with or assets within either state.

Of course, to the extent that the threat of U.S. intervention deters aggressive behavior, the same ends are preserved without damage to the global restraints on violence. *This is the crux of the long-term U.S. dilemma. U.S. participation in the hemispheric system of mutual defense certainly will continue to have some deterrent effect. But where deterrence fails, participation may suck the United States into conflicts in whose outcome it has no material or ideological interest, conflicts, moreover, that might not occur if subregional hegemonies were allowed to operate.*

If—pessimists would say when—nuclear weapons proliferate into Latin America, the dilemma will grow more vicious. The very danger of proliferation will give it a progressively sharper edge. On the one hand, the U.S. commitment to hemispheric peace may reassure states that might otherwise begin to consider acquisition of a nuclear deterrent. On the other, U.S. restraints on subregional powers, particularly Brazil, the leading candidate for Latin hegemony, may encourage acquisition as a means of restraining the United States and intimidating lesser lights.

The immediate risk of conflict is still quite low in most of Latin America. Even if it were higher, no one is going to advocate a sudden winding down of hemispheric defense commitments at a time when the United States is widely, albeit groundlessly, accused of loss of nerve. Now is not the time to act; it is the time to begin thinking whether, on balance, U.S. or Latin interests are best served by an arrangement under which the United States will indefinitely police the hemisphere.

The very factors that have reduced the ability of the United States to impose its will argue in favor of a broadened responsibility for peacekeeping. Japan and Western Europe now have economic stakes in Latin America hardly less than those of the United States. Responsibility could be shared by enlarging the system to receive these interested parties, if only they were inclined to be received. But such inclination will remain unlikely.

In the first place, these states, with very few exceptions, evince a strong distaste for peacekeeping roles, except perhaps in the context of UN operations undertaken with the consent of the belligerents, the Afro-Asian bloc, and the superpowers. Moreover, despite the growth of their economic ties with Latin America, for both economic and historical reasons they are far more concerned with developments in other parts of the Third World. So even if they decide to play the regional peacekeeping game, Latin America will not be the site of their exertions. Furthermore, they reasonably will assume that the multiple reasons—strategic, economic, sentimental—that make other parts of the world the primary focus of their concern will keep the United States functioning as the Western Hemisphere's peacekeeper. With that comfortable assumption in the background, prudence will incline them toward neutrality in most Latin American disputes, an inclination necessarily intensified by the highly concentrated focus of European and Japanese interests. Heavy investment and trade is limited to a handful of states, states at least as apt to be aggressors as victims. In short, the very fact that Euro-Japanese interests in the area are almost exclusively economic strongly militates against a comprehensive political involvement, especially one with military overtones.

If responsibility cannot be shared by coaxing other states into the regional system, one alternative is the gradual restoration of peacekeeping responsibilities to the United Nations, the institution from which they were wrenched at the very moment of its birth.

The outline of the United Nations Charter, negotiated by the Great Powers among themselves at the 1944 Dumbarton Oaks Conference, centralized peacekeeping activities. But in the course of the following year's San Francisco conference the Latin states, supported by their northern neighbor, prevailed on the other participants to incorporate in the charter an option for arguably autonomous peacekeeping, which the United States and its neighbors quickly exercised through the Rio Treaty and the Pact of Bogotá.

Nothing in the history of Chapter 8 ("Regional Arrangements") and the associated provisions of Chapters 6 and 7 of the UN Charter precludes an interpretation that would require a regional organization to secure Security Council authorization prior to taking or authorizing member states to take in collective, military and other sanctions on behalf of peace and security, except self-defense against aggression, pending Security Council action. Given the more natural meaning of the relevant language, the tendency of violence to have extraregional reverberations, and the difficulties of determining what states at particular times legitimately are subject to the authority of a regional organization, there is much to be said in favor of that interpretation.

The Soviet Union and its clients have said as much on every possible occasion but without seeming to influence the contrary conviction of the United States, its Latin allies, and its particular friends elsewhere in the world. The latter having a clear majority in the Security Council, that body has never chosen to reject U.S. claims for a kind of primary jurisdiction in the OAS and a merely residual one for the Security Council, to be exercised only if the regional organization plainly has failed to keep the peace.

Different arguments have been employed as seemed useful to accommodate the facts and political necessities of each case from Guatemala in 1954 to the Dominican intervention of 1965. At one point, for instance, the United States argued that when the OAS merely authorized member states to use force, that most certainly was not an "enforcement action" requiring prior Security Council authorization, because that phrase referred only to cases where states were ordered to act. In fulfilling its peacekeeping responsibilities under Chapter 7 of the Charter, the Security Council could issue such orders; no organ of the OAS was similarly empowered.

But at another point the United States seemed to rely rather more heavily on the view that, although Security Council authorization might be needed before the OAS could legitimate behavior that without OAS approval would violate charter principles restraining intervention and the use of force, that authorization could be both subsequent and tacit. In other words, if after the fact the Security Council did not condemn acts authorized by a regional organization, those acts were presumed to be approved.

Whether the Department of State's inner confidence about the juridical elegance of these interpretations has quite matched its outward displays of assurance is subject to some doubt. At least it must be said that in 1961 when the Cuban government proposed seeking an advisory opinion from the International Court of Justice on the powers of regional organizations, the United States found it desirable to marshal a vote against the Cuban proposal.

By its own force majeure, the United States has shaped a network of precedents, assumptions, and political reflexes that effectively deny the United Nations any real peacekeeping role in the hemisphere. What the United States has taken the lead in making, it now can unmake. This should not be done precipitously and certainly not unilaterally. Rather, the United States should begin a process of intergovernmental consultation about new ways to reflect the deepening involvement of the leading Latin states in the international system.

The United States can spread responsibility for keeping the regional peace without any change in the major legal texts. It simply could organize support for a revised interpretation of the UN Charter under which regional institutions would retain a mandate to promote the peaceful settlement of disputes. But once a dispute escalated into a threat to the peace, jurisdiction would spring to the Security Council. The council then would have the option of attempting to deal with the case directly or delegating responsibility to the OAS, subject to continuing Security Council review.

Since by this step policing and securing the Western Hemisphere would cease to appear as the special province of the United States, it would lay the psychological basis for eventually replacing the comprehensive obligation to join in the defense of every Latin state, which was imposed by the Rio Treaty, with defense commitments that more precisely reflect U.S. ideological, economic, and strategic interests.

Of course one cannot have the Security Council in without having the Soviet Union as well. Keeping the Soviets out of the hemisphere was a principal rationale for the security and peacekeeping features of the regional system. The same motive lay behind the prodigies of UN Charter interpretation produced by the United States. Since detente shows no signs of an early ripening into entente, why allow the Soviets to fish legitimately in hemispheric diplomatic waters during every serious storm?

We already have enumerated the primary advantages of slowly restoring responsibility to the United Nations. Does the potential Soviet role constitute an overbalancing cost? I think not. The Soviet Union, after all, is already through the psychological barriers to its presence, having become an arms supplier to Peru and a not trivial trading partner of Argentina. But although it is no longer an untouchable, the Soviet Union seems doomed to marginality other than as a possible supplier of arms and men to bear them, since it is short of capital, technologically retarded in almost every area relevant to economic development, and proponent of a development model hostile to the instincts and interests of most Latin elites.

Under the existing arrangements, the Soviets can use whatever assets they have to play diplomatic games in Latin America, relatively unencumbered by obligations to cooperate in promoting the peaceful settlement of disputes. There is no forum in which they can be compelled to take positions and chastised for acting irresponsibly. Hence, a shift of peacekeeping jurisdiction back to the Security Council might tend to reduce their freedom of action. In this respect, the Soviet factor actually could weigh in favor of such a shift.

But what about the Soviet veto so often invoked to support the containment of peacekeeping responsibilities within the hemispheric system? In answering that question, one usefully might begin by considering just what action would be subject to veto. Certainly not collective self-defense, for under Article 51 of the UN Charter one state may join in the defense of another without waiting for the Security Council to act. All that will be lost, then, is the putative OAS power to legitimate the use of force by member states for reasons other than self-defense.

The Cuban quarantine is a case in point. When the United States demanded removal of Soviet missiles from Cuba, it was not because of fear that they soon would be launched or that their emplacement was a prelude to attack elsewhere in the world. Rather, the United States feared longer-term political-military consequences that the UN Charter probably does not allow a state to reverse through the use of force.

Changes in the balance of nuclear power, in the range and characteristics of Soviet and U.S. weapon systems and strategies, and a host of other factors make it hard to visualize another case in which the United States would be justified in using force (as opposed to other kinds of sanctions) against the Soviet Union for actions in the hemisphere that did not amount to the threat of an armed attack against the United States or some other country. But even if such a case arose, the proposed shift in jurisdiction should not perceptibly affect U.S. capacity to marshal support for an appropriate riposte.

When U.S. allies in Europe and Latin America rallied behind the quarantine, it was not on the theory that OAS resolutions could legitimate interference with high seas navigation and dictation of the means that a state (in this case Cuba) could adopt for its self-defense. Norms, whether thought of as international legal principles or rules of the diplomatic game, no doubt influenced the perception of U.S. allies that the United States was behaving reasonably under the circumstances. By eschewing any intention of using the crisis to eliminate the Cuban regime, by using the minimum threat of force consistent with its ends, and by carefully limiting the impact of the quarantine's impact on international shipping, the United States appeared responsive to principles of proportionality, national independence, and freedom of navigation on the high seas. Conversely, by introducing nuclear weapons into an area perceived to be almost as much a U.S. preserve as Eastern Europe was a Soviet one, the Soviet Union was seen to be creating a threat to international peace for an end—protecting the Cuban regime—that could be achieved by less dangerous means.

If this analysis is accurate, perception of the hemisphere as a U.S. sphere of influence may have played some role in rallying support for the quarantine. And so it might be argued that any act that tended to blur that perception would weaken the future ability of the United States to "legitimate" the threat of force if the Soviet Union again were to behave in a manner considered provocative. One could so argue, but in this instance not persuasively, primarily because the shift in peacekeeping jurisdiction would coincide with and in large measure simply record the attenuation of U.S. hegemony and the integration of Latin America into the global system, a development springing from factors beyond U.S. control. Under these circumstances, the normative and psychological impact of the transfer would be inconsequential. Quite apart from that, the interest in minimizing the risk of war that the United States shares with all other major international actors may well be advanced by institutional arrangements restraining the use of force when it cannot plausibly be justified as anticipatory self-defense.

Chapter 12

NUCLEAR PROLIFERATION AND THE INTER-AMERICAN SYSTEM

Jo L. Husbands

One test of a system is its capacity to adapt, over time, to cope with changes in its environment. On Valentine's Day, 1967, a treaty establishing a new inter-American system was opened for signature.[1] This treaty, the Treaty for the Prohibition of Nuclear Weapons in Latin America (the Tlatelolco Treaty), created a system—a nuclear-free zone—to deal with the threat of nuclear proliferation in Latin America.[2] The ability of this system, just over a decade later, to cope with current proliferation issues in the region is the subject of this study.

A number of digressions are needed to provide background for the analysis. The first discusses nuclear-free zones as special systems of arms control and examines their success in other regions. The second deals with the history of the movement for a Latin American nuclear-free zone. The negotiations for the eventual treaty are only briefly considered,[3] but the treaty itself is described in greater detail. Finally, the current status of nuclear energy development in Latin America completes the information necessary to evaluate the Inter-American System and nuclear proliferation.[4]

NUCLEAR-FREE ZONES AS ARMS CONTROL

Although the idea of nuclear-free zones is relatively recent, the broader concept of withdrawing areas from certain conflicts or weapons is an ancient one:

> Areas of land and water may be used to serve disarmament and security purposes by either neutralizing or demilitarizing them. Neutral zones have a respectable and long history. Their purpose has been to avoid friction between states or tribes and thus to avoid accidental outbreaks of hostilities.[5]

Defining a nuclear-free zone quickly becomes a complex task. John Redick identified four essential features implied by the term:

> (1) nuclear weapons may not be manufactured or produced within the zone; (2) importation of nuclear weapons into the zone by a government within the zone is prohibited; (3) no extra-zonal nation may store nuclear weapons within the borders of any nation within the zone; and (4) nuclear weapons states pledge to respect the denuclearized status of the zone.[6]

At a minimum, then, the production, importation, storage, and use of nuclear weapons are prohibited within the boundaries of the nuclear-free zone. Issues such as the definition of a nuclear weapon, the permissibility of explosions for "peaceful purposes," and the system, if any, of verification and control, are all part of the specific characteristics of each zone.

Bertel Heurlin distinguishes further between "tension-zones," areas of serious major power conflict where denuclearization might defuse the confrontation, and "continent-zones," large, clearly and geographically defined regions that are to be kept free of nuclear weapons.[7] Heurlin notes that zones of either type are seldom proposed for their own sake but rather to serve other ends of a nation's foreign policy.[8] His point is hardly surprising but tends to be lost in detailed discussions of particular proposals.

The first proposals to make nuclear weapons the objects of special demilitarization efforts came from the Soviet Union and its allies in Eastern Europe. In 1957 the Polish foreign minister, Adam Rapacki, proposed a freeze on the production and stockpiling of nuclear weapons in Central Europe and a subsequent "denuclearization" of Germany, Poland, and Czechoslovakia.[9] The West rejected the Rapacki plan very quickly. The primary objection was that denuclearization would result in military imbalances by eliminating the tactical nuclear weapons on which NATO relied to offset the Warsaw Pact's conventional superiority. Remnants of the Rapacki plan and its offspring[10] still color the current negotiations on MBFR (mutual and balanced force reduction) in Europe.[11] As a rule, proposals for "tension-zones" in areas of primary concern to the nuclear superpowers have been singularly unsuccessful.

The urge to isolate certain areas from nuclear weapons so far has found the most fulfillment when the area in question was uninhabited: "The extent to which the world has been forced to retreat from the major battlefields of the cold war to find suitable geography to denuclearize is seen by the fact that the first nuclear-free zone was created in Antarctica by treaty in 1959."[12] In addition to the Antarctic Treaty, the Outer Space Treaty of 1967 and the Seabeds Treaty of 1971 create nuclear-free zones, although each covers an environment rather than a region. In the three cases, it was to the perceived benefit of the nuclear powers to ensure that the nuclear arms race did not intrude into a hitherto untouched area. Agreement may have been relatively simple because "essentially, everyone was willing to agree on banning weapons systems they never wanted in the first place."[13]

Beyond Europe and the environments, almost every portion of the Third World has been suggested at one time or another as a potential nuclear-free zone. These proposed zones usually have been continent- rather than tension-zones. In many cases, a local crisis or the sudden intrusion of Great Power conflict has been the spur to such plans. The Indian nuclear test in 1974 prompted a Pakistani suggestion to the UN General Assembly for a nuclear-free zone in South Asia. The test had raised the specter of a regional nuclear arms race, with Pakistan going nuclear, followed almost inevitably by Iran and Indonesia.[14] The Indians, repeating protestations that theirs was no more than a "peaceful nuclear device," rejected the Pakistani plan as mere opportunism.

Fears of similar local chain reactions lay behind Egyptian and Iranian proposals for a Middle East nuclear-free zone.[15] The political situation in the area was simply too tense to permit any serious consideration of the 1974 plan. Without the cooperation and support of all the significant near-nuclear states, plans for nuclear-free zones in any area are unlikely to prosper.

Several factors lay behind proposals for an African nuclear-free zone, first formalized in a UN resolution in 1961. The continent, just emerging from colonial rule, was unarmed by world standards, free from military commitments to the major powers, and had relatively little to gain from acquiring either.[16] A group of African leaders wished to keep the continent removed from the East-West conflict, and the nonaligned movement provided a strong base for such desires.[17] The series of French nuclear tests begun in the Sahara in 1960 only gave an added urgency; the first call for an African nuclear-free zone came immediately after the first French test.[18] An African-sponsored UN resolution in 1961 contained both a call for a nuclear-free zone and a plea to stop all testing in the area. The Soviet Union and its allies supported the resolution, but the Western nations found an uncontrolled and unverified moratorium on testing an unacceptable and undesirable precedent.

No formal treaty ever has been negotiated to denuclearize the region, but in 1974 another General Assembly resolution, sponsored by 26 African nations, reaffirmed the proposals of the previous resolution. This time the resolution passed unanimously, for by now France had shifted its nuclear testing to the South Pacific.[19]

The problem for the African efforts has been that each of the important near-nuclear countries, Egypt and South Africa, has reason to resist such agreements.[20] The other African nations do not wish to deal with South Africa for fear of seeming to confer some legitimacy and recognition on the continent's pariah. The South Africans do not wish to give up the technological edge, which is one of their most important strategic advantages.[21] Egypt, on the other hand, is an African nation by geography rather than affinity, and its security interests lie mainly in the Middle East. This makes the hope of adherence to an African nuclear-free zone without similar settlements in the other area very slight. The alternative would be a nuclear-free zone without the participation of the two major threshold powers, but such an agreement would have more ceremonial than political value. So far, the ceremonial appeals have not been enough to bring about a treaty.

THE SUPERPOWERS AND NUCLEAR-FREE ZONES

The attitudes of the nuclear superpowers toward the creation of nuclear-free zones developed quite differently. The Soviets introduced the concept and remained its consistent champion in international forums. In general, they have not set very high standards for their support: "The Soviet attitude is said to be based on two considerations: (1) the readiness of other nuclear powers to respect the demilitarized status of the area and (2) the completeness of the obligations of the contracting parties and the extent to which they insure the zone's denuclearized status."[22]

Most of the Soviet Union's attention has gone to tension-zones, for these better serve its own strategic interests. For example, the creation of a simple nuclear-free zone in Central Europe could give the Warsaw Pact a considerable initial military advantage. U.S. defense policy, which in the 1950s and 1960s depended on a series of foreign bases on the perimeter of the Soviet Union, could have been frustrated by nuclear-free zones: "In practice . . . almost all the proposals seek to prevent states outside the region from stationing weapons in the zone."[23]

Soviet support for nuclear-free zones beyond areas with heavy concentrations of nuclear weapons has been steady but less specific. The propaganda value of such advocacy must not be forgotten. However, there is

> no reason to doubt the seriousness of Soviet interest in formalizing, under international law, nuclear-free zones in areas where no nuclear weapons now exist. Such an attitude is congruent with Soviet interest in reducing the possibility of war, especially war instigated by third parties . . . .
>
> The Soviet advocacy of nuclear-free zones may include the expectation that they would serve to "educate" the United States to accept such arrangements, presumably in the hope of later extending them to areas around the perimeter of the USSR or its allies.[24]

U.S. views on nuclear-free zones have been less enthusiastic. Soviet support alone offers a reasonable explanation for U.S. wariness. U.S.

security interests, while tied to overseas bases,[25] would dictate further caution. In areas such as Central Europe, where nuclear weapons already were an integral part of the security system, proposals limited to nuclear weapons threatened to reduce Western security rather than to decrease tension.

The United States did not offer much more support for continent-zones, although "welcoming" regional arrangements "freely arrived at" by all the states in the area.[26] Rather than a blanket endorsement of the concept, the United States made clear that each proposal would be evaluated separately, according to the area and the measures involved:

> The position of the Western countries in regard to nuclear-free zones had been, generally, that they must meet three criteria. First, they should cover a clearly defined area with definite boundaries and all the countries within an area should subcribe. Second, the setting up of such an area should not confer a military advantage on any nation or group to the disadvantage of any other. Third, there should be some means of verification to ensure that all parties to the treaty or convention fulfill their obligations.[27]

A discussion of superpower attitudes toward nuclear-free zones points up one of the ironies of their popularity: A major appeal to the Third World is that such arrangements can be made without the direct participation of the nuclear powers. In negotiations for nuclear-free zones, the nonnuclear nations are able to take part as relative equals. Nuclear-free zones offer the opportunity for the nonmajor powers, usually an audience watching the interminable bargaining of the superpowers, to take a meaningful step toward arms control and simultaneously to demonstrate their initiative and independence. A certain satisfaction must come from showing that the nonnuclear nations could succeed where the nuclear powers had failed so completely.

But the question remains how meaningful any nuclear-free zone could be if it was not accepted by the nuclear nations. Western analysts generally have argued that no nuclear-free zone could survive without such acceptance.[28] The point is an obvious one but may be overstated. All that is required of the nuclear nations is acquiescence, not active support, and this may be easier to obtain. A more telling argument is that the effectiveness of a nuclear-free zone requires a consensus among the nuclear powers. This could be much harder to achieve. A perceived threat to the security of any major nuclear nation from a nuclear-free zone would make such an agreement impossible. Even though the nuclear nations are not direct participants in regional negotiations, they constitute a sort of presence beyond the talks that sets limits on any achievements.

The effectiveness of nuclear-free zones may be dependent on the major nuclear powers in another sense:

> Perhaps the most important single reinforcement of a rational approach to security through arms control would be evidence that the great powers were pursuing with equal vigor measures of arms control applicable to themselves.[29]

The bargaining over the Non-Proliferation Treaty illustrates how very bitterly the nonnuclear powers resented being asked to forgo nuclear weapons while the nuclear nations did nothing to check their own vertical proliferation. Convincing the near-nuclear nations in any region to sacrifice their potential without evidence of a comparable sacrifice from the nuclear powers is difficult. Holding them to any agreement as the technological gap between the nuclear "have" and "have not" nations widens might be even more difficult.

THE LATIN AMERICAN NUCLEAR-FREE ZONE: BEGINNINGS

Precedents for the movement toward a Latin American nuclear-free zone are found in a series of demilitarization agreements among various countries in the region.[30] In 1829, Peru and Colombia agreed to mutual troop reductions along their common border. In 1858, Costa Rica and Nicaragua pledged to permit no hostilities in a portion of the San Juan del Norte and Lake Nicaragua area "even in case of war." Chile and Argentina neutralized and demilitarized the Straits of Magellan in 1881 and went on in 1902 to limit their naval forces. The latter agreement was broken when Brazil began to build up its naval forces, sparking a regional arms race.

A comprehensive disarmament treaty covering aircraft, warships, and troops was signed in 1923 by five Central American nations: El Salvador, Costa Rica, Guatemala, Honduras, and Nicaragua. The lack of any inspection or enforcement mechanisms meant the treaty was completely ineffective, and it was allowed to expire 20 years later.[31] When the Rio Treaty was signed in 1947, the conference resolved that its creation should not be taken to justify "excessive armaments." The Latin American nuclear-free zone is not a direct descendant of any of these agreements, but the impulse to avoid conflict by setting certain weapons or territory aside is very much the same.

A more relevant proposal came from the Costa Rican ambassador to the OAS in 1958, calling for a "substantial reduction" in military expenditures and a treaty to renounce the acquisition of weapons "in excess of security requirements."[32] Nuclear weapons were included, making this the first proposal for a Latin American nuclear-free zone.

Unfortunately, the premises of the plan made it politically unacceptable from the start. The Costa Ricans argued that Latin American military forces could never play a meaningful role in the defense of the hemisphere, and that dependence on the United States for security should be acknowledged. Such an acknowledgement would free the way for genuine disarmament and the release of resources critically needed in the development effort. But such an admission of military impotence was universally rejected by the other Latin Americans. Costa Rica, which had no national military,[33] might be able to make such remarks, but most Latin American politicians could not:

> The primary obstacles to any arms agreements in Latin America grow out of internal rather than international factors. For the most part, anti-Communist, reform-minded political groups would favor the allocation of fewer resources to the armed forces; the major group in opposition would be the military establishment, which in nearly all the countries is an important element in the domestic political process.[34]

The United States was no happier than Latin America with the Costa Rican idea. Since World War II the United States had advocated the buildup of Latin American military forces, not their reduction.[35] The United States had a commitment, perhaps only rhetorical, to mutual regional defense in which widespread arms control played no part. Not surprisingly, the Costa Rican plan was referred to the OAS Council of Foreign Ministers for "study" and never seen again.

In 1959 a similar proposal surfaced, this time in the Christmas message of Chilean President Jorge Alessandri. He called for a halt in the development and purchase of new offensive weapons, including nuclear weapons. When President Dwight D. Eisenhower came to visit Chile, Alessandri presented the plan to him and "Eisenhower expressed support for the principle of arms control in Latin America after an equilibrium in military strength had been reached among the countries of the region."[36]

The proposal was brought to the OAS council in very vague form in 1960. A study group was set up but it never met and this plan, too, faded away. Proposals that included conventional forces and hence touched the immediate interests of the Latin American military appeared doomed:

> "Costa Ricanization," that is, disbandment of traditional armies in Latin America is Utopian. Furthermore, significant arms control measures, short of disbandment, are not now feasible and may very well be undesirable. This does not mean that Latin American force levels and military expenditures could not be reduced without endangering the effectiveness and legitimate responsibilities of the various military forces. But it is unlikely that this will happen.[37]

No one had yet thought to separate nuclear from conventional disarmament proposals.

One other Latin American country had acquired a strong interest in arms control: Brazil. There had been no well-formulated plan until the late 1950s when President Juscelino Kubitschek began to view regional arms expenditures and competition as siphoning off funds that were needed desperately for development. By the end of 1958 Kubitschek had become a forceful advocate of disarmament, but it was not until the presidencies of Jânio Quadros and João Goulart between 1960 and 1964 that Brazil sought a leading international and regional role.[38]

As a member of the 18-nation disarmament conference in Geneva, Brazil was especially concerned with the linkages between disarmament and the release of funds from the Great Powers for development. The "dollars for development" issue was very much its own. Brazil began to advocate the denuclearization of Latin America in 1961. The close ties being cultivated between Brazil and the Portuguese territories in Africa made the Brazilians aware of the African denuclearization movement. Brazil could be expected to play a leading role in any similar movement in Latin America in the early 1960s.

The real spur to the Latin American nuclear-free zone, however, came from the Cuban missile crisis. The sudden intrusion of the cold war, with the accompanying threat of nuclear conflict, profoundly shocked and frightened many Latin American leaders:

> Since Latin America so precipitously lost its nuclear virginity in 1962, many Latins have come to appreciate that their long-term security would be enhanced if nuclear weapons could be permanently kept out of the southern part of the hemisphere.[39]

In November 1962, Brazil, Bolivia, Chile, and Ecuador introduced a resolution in the UN First Committee stating that the Latin Americans would

> through the means and channels which will be found most appropriate negotiate arrangements whereby the countries in the area would: (a) agree not to manufacture, receive, store or test nuclear weapons or carrying devices; (b) agree to dispose forthwith of any nuclear weapons or nuclear delivery vehicles which may now be in their territory; (c) agree to make provision for verification of these arrangements.

The resolution also requested the cooperation of the nuclear nations in respecting the proposed nuclear-free zone. Action was deferred on the draft resolution at the request of the United States, but Brazil asked that the "denuclearization of Latin America" be included as an agenda item at the next General Assembly.

On March 21, 1963, President Lopez Mateos of Mexico proposed to the presidents of Chile, Brazil, Bolivia, and Ecuador that these five nations join forces to promote the denuclearization effort.[40] This led, on April 29, 1963, to a joint declaration in which they announced that "their governments are prepared to sign a multilateral Latin American agreement whereby their countries would undertake not to manufacture, receive, store or test nuclear weapons or nuclear launching devices.[41]

The campaign for a nuclear-free zone in Latin America began in earnest with that declaration. The issue was brought before the United Nations in the fall of 1963 in a resolution sponsored by 11 Latin American nations. The resolution was to be only an expression of endorsement from the United Nations, not a declaration. The Latin Americans wanted their own authority, not the international organization's, to be the clear source of denuclearization.[42] This was to be a Latin American project, carried out by the Latin Americans. Brazil and Mexico played leading roles in the UN discussions, but Argentina was too absorbed in its own domestic political problems to pay much attention to regional matters.[43] The project was endorsed by the United States, although not wholeheartedly. Ambassador Adlai Stevenson repeated the U.S. criteria for a legitimate nuclear-free zone without stating whether the United States felt Latin America could meet those standards.

Several factors favored the creation of a nuclear-free zone in Latin America. The first was the traumatic shock of the Cuban missile crisis and the profound desire of many Latin Americans to avoid all chances of a repetition.[44] Until the missile crisis Latin America had never figured as a major theater in the cold war, and most Latin Americans preferred to retain that isolation.[45] Nor was Latin America the victim of the significant national conflicts that plagued areas such as the Middle East. Suspicions and rivalries were plentiful, but there seemed to be a welcome lack of fundamental and irreconcilable divisions on the continent. Cuba, especially a nuclear Cuba, threatened to change that.

The introduction of nuclear weapons also would upset the regional security balance and perhaps trigger an arms race.[46] Any such competition would place tremendous strain on the resources of the Latin American countries: "Many development-minded Latins fear that an atomic arms race among rival Latin nations would be economically ruinous."[47]

Although six countries had small nuclear research reactors in the mid-1960s, none of them had a nuclear energy program of genuine military significance.[48] Plans for larger and significant reactors existed, but at the time there were no known plans to utilize their military potential.[49] A nuclear-free zone had some hope of success if it could be achieved before the military possibilities of nuclear energy gained a strong position.

A final appeal of the nuclear-free zone was that its successful creation would enable the Latin Americans to serve as a "model" to other nations and regions. Mexico's Alfonso García Robles[50] made extensive use of this argument in arousing support for the negotiations,[51] and this was a constant theme in the COPREDAL.[52] Beyond the prestige that success could bring to Latin America, there was "a genuine hope that establishment of a Latin American nuclear-free zone would have an impact on arms control negotiations elsewhere in the world and be a significant contribution to peace." [53]

The path to a nuclear-free zone in Latin America would not be smooth, however. Balanced against the security concerns that weighed in favor of the treaty were others opposing it. The primary concern came from a reluctance to give up nuclear weapons except as part of a global effort for disarmament. One might acquire prestige as the first nuclear-free zone in an inhabited region, but that also would place the area in a somewhat exposed position. Great Power, especially U.S. security guarantees, could assuage that fear, but this might be construed as another admission of weakness, which national pride could not tolerate.[54]

Concerns for prestige of another sort also figured in Latin American reluctance. There was a clearly perceived link between nuclear weapons and international prestige, making the search for status a major force behind the drive for nuclear capabilities.[55] Nuclear weapons appeared to be the surest ticket of admission to the ranks of the "Great Powers." Therefore, it was difficult for the nuclear powers and especially the United States "to be convincing on the horrors of nuclear war and the inadvisability of opting for nuclear weapons when the United States had used them in the past and is relying on such weapons as the backbone of the American defense system." [56]

Potentially powerful psychological factors thus operated from the first to dampen enthusiasm for the nuclear-free zone.

Another potential source of opposition came from the Latin American military. It is important to note that the Latin American military's position was based on internal political clout rather than national defense needs:

> Armed forces are needed in Latin America principally to maintain law and order, and to deter and eliminate subversion. There is little objective military need for any Latin American state to acquire a military capability to defend itself against other states in the region or to defend the region as a whole against attack.[57]

As another observer noted,

> For all their militarism, coups, caudillos, and juntas, Latin American armies simply do not do much fighting, they do not kill very many people, they do not engage in vicious propaganda, they rarely violate international frontiers, and they almost never engage in regional aggression.[58]

Opposition from the military to conventional arms control was "to be expected" as a direct perceived threat to its position.[59] Its opposition to nuclear arms control was less certain, however, and more likely to rest on prestige rather than political considerations. Assurances that a nuclear-free zone would not seek to press on to conventional arms control, and might even stimulate compensatory spending on conventional weapons, could give Latin American political leaders more latitude in the negotiations than initially would be expected. This generalization would not apply, of course, where the military had become enamored of nuclear energy and its military potential.

CREATION OF THE NUCLEAR-FREE ZONE

The establishment of the Latin American nuclear-free zone consumed four years of negotiations.[60] The year between the passage of the UN resolution endorsing the zone concept and the preliminary meetings on denuclearization (REUPRAL) saw changes in the executives of four of the five original sponsors of the denuclearization movement.[61] Of these changes, only the military coup in Brazil overthrowing President Goulart proved significant for the Tlatelolco negotiations.

There is no need for a detailed case study of the negotiations here; for that, one should see the work of John Redick.[62] However, certain choices made in the course of the bargaining affected the capacity of the system to deal with current proliferation problems. Perhaps the simplest method of treating the negotiations is to go over the treaty that emerged, pointing out the compromises and any remaining sources of controversy.

The Treaty of Tlatelolco is a relatively long document, with 31 articles and two additional protocols. The preamble sets out the purposes and principles of the treaty, reflecting ideas basic to Latin American and Third World views of arms control and disarmament:

> that the military denuclearization of Latin America—being understood to mean the undertaking entered into internationally in this Treaty to keep their territories forever free from nuclear weapons—will constitute a measure which will spare their peoples from the squandering of their limited resources on nuclear armaments and will protect them against possible nuclear attacks on their territories, and will also constitute a significant contribution towards preventing the proliferation of nuclear weapons and a powerful factor for general and complete disarmament.

Of interest are two passages added at the insistence of Brazil and Uruguay. Taken together, they represent a succinct statement of the major grievances of the nonmajor actors in international arms control negotiations:

> Recalling United Nations General Assembly Resolution 2028 which established the principle of an acceptable balance of mutual responsibilities and duties for the nuclear and non-nuclear powers . . . .

> [That] the Latin American countries should use their right to the greatest and most equitable possible access to this new source of energy in order to expedite the economic and social development of their peoples.

The desire to keep Latin America absolutely free from nuclear weapons, which prompted the nuclear-free zone effort, is reflected in the very comprehensive obligations laid out in Article 1. The nuclear programs of the Latin American nations are to be used entirely for peaceful purposes. The "testing, use, manufacture, production, or acquisition of nuclear weapons" are prohibited in the territories covered by the treaty, and the "receipt, storage, installation, deployment, and any form of possession" is forbidden to the parties. The "transport" of nuclear weapons through the zone is not prohibited, however, marking a concession to the wishes of the United States. It was clear the United States never would support a treaty denying its nuclear weapons-carrying warships the right to pass through the Panama Canal.[63] There also was the practical question of the difficulties of enforcing any ban on transporting nuclear weapons. Finally, the parties agreed to "refrain from engaging in, encouraging or authorizing, directly or indirectly, or in any way participating in the testing, use, manufacture, production, possession, or control of any nuclear weapon." Both proliferation and dissemination thus were covered by the treaty.[64]

Article 3 defines the treaty's concept of territory and points up several Latin American foreign policy interests that, although only marginally related to denuclearization, managed to be included in the treaty. Territory includes "territorial sea, air and any other space over which the State exercises sovereignty in accordance with its own legislation." This wording could be construed to support Argentine claims to the Falkland Islands, and it certainly permitted states that set a 200-mile limit for their territorial waters to claim the support of the treaty. The Tlatelolco Treaty thus was made to serve purposes beyond the removal of the threat of nuclear weapons. Article 4 defines the zone of application, using a definition based on longitude and latitude rather than history and culture.

The definition of a nuclear weapon is contained in Article 5, which relies on objective rather than subjective criteria. The supporters of subjective criteria, such as Brazil and Argentina, wanted the inclusion of intentions as a further rationale and support for peaceful nuclear explosives. Obviously, the definition of a nuclear weapon was intimately related to the permissibility of such peaceful devices, and nations such as Mexico sought objective criteria to avoid an "easy" distinction based on a nation's intentions.

Interestingly, "an instrument that may be used for the transport or propulsion of the device is not included in this definition if it is separate from the device and is not an indivisible part thereof." The early calls for a nuclear-free zone had included delivery vehicles, but that prohibition had been dropped. Brazil, Mexico, and Argentina all had rocket programs, although Brazil's was the most advanced. The task of defining and distinguishing between peaceful and warlike launching devices, especially those with conventional applications, proved too technically and politically complex. This also avoided a potential confrontation with the United States over any delivery vehicles stationed in its Latin American territories. The mere attempt to define a nuclear weapon, however, was a major accomplishment.[65]

Articles 7 through 11 outlined the structure and duties of an independent international organization (OPANAL) to oversee the Treaty.[66] The supreme organ of the OPANAL was its general conference, which would meet every two years. The decision to hold regular meetings and to permit special sessions "whenever the Treaty so provides or, in the opinion of the Council [a five-member board elected by the General Conference], the circumstances so require" represented the choice of a weak secretary general. Nations such as Brazil and Argentina had sought to limit the authority of the agency's permanent staff against the more political conference. OPANAL was to be headquartered in Mexico City, another tribute to Mexican leadership of the denuclearization efforts.

The treaty's system of verification and control is laid out in Articles 12 through 16 and part of Article 18. That system is one of the most comprehensive in any arms control agreement and was achieved only after considerable controversy. International Atomic Energy Agency (IAEA) safeguards will be fully applied through either bilateral or multilateral agreements. This represents a compromise that was necessary to win Brazilian support but offered partial satisfaction to nations such as Ecuador and Mexico, which wished to ensure strict and equal controls.[67] The system was to verify not only "that devices, services and facilities intended for peaceful uses of nuclear energy are not used in the testing and manufacture of nuclear weapons" (Article 12) but also that none of the activities prohibited in Article 1 are undertaken and that any peaceful nuclear explosions are compatible with the provisions of Article 18. There was to be a system, beyond the normal procedures and reports, whereby a nation suspecting a treaty violation could call for a special inspection. A nation suspected of a violation also could ask for a special inspection to clear its good name.

This approach prompted UN Secretary General U Thant to remark, "There is embodied in your Treaty a number of aspects of the system known as "verification-by-challenge," which is one of the more hopeful new concepts introduced into the complicated question of verification and control."[68]

The determination of Latin American nations such as Brazil and Argentina to ensure that nothing in the treaty should infringe on their national nuclear energy development finds expression in Article 17:

"Nothing in the provisions of this Treaty shall prejudice the rights of the Contracting Parties, in conformity with this Treaty, to use nuclear energy for peaceful purposes, in particular for their economic development and social progress."

This support for the peaceful uses of nuclear energy is one of the consistent themes of the COPREDAL. No Latin American nations argued against peaceful nuclear technology, but only Brazil and Argentina had the programs and capacities to encourage forceful advocacy.

Article 18 remains perhaps the most controversial in the treaty, for it deals with the issue of peaceful nuclear explosives. It is quite explicit in permitting the peaceful nuclear explosions (PNEs) that Brazil, Argentina, and Nicaragua,[69] among others, demanded. The controls included IAEA inspection and supervision of all use of such devices. The controversy centered around the ability to make a meaningful distinction between nuclear weapons and peaceful nuclear explosives. Brazil and Argentina claimed such a distinction could be made, Mexico contended that it could not and that Article 18 was subordinate to the definition of a nuclear weapon in Article 5. The controversy eventually was carried beyond the regional talks to the United Nations and the Geneva disarmament talks but never resolved: "Clearly ample groundwork has been laid for continuous and extended disputation on the meaning of these conflicting Articles."[70]

Articles 19 to 27 deal with relations with other international organizations and the procedures for dispute settlement. The United Nations and the International Court of Justice are to be the major avenues of settlement, although the United Nations and the OAS are to receive reports of any violations simultaneously. The sanctity of regional and international security systems is guaranteed in Article 21, reflecting the concern of some parties for the treaty's relationship with the Inter-American System.

This issue had placed Mexico on one side, Brazil and Argentina on the other. Mexico maintained denuclearization was not incompatible with the OAS or the Rio Treaty. At the same time, it was important to keep the treaty mechanisms separate from the Inter-American Security System, since the presence of a nuclear superpower, the United States, would destroy the treaty's regional character and purpose. In addition, non-OAS members might be unable or unwilling to adhere to a nuclear-free zone tied to the OAS structure. Mexico was adamant about the need to remove the threat of nuclear weapons from Latin America. None of the Western nuclear powers, it was noted, had argued a Latin American nuclear-free zone would weaken basic Western security. Latin America was peripheral to the East-West conflict but the only way to remain so, Mexico argued, was to ensure that nuclear weapons never intruded.

The response to the Mexican arguments was sharp. Brazil declared that a nuclear-free zone consisting of a patchwork of Latin American nations would be "ridiculous" and would reduce the entire effort to the elements of a farce. Success depended on universal adherence, and anything less was meaningless. The Argentines did not believe giving up nuclear weapons necessarily would increase Latin America's regional security since "the existence of an atomic void would not constitute a synonym with security."[71]

The treaty was open for signature to "all Latin American republics" and all other sovereign nations within the geographic zone (Article 25). But the same article declared: "The General Conference shall not take any decision regarding the admission of a political entity part or all of whose territory is the subject . . . of a dispute or claim between an extra-continental country and one or more Latin American States."

This was another instance of issues beyond denuclearization affecting the negotiations. Venezuela had carried old disputes with Great Britain over into new disputes with Guyana and had almost remained out of the negotiations as a protest. This prohibition was designed to reassure any nations with old territorial grievances.

The conditions of the treaty's entry into force (Article 28) provoked considerable controversy. The strong advocates of denuclearization, such as Mexico, wanted the treaty to take effect as quickly as possible for as many nations as possible. More cautious nations, such as Brazil and Colombia, argued a nuclear-free zone composed of only some of the states in the region would be ineffective and perhaps dangerous. They also argued that a nuclear-free zone could not win the support of the nuclear powers without universal membership.

The resulting compromise permitted each side to claim a partial victory. The treaty would enter into force for all signatories only when: (1) all the relevant Latin American nations had ratified the treaty; (2) all nations holding de facto or de jure control in the region had ratified Additional Protocol 1; (3) all nuclear nations had ratified Additional Protocol 2; and (4) multilateral or bilateral safeguards agreements had been concluded with the IAEA. This permitted the "universalists" to delay the full force of the treaty until it met their exacting standards. For those who wished faster action, however, a nation could waive, wholly or in part, the restrictions just described for entry into force. In essence, along with its ratification of the treaty, a nation deposited a declaration that the provisions were now in force for that nation.

To date, 23 Latin American nations have signed the treaty and 22 of those have ratified it. Of the latter, 20 have waived the full requirements of Article 28 and declared the treaty in force for their territory. These countries include Mexico, Colombia, and Venezuela, all threshold nations. Not included are Brazil, Argentina, and Chile.[72] Serious questions may be raised about the effectiveness of a nuclear-free zone in which three of the area's most important states, and its two near-nuclear nations, do not participate.

THE TREATY AND OUTSIDE POWERS

The two additional protocols to the treaty provide nations outside the region with the opportunity to adhere to its provisions. Protocol 1 concerns nations that exercise de facto or de jure control over territory within the geographic boundaries of the treaty. Such nations would agree to "undertake to apply the statute of denuclearization in respect of warlike purposes" to their territorial possessions. Adhering to Protocol 1 did not give these nations a voice in the OPANAL, but neither did it subject them to the treaty's control and verification procedures. France, the Netherlands, the United Kingdom, and the United States held territory within the zone of the Tlatelolco Treaty in 1967.

The United Kingdom and the Netherlands signed and ratified Protocol 1 relatively quickly, with the British adding only a reservation stating continued opposition to peaceful nuclear explosions. The United States did not sign Protocol 1 until the spring of 1977. France always has considered its territory an integral part of "the French nation" and raised constitutional and legal objections to the protocol.[73] Over time, however, the initially harsh refusal, which caused considerable anger among the Latin Americans, moderated to an attitude of "benign neglect."[74] None of the states holding territory in the region appears to be following policies that threaten the effective creation of the nuclear-free zone.

Protocol 2, which applies to the nuclear powers, sets three primary conditions on those nations: (1) to respect the statute of denuclearization; (2) not to contribute in any way to acts that would violate that statute; and (3) not to use or to threaten to use nuclear weapons against the parties to the treaty. The United States, the Soviet Union, the United Kingdom, France, and the People's Republic of China all were asked to adhere to Protocol 2.

The Latin American delegations consistently had sought the views and support of the nuclear nations. These views sometimes resulted in modifications of treaty drafts to meet nuclear power objections. Adroit propaganda also sought to create a climate in which nuclear power refusal would be difficult:

> The nuclear powers themselves are the first to insist on the urgent and pressing necessity of avoiding the proliferation of nuclear weapons. Since denuclearization is the most radical form of non-proliferation, it would only be logical that the nuclear powers readily agree to lend their fullest cooperation . . . . A different behavior would mean an open contradiction between statements and facts, between words and deeds.[75]

Great Britain is the only nation that has ratified both protocols. France, which refused to accept any limits on its nuclear policies in the Moscow Treaty, initially would not accept them from the Treaty of

Tlatelolco. France's signature and ratification were not obtained until March 22, 1974. The same pattern of initial rejection but eventual acceptance held for China as well. The Chinese had given favorable responses early in the denuclearization negotiations, at least to the general notion of a nuclear-free zone. At first the Chinese refused to sign Protocol 2 because the treaty was a UN-sponsored instrument and therefore unacceptable.[76] Once China was admitted to the United Nations, the basis of opposition was removed and China signed Protocol 2 on June 12, 1974.

The United States quickly signed and ratified Protocol 2. Vice President Hubert Humphrey went to Mexico City for a signing ceremony in 1968, but the furor over President Lyndon Johnson's decision not to run for a second term meant the event went unnoticed outside Latin America. The United States added a few reservations to its signature, but only the interpretation of Article 18 to forbid peaceful nuclear explosions in light of current technology is relevant.

The Soviet Union, on the other hand, resisted pressures to sign Protocol 2 for more than ten years. The "Cuban connection" was the major factor holding back Soviet acceptance of the Tlatelolco Treaty. Soviet objections to the Latin American nuclear-free zone went back to the presentation in the United Nations in 1963:

> When the U.N. General Assembly passed a resolution in late 1967 endorsing the treaty, the USSR abstained. The Soviet representative criticized the treaty for failing to prohibit nuclear explosions for peaceful purposes and to restrict the transit of nuclear weapons through the zone, and also objected to the inclusion of large areas of the Atlantic and the Pacific Oceans in the nuclear-free zone.[77]

Acceptance of the Treaty through adherence to Protocol 2 removes the hypocrisy of a rhetorical commitment to nuclear-free zones while opposing Latin America's in practice. García Robles had persistently chided the Soviet Union in the United Nations and in the Geneva disarmament negotiations for this lapse.

> Its position has been consistent but has been one of consistent error, in open contradiction to the position of enthusiastic theoretical support reiterated ad nauseum by the Soviet government. Moreover, this error challenges the ruling of the world conscience embodied in General Assembly resolutions . . . all of which were approved by about 100 votes in favor with none against.[78]

Despite the Soviet Union's signature on May 18, 1978, the Cubans continue to reject all Latin American overtures to accept the Tlatelolco Treaty and already have announced that the change in Soviet policy will not affect their own. The Cuban demand for removal of the U.S. presence from the Caribbean as a precondition for adherence is unlikely to be met in the near future. Normalization of relations between the United States and Cuba would be a minimum condition for Cuban adherence to Tlatelolco. The state of current Cuban-U.S. relations over Cuban involvement in Africa makes normalization improbable very soon. In light of the intense U.S. interest in and attention to Cuban foreign policy activism in Africa, it is interesting to note that in the case of Tlatelolco it is Cuba's inaction that has the significant impact. A successful nuclear-free zone in Latin America in the long run depends on Cuban participation or acquiescence. In the meantime, the Cuban refusal has become the primary rationalization for the continuing unwillingness of Brazil and Argentina to enter into full treaty participation.

NUCLEAR ENERGY IN LATIN AMERICA

Any discussion of the adequacy of the Tlatelolco Treaty to deal with nuclear proliferation must consider the nuclear energy programs of the Latin American nations. The scholarly work on nuclear proliferation is extensive, and most studies include lists of near-nuclear or "Nth" countries. Predicting Nth country status is a complex process and estimates vary. For example, William Epstein gives a list of near-nuclear and potential nuclear nations. Argentina is the only Latin American nation credited with the capacity to go nuclear "in one to two years." Brazil, Chile, Cuba, Mexico, and Venezuela all make the ten-year list, however. A Stockholm International Peace Research Institute (SIPRI) monograph (1972), on the other hand, profiled Brazil but ignored Argentina in its survey of supposed near-nuclear nations.[79]

In the mid-1960s, six Latin American nations had nuclear energy programs of potential significance: Mexico, Brazil, Argentina, Chile, Colombia, and Venezuela. The programs of the last three were minor, confined to research reactors and cooperative projects with the IAEA in such fields as desalinization and food production.[80] In March 1962 Mexico had unilaterally declared itself a one-nation nuclear-free zone, but neither Brazil nor Argentina made similar renunciations.

The current situation retains the gap between leading nuclear energy developers and nations just beginning to acquire nuclear technology, but the ranks of the minor nuclear energy developers are growing. Bolivia, Uruguay, Peru, Cuba, and Ecuador all have or soon will have research reactors.[81] Each also has announced its intentions of pursuing nuclear power development.

An especially interesting aspect of these developments is that Argentina will serve as a major source of technical information, advice, and equipment.[82] The new research reactor soon to go critical in Peru, for example, was designed and developed completely in Argentina; Argentina even is supplying the enriched uranium for the reactor.[83] This active intra-American cooperation is of relatively recent vintage and could pave the way for greater regional cooperation in nuclear energy development. In an interview, Mexican President Jose Lopez-Portillo suggested that

> there are some bottlenecks in nuclear development resulting from the high cost of some installations, which cannot be considered for every country, but which could be agreed upon by several. The case of enriching uranium is an example, but others can be studied: equipment, installations, technology, etc.[84]

The regional option deserves further consideration, but any discussion of potential proliferation must focus on Brazil, Argentina, and, as a contrast, Mexico.

Argentina

Argentina was the first Latin American nation to launch a nuclear energy program. Its National Commission for Atomic Energy (CNEA) was created in 1950 by the decree of President Juan Perón. Three years later the CNEA signed an Atoms for Peace development agreement with the United States, benefiting from U.S. financial and technical aid as well as enriched uranium. The turmoil that beset Argentine political and economic life kept the nuclear energy program from full development at the anticipated pace. Delayed funding, frustrations, and the consequent loss of trained personnel held back the program. But there was remarkably little direct political interference with CNEA. The agency had only three directors in 18 years, although all were retired admirals.[85]

At the time of the nuclear-free zone negotiations, Argentina possessed four research reactors, one of which had been the first on the continent.[86] A fifth went critical in May 1967. Four of these were designed and built by the CNEA alone. As early as 1957, Argentina decided not to purchase foreign reactors but to develop its own national capabilities. That desire for national independence later influenced Argentina's 1968 decision to purchase its first nuclear power plant from the West Germans. The plant, Atucha 1, although more expensive than comparable U.S. models, used natural uranium rather than the enriched uranium over which the United States exercised a virtual monopoly.[87] It went critical in 1974, and supplies 319 MWe.[88]

Simple nationalism, as much as any desire to develop nuclear weapons free from outside interference, could explain these policy choices. However, "it is difficult to escape the conclusion that the path chosen by Argentina in developing its civil nuclear capacity lends itself more easily to weapons development than others which it might have followed."[89]

Argentina currently is the leader in nuclear technology in Latin America. Beyond Atucha 1, four more heavy water reactors will be built by the Canadian firm AECL. Construction is scheduled to be completed on the final plant by 1986; each will have a 600 MWe capacity. Argentina has rather extensive uranium deposits[90] and in addition has agreements for joint mining exploration with Uruguay, Peru, Bolivia, and Ecuador.[91] The Argentine nuclear energy program is well established, relatively uncontroversial, and likely to maintain its technological edge for the near future.

The most likely route for eventual Argentine proliferation would be through a "peaceful nuclear explosion" comparable to India's. Argentina already has filed a reservation to the Tlatelolco Treaty reiterating its views that a useful distinction can be made between peaceful and other nuclear devices. The Argentines and Indians have signed a nuclear cooperation agreement; Argentina dismisses as an unfortunate coincidence the fact that the agreement was completed just as India exploded its first peaceful nuclear device. In terms of sheer technical capabilities, Argentina easily could acquire nuclear explosive devices by the end of the 1980s, far earlier if it undertook a crash program.

Brazil

Argentina's primary rival in Latin American nuclear energy development is Brazil, and the two nations watch each other's programs closely.[92] Brazil entered the nuclear field somewhat later than Argentina, stimulated primarily by the Atoms for Peace program. Its National Commission for Nuclear Energy (CNEN) was founded in 1956 by President Juscelino Kubitschek. The real boost to nuclear development came in 1964, however, when a coup ousted President Goulart and installed a military government.[93] The military leaders revived Brazilian ambitions to continental leadership and Great Power status internationally. Nuclear energy development, particularly nuclear explosions for peaceful purposes, appeared to be an integral part of the military's plans for growth.[94]

At the time of the Tlatelolco negotiations Brazil had three research reactors, all operating with U.S. enriched uranium under IAEA safeguards. The program to develop nuclear power plants was several years behind that in Argentina. The reactors all had been manufactured in Brazil by Brazilian companies and were staffed entirely by Brazilian technical personnel.[95] The same desire for indigenous development and control that motivated the Argentines also propelled the Brazilians. In 1967, Brazil signed an agreement for nuclear cooperation with the French[96] that would, it was claimed, transform Brasilia into the "atomic capitol of Latin America"[97] through eventual development of breeder reactor technology.

The basis of present Brazilian policy could be discerned during the period of the nuclear-free zone negotiations. Brazil already was seeking independence in nuclear energy development and had made such development an important part of a broader national policy for growth. The interest of the military government in peaceful nuclear explosives is a critical factor in Brazil's behavior. Brazil, which under Goulart had been very active in international affairs, including disarmament matters, withdrew after 1964 to concentrate on national economic development. The country's enthusiasm for disarmament and arms control cooled perceptibly.[98] The Brazilians also were seeking to keep their nuclear options open and increasingly were unwilling to risk a loss of technological advancement through an unconditional renunciation of nuclear weapons.

At present, Brazil still is awaiting completion of its first nuclear power plant, Angra 1. As of March 1978, the project was two years behind schedule, and reports of serious construction problems and safety hazards have appeared.[99] The plant is being built by Westinghouse and will have an eventual capacity of 626 MWe.[100] Unlike Argentina, Brazil is relying on enriched uranium reactor technology rather than natural uranium. Brazil claims to have one of the world's largest uranium reserve supplies.[101] It also has signed agreements with West Germany to work on high temperature reactor technology to make use of Brazil's extensive thorium deposits.[102]

Of much greater significance, Brazil has cooperative agreements with West Germany that culminated in 1975 in a deal for "the largest transfer ever made of nuclear technology to a developing country."[103] The arrangement "would satisfy the long-standing ambitions of both countries for greater nuclear self-sufficiency and would contribute toward Brazil's dream of becoming a major power."[104]

Under the agreements, Brazil will receive a full nuclear fuel cycle, including enrichment and reprocessing technology. Up to eight reactors, each with a 1,300 MWe capacity,[105] will be constructed by 1990, with Brazil assuming a greater and greater share of the construction and technical responsibilities as the projects continue.[106] Two reactors, Angra 2 and 3, already have been begun, and construction is starting on components of the enrichment process.[107]

The censorious reaction of the United States to the deal, and subsequent U.S. pressure on both Brazil and West Germany to give up the agreement, has done much to cool U.S. relations with each.[108] Brazil remains committed to acquiring the full fuel cycle. When asked if his country would consider forgoing recycling technology, the president of NUCLEBRAS[109] retorted:

> To give up recycling means to have no plutonium which is also ours, right? It would be like giving up our water, the energy of our rivers, our

oil, or our uranium. Plutonium is a fuel which will be produced in Brazil, in our country. There is no reason to give it up.[110]

Like Argentina, the probable Brazilian route to nuclear weapons would be through PNEs. Each nation, in its own way, is ensuring itself the independent technical capacity to produce nuclear explosive devices. At the moment Brazil is somewhat behind Argentina in nuclear technology, but an all-out effort could close the gap very quickly. If nuclear proliferation comes to Latin America in the near future, it will come through the actions of one or both of these nations. Given their long rivalry and suspicions, a peaceful nuclear explosion by one would trigger a comparable "test" by the other within a short time.

Mexico

After viewing the Brazilian and Argentine nuclear programs, Mexico's does not appear very dramatic. Part of this is due to Mexico's consistent statements that it has no ambitions for nuclear weapons. Nonetheless, Mexico's nuclear energy program was the third largest in Latin America at the time of the Tlatelolco negotiations and provides an interesting contrast to those of Brazil and Argentina.

Mexican policy is developed and controlled by the National Commission for Nuclear Energy (CNEN), founded in 1955. Mexico had three research reactors in the mid-1960s, and CNEN devoted most of its attention to the social and medical applications of nuclear energy. John Redick describes the pace of the Mexican program as "measured" but notes criticisms from a national manufacturing group that the "snail's pace" of development was hampering industrial growth.[111] Unlike Brazil and Argentina, Mexico had no bilateral nuclear cooperation agreements, and fuel for the reactors came primarily from the IAEA. IAEA also provided the major portion of technical assistance, although some technical personnel were trained in the United States.

The Mexicans had not, in the mid-1960s, made a firm commitment to proceed with the development of nuclear power plants, a further indication of the peaceful nature of the program. The Mexicans were running a comparative study of nuclear versus fossil-fueled plants of the same capacity against the overall needs of Mexican power development.[112] At least during the course of the Tlatelolco negotiations, Mexico did not even display an interest in keeping its options open.

A number of factors may have accounted for this lack of interest in nuclear energy development. Mexico's geographic proximity to the United States makes the desire for nuclear weapons faintly "ludicrous."[113] At the same time, the U.S. presence provides a "free" security umbrella. Unfortunately, that also places Mexico uncomfortably close to the most likely site of major nuclear warfare. The relatively minor role of the military in Mexican politics eliminated a powerful pressure group that has been active in Brazil and Argentina. Mexico's international ambitions also appear to be somewhat different from those of the other two countries. Mexico seems to lack traditional Great Power ambitions and instead aspires to leadership within the Third World bloc of nonaligned nations. Nuclear weapons may be less a mark of prestige among this group than successful economic development, which a heavy nuclear energy program could hamper.

Mexican interest in nuclear energy has picked up since the late 1960s, but it still does not resemble Brazilian and Argentine ambitions for major national programs. As of 1977 General Electric was building two moderate-sized power reactors of 654 MWe each in the state of Veracruz, and indefinite plans existed for seven others.[114]

Of greater importance are recent reports of a Mexican desire to acquire enrichment technology. The statement of President Lopez-Portillo suggesting regional cooperation has been cited. The subject evidently was raised during U.S. Vice President Walter Mondale's visit in the fall of 1977, but the United States reportedly refused to consider guaranteeing Mexican supplies.[115] Enrichment technology was discussed by President Lopez-Portillo and President Ernesto Geisel of Brazil during the latter's visit in the spring of 1978, but their conflicting views of the Tlatelolco Treaty make extensive joint efforts unlikely. A report has surfaced that Iran and France were willing to give Mexico a 30 percent share as co-owner of an enrichment plant,[116] but nothing more has been heard about the story.

Interest in enrichment technology does not mean Mexico suddenly has abandoned its long opposition to peaceful nuclear explosions or to nuclear proliferation in general. Instead, it demonstrates very clearly the strength of motives for energy independence, especially in the face of increasing U.S. restrictions on its nuclear exports. Along with Argentina's nuclear cooperation agreements, it also illustrates the amount of nuclear cooperation agreements, it also illustrates the amount of nuclear technology readily available to the Latin Americans. The number of routes to national nuclear energy programs has grown and is still growing.

NUCLEAR PROLIFERATION AND TLATELOLCO

The components of this analysis add up to one message: The Treaty of Tlatelolco was ineffective from the moment it was signed. In the years between the initial impetus of the Cuban missile crisis and the end of the negotiations, circumstances reduced its chances for success to close to zero. With the two leading potential proliferators, Brazil and Aregentina, choosing "open options" paths to nuclear energy development, a nuclear-free zone composed of countries with no plans and few capabilities for acquiring nuclear weapons had the elements of an international charade.[117]

In spite of zealous promotion by its advocates,[118] the Latin American nuclear-free zone never has been taken very seriously. Tlatelolco is hardly a household word, even among people familiar with arms control. Most analyses of the treaty, and there are not many, finally praise the efforts and the intentions rather than the results: "While the treaty is a limited step, it is not entirely an insignificant one. . . . No evidence exists, however, to suggest that the treaty is a prelude to further action in the field of arms control."[119]

In the end, the virtue of the Treaty of Tlatelolco is its existence. It cannot create disincentives for nuclear proliferation, but it could take advantage of any that occur. Should conditions in Latin America ever change sufficiently to make the nuclear-free zone workable, the system already is in place to control the region's nuclear energy development.

To say that if the nations of Latin America wanted their nuclear-free zone to work it could is hardly tumultuous acclaim, yet Tlatelolco remains a far more plausible instrument for solving Latin America's proliferation problems than the nonproliferation treaty or the full Inter-American System. As a Latin American system created by Latin Americans, it has the special advantage of avoiding the bitter character of many current north-south nonproliferation controversies, as well as the stigma of U.S. domination.

It also is well to remember that the vision of a Latin America bristling with nuclear weapons by the end of the century is implausible. As things stand now, Argentina and Brazil may very well have "peaceful" nuclear devices by 1990. A crash program could bring them to that goal much sooner. Latin America is not filled with extreme, irreconcilable conflicts, however, and PNEs need never translate into full nuclear weapons programs, nor into a regional nuclear arms race. There is still time to promote regional cooperation and to dampen national ambitions for acquiring PNEs.[120] Latin American interest in nuclear energy will not disappear, but it could prove manageable and the Treaty of Tlatelolco would be the means to that end.

NOTES

1. This chapter is thus not a study of the formal Inter-American System but of a smaller, separate inter-American system created by Latin Americans for their own purposes.

2. Tlatelolco is the district in Mexico City in which the negotiations were held.

3. *See* J. Redick, The Politics of Denuclearization: A Study of the Treaty for the Prohibition of Nuclear Weapons in Latin America (1970 unpublished dissertation, University of Virginia.)

4. This is a political rather than a technical analysis of the proliferation issues.

5. H. Forbes, The Strategy of Disarmament 58 (1962).

6. Redick, *supra* notes at 16.

7. Heurlin, Nuclear-Free Zones: An Attempt to Place Suggested and Established Nuclear-Free Zones Within the Framework of International Politics, 1 Cooperation and Conflict 11 (1966).

8. *Id.*

9. Dallin states that the question of whether the "Rapacki plan was unveiled with Soviet support or at Soviet behest remains in dispute." A. Dallin, The Soviet Union and Disarmament 228 (1964).

10. A variant, the Gomulka Plan, was put forward in the United Nations in 1964. It sought to meet Western objections by making a freeze on nuclear weapons the first stage of a more general reduction of military forces. T. Larson, Disarmament and Soviet Policy, 1964–68 186 (1969).

11. W. Epstein, The Last Chance 209 (1976).

12. Firmage, *The Treaty on the Non-Proliferation of Nuclear Weapons,* 63 Am. J. Int'l L. 715 (1971).

13. The recent controversy over Soviet "hunter-killer" satellites suggests outer space may not remain removed from the super power arms race much longer. A. Kramish, *The Proliferation of Nuclear Weapons,* 3 Future Int'l Legal Order 251 (1973).

14. W. Epstein, *supra* note 11, at 215.

15. *Id.,* at 214.

16. Smithies, *Regional Arms Limitation,* in Arms Reduction: Programs and Issues 79 (D. Frisch ed. 1961).

17. J. Redick, *supra* note 3, at 25.

18. W. Epstein, *supra* note 11, at 209.

19. The change in testing sites provoked a series of protests from nations in the new area, so the French did not escape censure by the move from Africa.

20. W. Ansberry, Arms Control and Disarmament 80 (1969).

21. Finance Minister Owen Horwood, leader of one faction of the ruling party in South Africa, remarked in summer 1977 that if that nation wanted to develop nuclear weapons, it "will jolly well do so." Wash. Post, Aug. 31, 1977.

22. J. Redick, *supra* note 3, at 23.

23. T. Larson, Disarmament and Soviet Policy, 1964–68, at 167 (1969).

24. A. Dallin, *supra* note 9, at 139.

25. The development of ICBMs and submarine technology has changed this dependence, although many bases retain a symbolic value to the United States.

26. W. Ansberry, *supra* note 20, at 83.

27. Burnes, *Can the Spread of Nuclear Weapons Be Stopped?* Int'l Organization 867 (1965).

28. Among these analysts are Edward Glick, Arthur Smithies, Ian Brownlie, William Ansberry, and Lynn Miller.

29. Bloomfield and Leiss, *Arms Control and the Developing Countries,* 18 World Pol. 19 (1965).

30. *See* Glick, *The Feasibility of Arms Control and Disarmament in Latin America,* 9 No. 3 Orbis 743 (1965).

31. Only Honduras bothered to go through the motions of a formal renunciation of the treaty before its expiration.

32. Stinson and Cochrane, *The Movement for Regional Arms Control in Latin America,* 13 J. Inter-Am. Stud. World Aff. 2–3 (1971).

33. The Costa Rican army was disbanded and replaced by a national guard force in 1949.

34. Bloomfield and Leiss, *supra* note 29, at 8.

35. Stinson and Cochrane, *supra* note 32, at 3.

36. *Id.* at 4.
37. Glick, *supra* note 30, at 751.
38. ROSENBAUM and COOPER 75 (1970).
39. Barnes, *Latin America: The First Nuclear-Free Zone?*, 22 BULL. ATOM. SCI. 37 (1966).
40. For the politics behind the choice of these nations, *see* J. Redick, *supra* note 3, at 98–99.
41. For a translation of the declaration, *see* A. GARCÍA ROBLES, THE DENUCLEARIZATION OF LATIN AMERICA 69–70 (1967).
42. U.N. 335 (1971).
43. This early leadership may have given the Brazilians an initial tie to the denuclearization movement the Argentines never felt. *See* J. Redick, *supra* note 3, at 98–99.
44. Browser, *Denuclearization in Latin America*, 50 SAT. REV. 32 1967, at 32.
45. Robinson, The Treaty of Tlatelolco and the United States: A Latin American Nuclear Free Zone, 64 AM. J. INT'L L. 282 (1970).
46. *Id.*
47. Barnes, *supra* note 39, at 37.
48. J. Redick, *Military Potential of Latin American Nuclear Energy Programs*, in 1 SAGE PROFESSIONAL PAPERS IN INT'L STUD. 51 (1972).
49. Barnes, *supra* note 39, at 38.
50. García Robles has been the Mexican ambassador at the Conference of the Committee on Disarmament negotiations in Geneva, and served as the chairman of the Tlatelolco negotiations. He is often referred to as the father of the Latin American nuclear-free zone.
51. Stinson and Cochrane, *supra* note 32, at 16.
52. REUPRAL stands for the Preliminary Meeting on the Denuclearization of Latin America; COPREDAL for the Preparatory Commission for the Denuclearization of Latin America.
53. Barnes, *supra* note 39, at 37.
54. Glick, *supra* note 30, at 755.
55. *See* W. ANSBERRY, *supra* note 20; Harrison, *Nth Nation Challenges: The Present Perspective*, 9 ORBIS (1965); Halle, *Any Number Can Play Nuclear 'Chicken'*, N.Y. Times, Nov. 8, 1964 (magazine); C. Barnaby, *Political Aspects*, in PREVENTING THE SPREAD OF NUCLEAR WEAPONS (1969).
56. W. BADER, THE UNITED STATES AND THE SPREAD OF NUCLEAR WEAPONS 16 (1968).
57. Bloomfield and Leiss, *supra* note 29, at 7.
58. Glick, *supra* note 30, at 745.
59. Stinson and Cochrane, *supra* note 32, at 15.
60. REUPRAL held its deliberations in 1964; COPREDAL lasted from 1965 to 1967.
61. There were newly elected chief executives in Chile, Mexico, and Venezuela. Military coups produced new leaders in Brazil and Ecuador.
62. Redick, *supra* note 3.
63. It also is U.S. policy never to acknowledge publicly which of its warships or submarines carries nuclear weapons.
64. Proliferation involves the more or less independent development of a nuclear capability while dissemination involves the direct aid of another, nuclear nation.
65. The nonproliferation treaty (NPT), for example, does not define a nuclear weapon.
66. OPANAL stands for Organization for the Prohibition of Nuclear Weapons in Latin America.
67. It is worth noting that neither of the nuclear superpowers accepts IAEA controls.
68. U Thant, OPANAL, 1969.
69. Nicaragua was interested in the possibility of a second canal across the Isthmus of Panama.
70. A. Kramish, *supra* note 13, at 238.

71. Argentina, COPREDAL/AR 24.

72. Chile and Brazil have ratified but refuse to waive Article 28 to permit the treaty to enter into force for them. Argentina has announced it will ratify the treaty but also will not waive it. *See* W. EPSTEIN, *supra* note 11, at 59.

73. Stinson and Cochrane, *supra* note 32, at 12.

74. J. Redick, *supra* note 3, at 291.

75. García Robles, *The Denuclearization of Latin America,* 17 NO. 398 REV. INT'L AFF. 10 (1966).

76. Stinson and Cochrane, *supra* note 32, at 12.

77. T. LARSON, *supra* note 23, at 168.

78. Conference of the Committee on Disarmament PV 553. (March 28, 1972).

79. W. EPSTEIN, *supra* note 11, at 234.

80. J. Redick, *supra* note 3, at 80–81.

81. Only Peru, Cuba, and Uruguay are close to research reactors; Bolivia and Ecuador are just launching programs.

82. The Ecuador-Argentina agreement was signed April 5, 1977, and updated in the spring of 1978. Ecuador also has recently signed a nuclear cooperation agreement with Spain. Argentina and Uruguay have signed a plan of action for 1978 that follows on their 1968 cooperation agreement. A new cooperation agreement between Argentina and Bolivia was announced in April, 1978 involving development of a research reactor at Viacha, 70 km. from La Paz. The first Peruvian-Argentine agreement was signed in 1969, and Peru's first research reactor is reported ready to go critical.

83. Reports from Buenos Aires note that its decision to send 15 kg. of enriched uranium to Peru generated inquiries from a number of other countries (Buenos Aires Domestic Service, quoted in Foreign Broadcast Information Service, March 1, 1978).

84. Lopez-Portillo was careful to rule out the sort of regional arrangements to replace national programs that the United States has recently suggested as part of its nonproliferation strategy. *See* Jornal do Brazil, Jan. 13, 1978.

85. J. Redick, *supra* note 3, at 42.

86. Gall, *Atoms for Brazil, Dangers for All,* 23 FOREIGN POL. 182 (1976).

87. J. Redick, *supra* note 3, at 45.

88. NUCLEAR PROLIFERATION FACTBOOK 239 (1977).

89. J. Redick, *supra* note 48, at 17.

90. NUCLEAR PROLIFERATION FACTBOOK, *supra* note 88, at 158.

91. The mining exploration agreements are part of each bilateral cooperation agreement.

92. Gall, *supra* note 86, at 177.

93. *Id.* at 178.

94. ROSENBAUM and COOPER, *supra* note 38, at 79.

95. J. Redick, *supra* note 3, at 52.

96. Brazil had by the late 1960s acquired nuclear cooperation agreements with 12 nations and international organizations.

97. J. Redick, *supra* note 3, at 54.

98. ROSENBAUM and COOPER, *supra* note 38, at 77.

99. A series of reports appeared in March 1978, first in *O Estado do Sao Paulo,* of major construction accidents and flaws. A total of 71 fires were reported between June and November; one $4 million warehouse blaze destroyed equipment for all parts of the Angra 1 project. Beyond this, foundation cracks were reported, and slight tilting of the turbogenerator building cast doubt on the geological soundness of the site. There also was a report of a seven-meter tide almost flooding the reactor building, and various hints of industrial sabotage. Official comments have been confined to downgrading the seriousness of the accidents, and pointing out that other nations' nuclear projects have troubles, too.

100. NUCLEAR PROLIFERATION FACTBOOK, *supra* note 88, at 240.

101. O Globo, Jan. 8, 1978, at 6.

102. Jornal do Brazil, Feb. 28, 1978, at 23.

103. Gall, *supra* note 86, at 155.

104. *Id.*

105. NUCLEAR PROLIFERATION HANDBOOK, *supra* note 88, at 240.

106. At present, 40 percent of the nuclear engineers with NUCLEN, the national nuclear engineering project, are German; plans are to reduce this to 10 percent by 1982. More and more of the reactor components are to be constructed in Brazil by Brazilian firms.

107. Brazil's plans to purchase enriched uranium from URENCO, the British-French-Dutch consortium, until its own enrichment facilities are completed, have recently hit a snag. The Dutch parliament has refused to permit URENCO exports until Brazil agrees to extensive safeguards; the Brazilians consider their arrangements with the West Germans for IAEA safeguards sufficient and refuse to sign stricter agreements. Brazilian newspapers report British, French, and even Soviet offers to replace the enriched uranium if the URENCO deal collapses.

108. One N.Y. Times editorial spoke of "nuclear madness". N.Y. Times, June 13, 1975.

109. The Brazilian national nuclear energy corporation.

110. O Globo, *supra* note 102.

111. J. Redick, *supra* note 48, at 30.

112. J. Redick, *supra* note 3, at 69–72.

113. G. QUESTER, THE POLITICS OF NUCLEAR PROLIFERATION (1973).

114. NUCLEAR PROLIFERATION FACTBOOK, *supra* note 88, at 245.

115. *INFORMEX* quoted in Foreign Broadcast Information Service, Jan. 30, 1978.

116. *Mexico City International Service* quoted in Foreign Broadcast Information Service, April 24, 1978.

117. One should not lump all other Latin Americans into one group of less likely nuclear nations. The point is to emphasize the gap between Brazil and Argentina (perhaps Mexico) and the other nations.

118. Alfonso García Robles has been its greatest champion.

119. Stinson and Cochrane, *supra* note 32, at 17.

120. See Redick, *Nuclear Proliferation in Latin America* in LATIN AMERICA'S NEW INTERNATIONALISM: THE END OF HEMISPHERIC ISOLATION (R. Fontaine and J. Theberge eds. (1976) for suggestions on how to control nuclear proliferation through upgrading and revamping of OPANAL.

III

EMERGING REGIONAL HEGEMONS: BRAZIL AND VENEZUELA

Chapter 13

BRAZIL AND THE INTER-AMERICAN SYSTEM

Riordan Roett

INTRODUCTION

The Brazilian view of the Inter-American System—both the institutions of the Organization of American States and the overall "system" of attitudes and expectations that characterizes the relationship among the states of the Western Hemisphere—is a relatively simple one. The System has had and will continue to have low priority in the ordering of Brazil's foreign policy objectives. Brazil prefers bilateral relations with the United States, and the U.S. role in the formulation of overall Brazilian foreign policy is a key to understanding Brazil's role in the System. The determination to avoid a Spanish American bloc, opposed to Brazil, has deeply colored Brazil's view of the System and of its linkage to the United States. A traditional rivalry with Argentina has suggested the Inter-American System as a first line of defense against that country's hemispheric pretensions.

Since 1964, and the institutionalization of the military regime now in power, the economic dynamics of Brazilian growth have created a series of international ties and interests that are not incompatible with hemispheric relations but increasingly more significant. Brazil's international outreach, economic and political, today is more important than its historical role in the Americas, except in the internal security area. Any threat to the existing political order from the radical or Marxist left legitimates the activation of inter-American security procedures. That concern for subversion has tied Brazil and the United States together throughout the postwar period and has facilitated Brazil's image in the United States as a responsible member of the inter-American community, in contrast to more hostile Spanish American states in Latin America.

This study traces the evolution of Brazil's view of the Inter-American

System, which is essential to understand the country's contemporary role in the Americas. Attention is given to Spanish American suspicions of Brazil's goals in foreign policy and of the special relationship with the United States, which has its origins in the nineteenth century. Brazil's utilitarian view of the Inter-American System continues today, but its unique link with the United States may be on the verge of a fundamental reassessment, given significant changes in the priorities of United States foreign policy in Latin America set by the Carter administration.

BRAZIL AND SPANISH AMERICA

The realities of geography have dictated a permanent concern in Brazil about Spanish America. The borders between the Spanish and Portuguese Americas were vague from the time of colonization. The treaties of Tordesillas (1494), Madrid (1750), and San Ildefonso (1777) were general statements about hemisphere boundaries. Uruguay was created as an independent nation to serve as a buffer between Brazil and Argentina (1828). A good deal of Brazilian imperial diplomacy in the nineteenth century concentrated on clarifying boundaries with Spanish American neighbors. Treaties with Peru in 1851, Uruguay in 1851 and 1852, Venezuela in 1859, and Bolivia in 1867 were preliminary agreements. At the end of the empire (1889), only two of 11 frontiers had been marked.

In 1895 the frontier with Argentina was settled; in 1900 with French Guyana. The baron of Rio Branco, José María da Silva Paranhos, foreign minister from 1902 to 1912, undertook the essential task of stabilizing Brazil's frontiers with the countries of Spanish America. In a series of treaties—Bolivia (1903), British Guyana (1904), Colombia (1907), and Peru (1909)—the potentially explosive issue was settled.

Rio Branco delineated nearly 9,000 miles of frontier; 342,000 square miles were added to the national territory, an area larger than France. Making pragmatic use of the principle of uti possidetis, Brazil gained its objectives without bloodshed, and in the process gained a reputation for hard bargaining and diplomatic competence.[1]

Cultural, linguistic, and racial differences have separated Brazil from Spanish America. Brazil's image, even in the nineteenth century, as a potentially aggressive continental force remained—and remains—a reality of intra-Latin American relations. The Brazilian role in the War of the Triple Alliance (1865–70) against Paraguay, and the subsequent occupation of that country by Brazilian forces, further emphasized the warrior image of Brazil.

From Brazil's perspective, Spanish American hostility was a given in its international relations. While momentary alliances were necessary for diplomatic purposes, the natural antagonism of its neighbors required a strong military capability and a clear indication of support from the United States. Spanish American doubts about Brazil's good intentions in Latin America were exacerbated by continuing, if low level, conflicts with Argentina, Peru, Venezuela, and Colombia over spheres of influence in countries such as Paraguay and Bolivia, natural resources, and compliance with established frontiers.

Much of the Brazilian view of Spanish America has been colored by relations with neighboring Argentina. The traditional rival of Brazil on the continent, Argentina also has been the leading antagonist of U.S. involvement in hemispheric affairs. The rivalry between the two countries stems from the colonial period when the boundary between the empires of Spain and Portugal were not clearly marked or accepted. At independence, in the early nineteenth century, armed conflict led to the creation of an independent buffer state, Uruguay. Argentina and Brazil have vied for influence in neighboring Paraguay and Bolivia, as well as Uruguay, throughout the nineteenth and twentieth centuries. Disputed territory between the two countries was awarded to Brazil in an 1895 arbitration settlement by U.S. President Grover Cleveland.

Argentina always has seen itself as culturally and socially more advanced than Brazil. At times, intimations of racial inferiority have poisoned the relationship. All in all, the tension between the two countries generated a feeling of suspicion in Brazil about Argentine pretensions as the self-appointed leader of the Spanish American states in the hemisphere. Only since the death of Juan Perón in 1974 and the removal of his wife as president in 1976 has there been the possibility of a realistic rapprochement between the two states. The conservative ideological bias of both military establishments, and their determination to destroy radical or Marxist subversion, have provided a basis for accommodation that may overcome centuries of rivalry and mutual suspicion.

Momentary pragmatic interests have led Brazil to cooperate with its Spanish-speaking neighbors but without any intent to limit its freedom. The formation of SELA—the Latin American Economic System—in October 1975 demonstrates Brazil's approach to Spanish America. SELA grew out of the Third World initiatives of Mexico and Venezuela. Brazil was reluctant to join any grouping that might be perceived in Washington as hostile to the United States. After a year of discussion Brazil agreed to join SELA but has not attempted to play an active role in the organization.

Brazil and the Spanish American nations maintain proper but distant relations within the Inter-American System. Brazil does not want the System to provide an opportunity for its neighbors to attempt to limit its world outreach, economically or politically. The possibilities of dialogue about common problems provided by the System are acceptable to Brazil, on its own terms. There is little that Brazil has not been able to achieve in the hemisphere by relying on its close ties with the United

States and its economic and political power. Respectful of the System, Brazil supports it without question. But still, the System is viewed in Brasilia as but one of many avenues through which Brazil must deal with the international system.

BRAZIL, THE UNITED STATES, AND PAN AMERICANISM

The Early Period

The foundations of Brazilian policy in the Americas have been a close relationship with the United States and strong support for the concepts of Pan Americanism. The Pan American emphasis in Brazilian foreign policy has been a way of reinforcing the special relationship with the United States. Brazil's early endorsement of the Pan American idea drew welcome and positive reactions from the United States. The period prior to World War I often saw the United States and Brazil as militant advocates of inter-American collaboration, often against the strong opposition of major Spanish American states, especially Argentina, Chile, and Mexico.

The United States was the first government to recognize the new Brazilian state after its independence in 1822, and Brazil negotiated a commercial treaty with the United States in 1828. While Great Britain retained a strong position in Brazilian trade throughout the nineteenth century, U.S. commercial relations grew in importance. By the time of the overthrow of the empire in 1889, U.S.-Brazilian ties were well established.

With the advent of the Old Republic (1889–1930), relations between the two countries became stronger. In April 1892, Brazil and Argentina submitted to President Cleveland the arbitration of the dispute regarding the territory of Misiones. The boundary between the two countries never had been clarified in this region. President Cleveland established the boundary in Brazil's favor in February 1895, and U.S. popularity escalated.

Close ties with the United States were pursued by the Baron of Rio Branco from the time he assumed the foreign ministry in 1902. His efforts to consolidate ties with the United States were based on four principles: increased international prestige; leadership in South America; Pan Americanism; and close alignment with the United States. Rio Branco's initiatives in foreign policy became the framework for Brazilian diplomacy for the next half-century:

> With the Baron of Rio Branco at the front of the Ministry Brazil turned openly toward the United States, with which it should march in accord *if possible*. . . . Brazilian foreign policy from 1912 to 1960, without major alterations, has consisted in accompanying the United States in

its programs of Pan Americanism and world solidarity and collaboration. It has continued to revolve around the principle of approximation with the United States in order not to become isolated in the midst of a united Hispanic America or in order to serve as an intermediary between the first and the second.[2]

As one commentator on Brazilian foreign policy has indicated, Rio Branco's decision was not taken lightly, nor did it derive from any romantic misconceptions about the U.S. role in Latin America. It was a pragmatic decision that recognized U.S. power; noted the growing commercial and trade links between the two countries; and lent support to Brazil's desire to be recognized by the United States and Latin America as a major actor on the continent. The understanding served Brazil's national interests at the time without doubt.

Pan Americanism

Brazilian support for the Pan American movement provided early endorsement for the Inter-American System and helped to consolidate the emerging linkage between Washington and Rio de Janeiro. The support by Brazil for the Pan American movement and its successor after World War II, the Organization of American States, united the hemisphere's two largest nations in a common cause.

The First International Conference of American States, held in Washington in 1889–90, formally opened the era of Pan Americanism. Under the inspiration of Secretary of State James G. Blaine, the short-run purpose was to foster harmonious political relations; the long-range goal was to increase investment and trade between North and South America.[3] Blaine's purpose in convening the meeting combined the moral rectitude of U.S. foreign policy of that era and a keen sense of economic opportunity—and opportunism.

Out of the conference emerged the Bureau of the American Republics (renamed the Pan American Union in 1910), funded by the United States and located in Washington. Its purpose was the "prompt collection and distribution of commercial information."[4]

The success of the first conference in Washington led to a U.S. commitment to participate in succeeding meetings of the American states. The meetings did not reduce Spanish American suspicion of U.S. motives, nor did substantive progress emerge on international commercial and legal issues. It soon became clear that Brazil and the United States were the principal supporters of the emerging Inter-American System.

In 1906 the Third International Conference of Inter-American States was held in Rio de Janeiro. Rio Branco had worked diligently to attract the meeting to Brazil. U.S. Secretary of State Elihu Root shattered tradition and attended the meeting in an effort to overcome Latin American concern about U.S. intentions in the hemisphere. The meeting in Rio was held against a backdrop of ten years of forceful U.S. confirmation of the Monroe Doctrine. The Venezuelan boundary crisis of 1895 led to the "Olney Extension" of the Monroe Doctrine by Grover Cleveland's secretary of state, in which the United States defended its right to intervene in the hemisphere and its power to protect U.S. interests against hemispheric and European opponents. Theodore Roosevelt, in his annual message of December 6, 1904, issued his corollary to the Monroe Doctrine and informed the world of North America's prerogative to exercise an "international police power" in its sphere of influence, the Western Hemisphere.

Brazil's view of the Monroe Doctrine had been far more positive than that of its Spanish American neighbors, many of whom had felt the weight of U.S. occupation or interference in their internal affairs, especially in Central America and the Caribbean. Brazil viewed the doctrine, early in the nineteenth century, as a measure of protection against European interference. The Brazilians believed that the doctrine was a multilateral, not a bilateral, declaration. It was the responsibility of all the nations in the hemisphere to follow the U.S. initiative and protect the hemisphere from outside intervention. The multilateral interpretation of the doctrine was stated frequently and publicly by Brazilian statesmen in the nineteenth and early twentieth centuries.[5]

The 1906 Rio meeting also coincided with the emergence of "Progressive Pan Americanism":

> a United States program primarily aimed at expanding trade, building investment opportunities, and tapping sources of agricultural and mineral raw materials in Latin America. It appealed to leaders in the American republics who viewed economic progress as crucial for their states, recognized the need for the participation of foreign interests and capital, and seemed to accept the secondary status to which Progressive Pan American policies relegated their countries.[6]

Progressive Pan Americanism dominated U.S. policy making through the Hoover administration (1928–32). It provided a comfortable framework within which progress could be defined in both economic and political terms and nations that supported progress would support the Pan American ideal. Brazil became a strong supporter. Progressive Pan Americanism provided an important link with the mainstream of U.S. political thinking prior to World War II. It explained the dependent economic ties between the two countries, and it provided Brazil with the image of a leader in the hemisphere and a peaceful participant in the steady progress of Latin America—under Washington's leadership.

The Brazilian response to Elihu Root's formulation of Progressive

Pan Americanism was most enthusiastic. The building in which the conference convened was renamed the Monroe Palace. Soon after the termination of the meeting, Rio Branco published a strong defense of the Monroe Doctrine entitled *Brazil, the United States and Monroeism* in which he defended the U.S.-Brazilian relationship and the need for a doctrine that protected Latin America from outside encroachment and encouraged progressive development.[7]

As one commentator has noted:

> Brazil's rivalry with Argentina for diplomatic leadership in South America encouraged friendship with the United States. Moreover, the latter provided the best market for Brazil's principal exports. From the United States viewpoint, the friendship of the largest Latin American state was important in the pursuit of her overall objectives in the region, especially in view of Argentina's attitude towards the developing inter-American System. Brazil did not feel threatened, as did some of the Spanish American states, by United States ambitions and policies.[8]

At succeeding conferences, Brazil supported the U.S. position. At the 1910 Buenos Aires conference, for example, the Brazilian delegation attempted to introduce a motion in praise of the Monroe Doctrine; it was withdrawn when vociferous Spanish American opposition surfaced.

The Spanish American states found themselves in an adversary relationship, with Brazil choosing to pose as the willing ally of the United States, sharing its goals in the hemisphere.[9] The Spanish Americans, on the other hand, saw the Brazilian policy as one of rank opportunism. Spanish American demands for recognition of the Calvo and Drago doctrines went unheeded. The United States continued to claim the right of diplomatic and/or military intervention in the internal affairs of Latin American nations. The Pan American Union was increasingly viewed, by Spanish America, as U.S.-controlled and therefore an improbable forum for criticism of U.S. policy. The Platt Amendment, the Roosevelt Corollary, and the Olney Extension all were explicit reminders of the dominance of U.S. power in the hemisphere.

The antagonism that existed between the United States and Argentina, and at times Chile, benefited Brazil. Although specific policy issues created discussion and negotiation between the two countries, such as the issue of coffee exports and prices during the 1920s, these differences were resolved amicably. Brazilian foreign policy elites clung to the belief that a close working relationship with the United States and with Pan Americanism best served Rio de Janeiro's interests.

Argentina's strong reluctance to accept U.S. hegemony in the hemisphere is long-standing. Argentina saw itself as the leader of Latin America; neither the United States nor Brazil was entitled to play that role. Argentina's elite always had maintained close ties with Europe—

both cultural and economic—and its geographic remoteness from the United States reinforced its defense of extracontinental linkages. It was hoped in Buenos Aires that those linkages would control U.S. ambition in the hemisphere. The Calvo Doctrine, named for the Argentine lawyer who had proposed the concept of indefeasible sovereignty, met U.S. opposition. The Argentine foreign minister, Luís Maria Drago, in a restatement of the Calvo Doctrine, was spurned by the United States as well.[10]

The attitude of Brazil contrasted sharply with Argentina during World War I. Argentina maintained a policy of strict neutrality. When the United States broke diplomatic relations with Germany in 1917, President Woodrow Wilson called on all neutral states to do the same. Argentina refused and went so far as to propose a conference, excluding the United States, to assert Argentine leadership in hemispheric affairs. Many countries accepted invitations but withdrew after entertaining second thoughts. Brazil, on the other hand, declared war. Brazilian ships patrolled the South Atlantic, and Brazilian foodstuffs and supplies aided the Allied cause. President Wilson stated that Brazil's "action in this moment of crisis, tightens the bonds of friendship which have always held the two republics together."[11]

Brazil, as a result of its declaration of war, became one of the signatories of the Treaty of Versailles. The government of Brazil ratified the peace treaty and became an original member of the League of Nations. Brazilian withdrawal from the League in 1926 ended a brief period of involvement in international politics and marked a return to the more traditional hemispheric focus—and U.S. leadership.

Thus, by the time the Old Republic ended in 1930 with a bloodless coup and Getúlio Vargas began his 15-year domination of Brazilian national life, the pattern established by Rio Branco at the beginning of the century had been followed with little divergence. Brazil embraced Pan Americanism as a mechanism for consolidating its ties with Washington and for extending its influence on the South American continent. U.S.-Brazilian commercial and trade relations flourished and aided the relationship. The obvious hostility of Argentina, Brazil's traditional rival, to both Pan Americanism and to the United States proved auspicious in Brazil's deliberate policy of linking its foreign policy to that of the United States—from supporting the Monroe Doctrine to declaring war against Germany.

By 1930, the broader Inter-American System that began with Secretary of State Blaine's initiatives in 1889 had won one firm adherent in Latin America—Brazil. The relationship between the United States and Brazil is crucial for understanding the latter's role in the Inter-American System. The next section discusses the period from 1930 to 1955, a period of change but also of continuity in the basic relations of Brazil and the Inter-American System.

The 1930-55 Period

The decade of the 1930s was characterized by the Good Neighbor Policy of Franklin D. Roosevelt and the growing hostility of Argentina toward the United States and Pan Americanism. Conversely, the ties between the United States and Brazil grew stronger.[12]

The Seventh International Conference of American States held in Montevideo, December 1933, resulted in the Convention on the Rights and Duties of States, which the United States signed with some reluctance and with a clear escape from the full implications of the agreement. The Reciprocal Trade Agreements Act of 1934 further demonstrated a U.S. willingness to respond to Latin American problems. At the December 1936 Inter-American Conference for the Maintenance of Peace, held in Buenos Aires at President Roosevelt's instigation to discuss inter-American security, a consultative pact was approved. The pact provided a mechanism for consultation among the states of the hemisphere in the event of a foreign attack. In Lima, Peru, in December 1938, the Eighth International Conference of American States reaffirmed the Buenos Aires Consultative Pact, although in a version far weaker than desired by the United States.

Throughout the series of Pan American meetings in the 1930s, the Argentines opposed and the Brazilians supported the U.S. position. The theme of nonintervention and autonomy from U.S. pressure for Latin America, permeated the declarations of the Argentine delegation. Argentina saw itself in an adversary position vis-a-vis the United States, in part due to its perception of a U.S. preference for Brazil and in part due to its historical claim to the leadership role in the Americas. Other issues exacerbated the situation. The Smoot-Hawley Tariff Act of 1930 had a particularly harsh impact on the Argentine economy. A series of disputes over Argentine corned beef exports marred the relationship as well. Late in the 1930s the Argentine government's attitude toward the growing conflict in Europe was clearly pro-Axis. The Argentines were instrumental in weakening the Lima Declaration in December 1938 and, after the outbreak of hostilities in Europe, Argentina's "neutrality" was judged to be distinctly favorable to Germany and its allies.

In contrast, Brazilian-U.S. relations flourished. Ambassador to the United States and Foreign Minister Oswaldo Aranha, a strong supporter of the United States, was instrumental in consolidating Brazilian support for the U.S./Allied position. After a period of flirtation with Germany and Italy over trade and armaments purchases, Brazil opted for a clear policy of cooperation with and support for the U.S. position.[13]

Brazil and the United States signed the first of Cordell Hull's cherished reciprocal trade agreements, which became effective on January 1, 1936. In October 1941, the two countries agreed on a comprehensive war effort that included U.S. access to bases in the Brazilian northeast, a military missions program, a Joint U.S.-Brazil Defense Commission, lend-lease arrangements, and so on. A series of important economic agreements followed. Brazil endorsed the U.S. position at the January 1942 Meeting of Foreign Ministers of the Americas and immediately thereafter broke diplomatic relations with the Axis; Brazil declared war in August 1942. Most important, substantively and symbolically, Brazil organized an expeditionary force that fought with the Allied armies in Europe, the only Latin American state to commit its men to the war effort.

In contrast, Argentina attacked the lend-lease agreements between the United States and Brazil, alleging that they upset the balance of power in South America. The allegation was rejected. Argentina's pro-Axis bias led the United States to withdraw its ambassador from Buenos Aires in June 1944. Argentina did not attend the Inter-American Conference on Problems of War and Peace, in Mexico City in early 1945; only on March 27, 1945, did Argentina declare war in order to be eligible to join the United Nations. By contrast, Oswaldo Aranha's remarks capture the Brazilian position: "We were, are, and desire to be Pan Americans. We go along with America and will follow the destiny of America. We will not remain neutral if an American nation takes part in the war."[14]

Getúlio Vargas's government was overthrown in a bloodless coup in 1945. A new constitution and national elections brought his former war minister, General Eurico Dutra, to the presidency. Dutra and his colleagues strongly endorsed the new Inter-American System. At the meetings of the United Nations and at the special inter-American meetings in Rio de Janeiro in 1947 and Bogotá in 1948, which created the postwar economic and political institutions of the Inter-American System, Brazil supported the U.S. position. Brazil and the United States signed the first Latin American military assistance agreement after the termination of the war. A series of bilateral economic commissions, meeting throughout the 1940s and 1950s, provided additional incentive for Brazilian collaboration with the United States. by contrast, the U.S. government once again entered a period of conflict with the government of Argentina during the Perón years (1945–55), which sharply contrasted with more amicable relations with Rio de Janiero.[15]

It should be pointed out that the Brazilian-U.S. relationship was not entirely smooth. The Brazilians complained about insufficient economic support for development purposes, as did the rest of Latin America. With Getúlio Vargas's return to the presidency in 1951 (he committed suicide in 1954), a period of apparent conflict opened with the emergence of Brazilian nationalism, but Foreign Minister João Neves da Fontoura maintained the traditional sympathetic support of Brazil for both the United States and the Inter-American System. At the Tenth Inter-American Conference, held in Caracas in March 1954, Brazil once again opposed the Spanish American nations in voting with the United States, in the Declaration of Caracas, to proclaim that the appearance of international communism in any of the hemispheric states would be a threat to the peace that would activate the collective action section of the Rio Treaty. Argentina and Mexico abstained in the vote (and Guatemala voted against).

Brazil joined the United States in calling for a consultative meeting under the terms of the Rio Treaty in 1954 to deal with the alleged communist threat in Guatemala. As a Latin American member of the U.N. Security Council in the Same year, Brazil referred a protest from Guatemala about Honduran aggression to the organization of American States and voted not to discuss the case in the United Nations. At least one commentator noted "Brazil's practically never-failing allegiance to the cause supported by the United States" in the first decade following the establishment of the United Nations, in contrast with the "frequent and conspicuous" dissents of Argentina.[16] A statistical voting analysis of the period 1945-54 ranks Brazil second only to Nicaragua in its voting support in the United Nations for positions taken by the United States.[17]

Through the end of the first postwar decade, Brazil maintained its deep commitment to the concept of Pan Americanism and the inter-American security system under U.S. leadership. The conservative, anticommunist view of the dominant elite in control of the government was an important factor in support of that position. The strong ties between the Brazilian armed forces and the United States as a result of the Expeditionary Force experience was another. Brazil's fear of and rivalry with Argentina prompted a close relationship at a time when the United States encountered continuing skepticism among the Spanish American states in its efforts to weld a strong, anticommunist bloc in the hemisphere. Even during Getúlio Vargas's second period in power, 1951-54, Brazilian economic nationalism did not seriously disturb the international thrust of its foreign policy and the deep ideological opposition of the conservative political and military elites to the threat of communism.[18]

The period following Vargas's suicide, and after the brief transition period in which traditional policy continued, opened an era of political as well as economic nationalism that posed a threat to the Brazilian-U.S. solidarity in employing the Inter-American System as a forceful and effective weapon against communism. A relatively brief period in perspective, it stands today as an anomaly in the pre-1964 history of Brazil.

Brazil's "Independent" Foreign Policy

The presidencies of Juscelino Kubitschek, Jânio Quadros, and João Goulart (1955-64) represent a decade of experimentation in international affairs for Brazil. By the middle of the 1950s, Brazil was a society undergoing significant socioeconomic and political change. Members of a strong intellectual and nationalist elite had begun to argue in favor of a more distant position for Brazil from the United States.[19] They wanted an "independent" foreign policy. Brazilian politics had moved into a period of populism in which the multiparty system produced a new generation of politicians to whom the independence theme was appealing personally and at the polls. The import substitution industrialization championed by Kubitschek created a growing middle class and literacy, urbanization, and mobility generated greater awareness about international affairs and opened discussion about Brazil's international options. University students and church groups argued in favor of a more vigorous and modern Brazil, with less dependence on the capitalist world led by the United States. Brazilian societal change accompanied significant transformations throughout the hemisphere of which the advent of the regime of Fidel Castro in Cuba in January 1959 was but the most dramatic.

Kubitschek's support for the new approach to foreign policy was more rhetorical than real. At the opening of his presidential term, he reaffirmed the friendship between the United States and Brazil, terming it "a constant of our foreign policy."[20] The Brazilian foreign minister, José Carlos de Macedo Soares, a member of a prominent and old family, spoke of the continuity of the country's foreign policy. In 1957, Brazil agreed to allow the United States to build and maintain a missile-tracking station on the island of Fernando de Noronha; the administration found the agreement in harmony with previous commitments to the Inter-American System.

Operation Pan America, launched in 1958 by Kubitschek, was an effort to generate new debate about Latin America's development needs. It followed the disastrous visit by Vice President Richard Nixon to Latin America in the same year and was transmitted to President Dwight D. Eisenhower in a letter "inspired by the best and most sincere fraternal sentiments that have always linked my country to the United States."[21] The proposal was received politely but did not inspire any positive reaction from Washington, although the initiative became part of the backdrop in 1960 to the U.S. Alliance for Progress.[22]

The Committee of 21, a Latin American group of consultation, was created as a result of Kubitschek's diplomatic efforts in the hemisphere. Viewed by some as anti-United States, it accomplished little although it did maintain Latin American interest in exploring new forms of collaboration. The committee continued to function technically and in September 1960 the Act of Bogotá was signed as part of its activity. The act committed the United States to support social and economic development in the hemisphere, but the impetus came more from the Cuban Revolution than from Operation Pan America.

There remained lingering fears among the Spanish American states that the Brazilian initiative was one in support of that country's expansion of influence in the Americas. As well, there was a belief that the United States and Brazil, in collaboration, would use Operation Pan America to consolidate their view of hemispheric development, to the detriment of the other states. Some saw it as an attempt to replace the OAS and others to repress communism, pure and simple. Some commentators viewed the policy as one ultimately unfriendly to the United States and its responsibilities in the Americas.

At the Seventh Consultative Meeting of the Foreign Ministers of the OAS in San José in August 1960, Brazil supported the United States in its policy toward Cuba. President Eisenhower's visit to Brazil in 1960 was an opportunity for effusive reaffirmation of traditional ties between the two countries. If the Kubitschek years were notable for their dynamism in economic policy, the initiatives in foreign policy were less notable and less successful. In a changing international context, Kubitschek clung to accepted foreign policy alliances. Operation Pan America, focused as it was on Latin America, aroused suspicion among some and resentment among others. Until 1960, the bedrock of Brazilian inter-American policy was a close working relationship with the United States. Kubitschek's conception of a new relationship was sufficiently unsettling to both North and South America that it had little chance of success. It did open a debate about the future of the Pan American idea, which would be transformed radically in response to the perceived security threat from Cuba—which activated and revitalized the old, postwar machinery as well as the new alliance.

The election of Jânio Quadros in late 1960 as president of Brazil signaled the opening of a period of friction between the United States and Brazil unimaginable to Rio Branco or Oswaldo Aranha. Elected as an unorthodox reformer, Quadros quickly moved to "reform" Brazilian foreign policy. In a *Foreign Affairs* article published after his sudden resignation in August 1961, Quadros stated that "the idea behind the foreign policy of Brazil, and its implementation, has now become the instrument for a national development policy. As part and parcel of our national life, foreign policy has ceased to be an unrealistic academic exercise carried out by oblivious and spellbound elites; it has become the main topic of daily concern."[23]

The main components of Brazil's independent foreign policy were closer ties with the emerging Third World; increased diplomatic and trade linkages with the communist countries; strong support for Africa and its fight for independence; and a movement away from the traditional Brazilian position for Portugal in Africa.[24] Quadros acknowledged the importance of the Inter-American System but claimed that Brazil, as a nation destined for greatness, could not be confined by it. He warned the United States that it must change its policies toward the socialist and Third World countries. He envisioned Brazil as an important go-between, mediating what today we term north-south conflicts.

Quadros's position, and the even more radical version of his vice president and successor, João Goulart, created a severe polarization in Brazilian political circles. The industrial and commercial elites by and large were concerned over the policy's impact on foreign investment, credits, and export markets; the majority of the armed forces clung to the pro-U.S. position of the early postwar years and feared communist subversion as a result of the apparent movement away from a close if dependent relationship with the United States; public opinion, as well as it could be judged, split, with support somewhat correlated with socioeconomic position and the wealthier, more conservative groups denouncing the independent foreign policy and its implications of a different strategy of economic development and diplomacy. University groups, intellectuals, a minority of the armed forces, and urban middle and lower-middle class groups tended to favor the new policy, with its allure of international greatness. They were attracted by the idea of a rapidly developing Brazil, not tied to the United States, widely respected, and playing a central role in international affairs. For them, mundane ties to a poorly understood Inter-American System were not sacrosanct.[25]

Quadros's world tour prior to taking office had left a strong impression of the apparent autonomy in world affairs of the Bandung generation of leaders such as Nehru and Nasser. His visit to Cuba in March 1960, and his praise for the regime of Fidel Castro, created a sensation. Perhaps to offset the impression that he would lead Brazil into a neutralist foreign policy, Quadros appointed a respected moderate as his foreign minister, Afonso Arinos de Melo Franco. It soon became clear that Quadros would control foreign policy. It was announced that Brazil would vote in favor of the admission of "Communist" China to the United Nations; Brazil established diplomatic and trade relations with Eastern European countries; diplomatic relations were restored with the Soviet Union; Afro-Brazilian cultural and diplomatic ties were vastly expanded; Quadros defended self-determination and sovereignty at the time of the U.S.-backed Bay of Pigs invasion of Cuba; and in August 1961 Quadros met and decorated Che Guevara.

The Cuban incident fragmented the president's political support. Denounced by the conservative wing of his coalition, he resigned and left the country. After a brief succession crisis, Vice President João Goulart assumed the position of chief executive. His term of office, from September 1961 through the coup of March 31, 1964, represented the nadir of Pan Americanism in Brazilian foreign policy and the emergence of a strong independent posture on international affairs.

The dynamics of Brazilian politics determined the course of the nation's foreign policy to a large degree. A populist politician, Goulart posed as the enemy of class privilege in Brazilian society. His erratic administration provided opportunities for a range of radical and neo-

Marxist activities by urban and rural groups that quickly polarized national debate. By early 1964, the armed forces, the land-owning oligarchy, industrial and commercial interests, and a large segment of national politicians coalesced. With implicit U.S. forbearance, the national elite overthrew Goulart and his cacophonous following.[26]

Goulart's presidency witnessed a series of important deviations from Brazil's traditional role in the Inter-American System. The most important was Brazil's failure to adopt the U.S. position regarding Cuba. Determined to defend the independent foreign policy position, the Brazilian delegation led the opposition at the Eighth Meeting of Consultation of Foreign Ministers, held at Punta del Este, Uruguay, in January 1962. Self-determination and nonintervention were the key words employed by Brazil to oppose the expulsion of Cuba from the OAS. Six states (Brazil, Argentina, Chile, Mexico, Bolivia, and Ecuador) abstained on the final vote, although the resolution received the necessary two-thirds required for passage. The Brazilian abstention caused a strong reaction in Brazil as well as the United States.

Brazil's hostility toward the United States was very apparent at the São Paulo meeting of the Inter-American Economic and Social Council in November 1963, when the Brazilians made little reference to the Alliance for Progress and called for a common Latin American policy against the industrialized world, saying that policy should be shaped by the Latin nations in preparation for the first meeting of the UN Conference on Trade and Development (UNCTAD), scheduled for 1964. At Brazil's urging, the São Paulo meeting established a Special Commission for Latin American Coordination (CECLA), which did not include the United States, to coordinate Latin American development policies and to establish a Latin American bargaining position vis-a-vis the industrialized world, particularly the United States. Prior to the March 1964 coup, Brazil took a leading role in UNCTAD preparations and continued to ignore the Alliance for Progress.

But Brazil's independent foreign policy ended abruptly. Its principal tenets have been summarized elsewhere, but for our purposes the most important aspects were the marginalization of the United States in the formulation of foreign policy objectives; a determination to integrate Brazil within the Third World; an unwillingness to become involved in what were viewed as East-West power politics; and a strong respect for "political pluralism" at home and abroad. The adoption of these principles brought Brazil into conflict with the U.S. immediately; moreover, they were principles not supported by significant and powerful elements in the national political elite, most importantly the armed forces. Without endorsement from the military and the foreign policy elites in Brazil, the pursuit of an independent, Third World foreign policy was impossible prior to 1964. Only after the Revolution of March 1964, and the creation of a strong economic base, would the military regime explore the themes of autonomy and Third World solidarity—but in a very different international context.

The Military Republic

The Military Republic has been led by four generals: Humberto Castello Branco (1964–67), Arturo do Costa e Silva (1967–69), Emílio Garrastazu Médici (1969–74), Ernesto Geisel (1974-present). Until recently, the revolutionary governments have stressed Brazil's traditional relationship with the United States, reverting to the Rio Branco principle of close collaboration with Washington in international affairs. By the time of the presidency of Médici, economic issues, often associated with strategic concerns, provided some divergence, but not of an ideological nature. As Brazil's presence in international affairs increased in the years following the March 1964 change in government, and as the north-south debate about development alternatives opened, Brazil increasingly looked beyond the Inter-American System in defining its foreign policy.[27]

Castello Branco and his foreign ministers frequently reiterated the close relationship between the United States and Brazil. The independent foreign policy of Quadros and Goulart was dropped, both rhetorically and substantively. While trade and commercial relations with the Soviet bloc were pursued, political contact was correct and no more. Brazil's radical posture at UNCTAD in 1964 changed immediately after the change in government, and the Third World support endorsed by the pre-1964 governments subsidied.

Brazil broke diplomatic relations with Cuba in May 1964. At the Ninth Meeting of Consultation of Foreign Ministers of the OAS in July 1964 in Washington, called to consider Cuban intervention in Venezuela, Brazil sided with the majority in imposing a mandatory suspension of diplomatic and economic relations. In April 1965, at the Tenth Meeting of Consultation of Foreign Ministers, called to consider the crisis in the Dominican Republic, Brazil supported the concept of a multi-nation inter-American peace force to legitimate U.S. peacekeeping efforts. A Brazilian general was appointed as commander of the force.

General Costa e Silva visited Washington in January 1967, immediately prior to his March inauguration, and received a pledge of support from the United States. In turn, the new chief executive stressed that Brazil's foreign policy would remain pro-Western and supportive of the Inter-American System. The dramatic change in Brazilian economic development, which began during the Costa e Silva government and continued through the Médici administration, introduced a new element into Brazil's role in the hemisphere and relations with the United States. While the Castello Branco government had been preoccupied with economic stabilization after the chaos of the early 1960s, the post-1967 governments turned to export-led growth policies that soon produced an economic "miracle" in Brazil.[28] The political consolidation of the Military Republic, with the Constitution of 1967 and its almost total control of the political environment, allowed for state-directed development. As Brazil's economic influence increased, its international trade and commercial relations diversified. Friction over economic issues, and a desire by Brazil for access to markets and international financing for development purposes, justified a strong role in the north-south debate that emerged in the late 1960s and early 1970s.

One area of deep and continuing concern is energy. A petroleum importer, Brazil long has sought alternative energy sources. As a drive began in the mid-1960s to control nuclear proliferation in the hemisphere, spearheaded by Mexico, Brazil refused to participate unless the rights of southern countries were recognized. In 1967 Brazil signed the Tlatelolco Treaty prohibiting nuclear weapons in Latin America, but with a reservation that its adherence did not restrict the possible development of nuclear energy for peaceful uses. Brazil did not become a signatory to the Nuclear nonproliferation Treaty. Most significant, the Geisel government entered into a 1975 agreement with West Germany for nuclear energy technology, over the vigorous protests of the United States.[29]

In the early 1970s, Brazilian concern for its fishing interests and coastal security led President Médici to declare unilaterally the establishment of a 200-mile territorial sea, thus placing Brazil in opposition to the prevailing U.S. position on the law of the sea at that time. The U.S. Trade Act of 1975, the international coffee agreement, and other trade issues have opened a new phase in Brazil's international economic relations that has justified growing participation in southern discussions about the New International Economic Order (NIEO). Brazil, for example, was a strong defender of the 1969 Consensus of Viña del Mar, adopted at a meeting of CECLA in May 1969 and then presented to the Nixon administration. The document stated a unified Latin American position on trade and development questions.

In contrast with its growing activism in north-south meetings, Brazil has retained its historical reticence toward Latin American organizational initiatives in the hemisphere. The recently created Latin American Economic System (SELA), sponsored by Venezuela and Mexico, does not include the United States. Brazil has joined SELA but has not taken an active role, nor will it do so in the future. Brazil's policy in the Americas remains bilateral in emphasis and it prefers to seek international remedies to its economic needs and problems.[30]

It is in the international security area that the Inter-American System has been most valued by Brazil. And it is the strong conservative flavor of the four military governments of the revolution that has provided the basis for an amicable working relationship with the United States. Concerned about subversion and Marxism in the hemisphere, the United States has valued Brazil's anticommunism. In turn, Brazil, since 1964, has argued for a strong, security-conscious OAS and has looked to the Inter-American System as a line of defense against internal subversion as well as hemispheric challenges to the existing order. One commentator has recognized the autonomy of Brazil in confronting the United States on economic issues, which the United States accepts, in exchange for a mutual view of defense and security issues:

> the position and policy of Brazil, distinct from the Spanish American countries and closer to the United States, further weakened the prospects for unity in Latin America. Although not infrequently opposed to the United States on particular economic issues, and subscribing in principle to the concept of a "Latin American personality" (as presented in the Consensus of Vina del Mar), Brazil's military government firmly supported the overall United States position within the Inter-American system.[31]

Throughout the Nixon-Ford years, the special bilateral relationship between the two countries rested securely on the mutual perception of potential subversion in the hemisphere. Economic disagreement was susceptible to negotiation or to agreement to disagree amicably. The spirit of that relationship was captured by then President Nixon during the state visit of President Médici to Washington in December 1971 when he commented that Latin America would go as Brazil went, prompting the expected cry of disbelief from the Spanish American countries.

The Kissinger-Silveira agreement, signed in Braśilia in 1976, established a formal consultative relationship between the two countries and further confirmed the pattern of mutual respect and cooperation. By the middle of 1976, relations between the two countries were at an all-time high. The presidential campaign in the United States, which ultimately saw Jimmy Carter elected, changed the tone and substance of the relationship dramatically. Carter's commitment to control of nuclear proliferation and to outspoken support for human rights created dismay, resentment, and outright hostility among the Brazilian political elites.

Through 1977, the bilateral relationship deteriorated. Trade questions, human rights, and nuclear questions dominated the diplomatic agenda. Little substantive progress resulted from intermittent talks. By the end of 1977, Brazil had undertaken a new hemispheric initiative in calling for an Amazon pact among countries with Amazonian borders. A series of meetings in Brazil brought together representatives from the countries to initiate conversations about future Amazon basin development and the exclusion of foreign interests from the region.

The Amazon pact undertaking was a multilateral decision taken outside the OAS. Nothing in 1978 indicated a shift in Brazil's attitude and orientation toward the Pan American System. Brazil, now the second largest contributor to the OAS budget, after the United States, supported U.S. efforts to reduce the size of the OAS permanent staff and to introduce more efficient methods for conducting OAS business. Brazilian views of the organization continued to indicate a marginal role for the OAS in Brazilian diplomatic activity in the hemisphere. Nor did the deterioration in Brazil's relations with the United States indicate that either state saw the organization as a means of outflanking the other.

CONCLUSION

Brazil's traditional political/security relationship with the United States flourished after 1964 and through the end of the Nixon-Ford years. Growing international economic policy differences did not obscure the complementarity of interests between the two nations in maintaining a Marxist-free hemisphere. The similar views of both countries about Cuba and Salvador Allende's Chile, for example, confirm that statement. The Inter-American System exists, for both countries, to protect vital national and international interests. The employment of the OAS system for primarily security purposes has eliminated potential friction for Brazil with its Spanish American neighbors and has cemented a long-standing relationship with the United States. In turn, the United States never has viewed Brazil as a security problem, save during the early 1960s, and the Brazilian armed forces dealt with the deviant conduct with relative ease.

The authoritarian regime in power since 1964 has grown increasingly confident. Its economic might through 1974 gave it degrees of freedom possessed by few other Latin American states. The petroleum price increase has taken its toll on Brazilian economic growth, but experts believe the period of recuperation will not be lengthy, particularly with the search for alternative energy sources now under way and the continuing international creditworthiness of Brazil—despite the size of its foreign debt.[32]

Brazil's low level of participation in the educational, cultural, and scientific work of the OAS undoubtedly will continue. Brazil does not look to the Inter-American System as a suitable arena for the settlement of economic issues. The security functions of the Inter-American System will continue to be of preeminent interest to Brazilian elites, military and civilian. Brazil will cooperate within the OAS structure with its Latin American neighbors, to avoid accusations of elitism or imperialism, but it rarely will take the lead on issues that do not directly relate to political/security questions. With its growing international prominence, the fundamental strength of its economy, and the apparent stability of its political system, Brazil will continue to view the Inter-American System pragmatically.

The tension between Brazil and the Carter administration over a series of foreign policy issues has not affected Brazil's view of or role in the OAS. The Inter-American System generally, and the organization specifically, remain marginal to the accomplishment of Brazilian international objectives. No new security threat has arisen in the hemisphere to necessitate a more active military role for the organization. The Panama Canal question, for example, had little impact in Brazilian foreign policy circles. While the Cuban presence in Africa is deplored on ideological grounds, it is not viewed as offering an immediate or medium-run threat to continental stability. Brazil's initiatives toward Venezuela especially, on the continent, have given Brazilian foreign policy elites alternative paths for the exploration of topical hemispheric issues. Bilateral presidential visits and frequent exchanges between the foreign ministers of the Latin American countries remain the preferred mechanisms for exchanging views on a series of questions.

While the Brazilian view of the Inter-American System has changed little of late, it remains to be seen whether the Brazilians will take a greater role in attempting to redirect or restructure the organization, given their share of the annual operating budget. If the operations of the Inter-American Commission on Human Rights, for example, were to become particularly embarrassing or vexatious to Brazil, there well might be an effort to depoliticize the work of that entity. If the OAS were indeed to become a forum for the serious discussion of trade and development issues, Brazil's interest would grow. Mere budgetary support for the System does not indicate greater interest in or concern for its role in the hemisphere. That financial responsibility is seen in Brazil as a natural burden of the country's emerging hemispheric and international status that must be carried regardless of the immediate return to the country itself. It remains too early to speculate seriously on a new approach to the Inter-American System by Brazil; current indications are that the traditional view will dominate for the foreseeable future.

NOTES

1. For a standard analysis of the boundary settlement procedure and the role of the Rio Branco, *see* E.B. BURNS, THE UNWRITTEN ALLIANCE (1966).

2. J. HONORIO RODRIGUES, INTERESSE NACIONAL E POLITICA EXTERNA, 184–86 (1966), *quoted in* K. STORRS, BRAZIL'S INDEPENDENT FOREIGN POLICY: 1961–64 (Dissertation Series, Latin American Studies Program, Cornell University, 44, 1973).

3. For a good overview of this period, *see* R. SEIDEL, PROGRESSIVE PAN AMERICANISM: DEVELOPMENT AND THE UNITED STATES POLICY TOWARD SOUTH AMERICA 1906–1931 (Dissertation Series, Latin American Studies Program, Cornell University, 45, 1973) and H. LOBO, O PAN-AMERICANISMO E O BRAZIL (1939).

4. *Id.*, R. SEIDEL, *supra* note 3, at 20.

5. A standard reference for this period is J. MECHAM, A SURVEY OF UNITED STATES-LATIN AMERICAN RELATIONS (1965).

6. *See* SEIDEL, *supra* note 3 at 2.

7. L. HILL, DIPLOMATIC RELATIONS BETWEEN THE UNITED STATES AND BRAZIL 292 (1932).

8. G. CONNELL-SMITH, THE UNITED STATES AND LATIN AMERICA 125 (1974).

9. Prior to the 1889-90 meeting in Washington, the Spanish American states had held a series of conferences that excluded both the United States and Brazil. Meetings were held in Panama, 1826; Lima, 1847-48; Santiago, 1856; and Lima, 1864-65. The conferences were limited in scope and achieved little in policy terms.

10. For an overview of U.S.-Argentine relations, *see* G. STUART and J. TIGNER, LATIN AMERICA AND THE UNITED STATES ch. 16 (6th ed. 1975).

11. *Quoted in* MECHAM, *supra* note 5, at 447.

12. G. CONNELL-SMITH, THE INTER-AMERICAN SYSTEM (1966) provides an overview of this period.

13. F. MCCANN, JR., THE BRAZILIAN-AMERICAN ALLIANCE, 1937-1945 (1973) discusses this period.

14. MECHAM, *supra* note 5, at 139.

15. *See generally* RODRIGUES, *Interesse Nacional*; D. DE CARVALHO, HISTORIA DIPLOMATICA DO BRASIL (1959); H. VIANNA, HISTORIA DIPLOMATICA DO BRASIL (1958). In English, *see* N. da Sousa Sampaio, *The Foreign Policy of Brazil*, FOREIGN POLICIES IN A WORLD OF CHANGE 617-41. (J. Black and K. Thompson eds. 1963).

16. STORRS, *supra* note 2, at 145-46.

17. R. RIGGS, POLITICS IN THE UNITED NATIONS (1958). For Brazil's role in the United Nations generally, *see* J. HOUSTON, LATIN AMERICA IN THE U.N. (1956).

18. T. SKIDMORE, POLITICS IN BRAZIL, 1930-64 (1967) discusses this period.

19. *See* H. JAGUARIBE, *The Dynamics of Brazilian Nationalism*, OBSTACLES TO CHANGE IN LATIN AMERICA 165-72 (C. Veliz ed. 1965).

20. STORRS, *supra* note 2, at 148.

21. *Id.* at 153.

22. A. DE SOUZA E SILVA, *Operacão Pan-Americana: Antecedentes e Perspectivas*, 3 REVISTA BRASILEIRA DE POLITICA INTERNACIONAL 41-59 (March 1960).

23. J. QUADROS, BRAZIL'S NEW FOREIGN POLICY, *reprinted in* LATIN AMERICAN INTERNATIONAL POLITICS 258 (C. Astiz ed. 1969).

24. *See* J. HONORIO RODRIGUES, BRAZIL AND AFRICA (1965) for a typical formulation of the "new" view of Brazil's role in Africa.

25. *See* J. AUGUSTO DE ARAUJO CASTRO, *The United Nations and the Freezing of the International Power Structure*, 16 INT'L ORG. 158-66 (winter 1972) for an authoritative statement about Brazil's aspirations.

26. For an overview of the Brazilian political system, *see* R. ROETT, BRAZIL: POLITICS IN A PATRIMONIAL SOCIETY (1972).

27. For an overview of the issues discussed here, *see* R. ROETT, *Brazil Ascendant*, 29 J. INT'L AFF. 139-54 (1975) and W. PERRY, CONTEMPORARY BRAZILIAN FOREIGN POLICY (2 The Foreign Policy Papers, 1978).

28. *See* W. BAER AND I. KERSTENETZKY, *The Brazilian Economy*, BRAZIL IN THE SIXTIES 105-46 (R. Roett ed. 1972).

29. N. GALL, *Atoms for Brazil, Dangers for All*, 23 FOR. POLICY (summer 1976).

30. Two recent statements about Brazilian foreign policy interests are T. SKIDMORE, *United States Policy Toward Brazil: Assumptions and Options*, LATIN AMERICA: THE SEARCH FOR A NEW INTERNATIONAL ROLE 191-203 (1975); and B. TYSON, Brazil, LATIN AMERICAN FOREIGN POLICIES 221-58 (H. Davis ed. 1975).

31. CONNELL-SMITH, *supra* n. 8 at 260.

32. For an overview of Brazil's international economic position and its foreign policy goals in the immediate future, see BRAZIL IN THE SEVENTIES (R. Roett ed. 1976).

Chapter 14

VENEZUELA AND THE INTER-AMERICAN SYSTEM

Franklin Tugwell

Venezuela is a young, vulnerable, oil-dependent, newly rich democracy, and in recent years it has been, among Latin American countries, one of the most assertive and independent in international affairs. In assessing the country's foreign policy goals and the broader implications of its likely future international conduct—for the United States and for the Western Hemisphere as a region—it is helpful to begin with some observations about the country's rather distinctive pattern of development and corresponding elite views concerning the national interest.[1]

Put succinctly, Venezuela's international role and aspirations can be explained in large part by its status as an oil exporter and beneficiary of recent price increases and by the deep and continuing commitment of its political elites to the twin goals of (1) consolidating and institutionalizing the democratic political system and (2) freeing the country from oil dependency by domesticating the petroleum industry and using oil-derived income to build an economic infrastructure independent of petroleum. In the years immediately after the 1958 overthrow of the Pérez Jiménez dictatorship, the first of these goals took precedence—by necessity. More recently, however, as the polity has grown more secure, Venezuelan leaders have turned their attention increasingly to policy areas with a tangible bearing upon the success of the country's economic development program. These include oil matters, OPEC (the Organization of Petroleum Exporting Countries), the legitimization of cartels generally, and U.S. bilateral trade relationships.

The nationalization of the oil industry on New Year's Day 1976 was an important first step in placing greater control over the economy in Venezuelan hands. But the larger, more important objective of building an economic infrastructure independent of petroleum remains. Indeed, in recent years if anything the country has become more firmly addicted to large and growing fiscal revenues from the oil sector.

Accordingly, the current government, led by Carlos Andrés Pérez, has launched an ambitious development program, drawing on the income provided by the post-1970 price jump in petroleum. As the Venezuelan government itself has recognized, however, this is likely to be the last opportunity to use oil income to build a balanced economy without the need for harsh measures that may provoke severe social and political turbulence, perhaps even threatening the survival of the democracy.

The recent influx of oil weatlh, combined with the country's growing experience and success in international economic negotiations, also has nourished among Venezuelan leaders a long-held dream of leadership in global and regional affairs. This dream perhaps can best be understood in terms of the pervasive influence within Venezuela of the legend of Simón Bolívar, the country's principal hero, who is pictured there not simply as a Venezuelan by birth but as a statesman of continental stature whose mission (unaccomplished, obviously) was to bring Latin America together in a system of constructive political relationships. Venezuela's oil wealth has provided important new resources with which to pursue this dream and also has brought the added encouragement of an unaccustomed but welcome degree of international public recognition.

The specific goals of Venezuelan diplomacy may be summarized as follows:

1. To secure the oil lifeline: maintain OPEC; keep prices high; justify cartels; and market oil.
2. To consolidate the national boundaries, including the maritime boundaries, where possible in favor of Venezuela.
3. To lead the way in shaping the emerging new system of hemispheric international relations.
4. To establish Venezuela firmly as a leader or coleader within several key subregional geopolitical frameworks.
5. To serve as an example and leader in the forging of a new global economic order that will grant an enhanced status and role in the developing nations.
6. To obtain satisfactory status and influence in the overall U.S. oil import system.

SECURING THE OIL LIFELINE

The oil lifeline means many things, and it has come to mean even more since the nationalization of the industry. In the broader sense, it means doing what is necessary at the international level to keep oil income flowing to the treasury. Given the current commitment to a massive and expansive developmental leap forward, this is even more critical.

At the heart of Venezuela's oil diplomacy, of course, is OPEC, an organization that was in large part the original idea of a Venezuelan petroleum minister, Juan Pablo Pérez Alfonzo, and that since 1970 has become the key to the new wealth of the oil producers. Venezuela's particular profile of resource endowment places it as the OPEC member with the strongest overall commitment to the full range of OPEC objectives: price control at high levels, perhaps even leading to a common pricing system in the near future; production control, if possible through organized as opposed to spontaneous proration; and joint agreement on secondary obligations, such as supporting other cartelizations and providing a portion of the windfall from price increases as development aid to oil-poor developing countries.

Since the production lifetime of Venezuela's regular oil reserves is relatively limited, the government is committed very strongly to maintaining prices. In the past, this was true even if it meant some sacrifice in terms of production quantities. Indeed, hoping to conserve oil for the future and at the same time to help OPEC handle the recent market surplus, Venezuela has made significant reductions in production rates on a voluntary basis. Another reason for Venezuela's commitment to high prices, probably more important in the long run, is the fact that the utilization of the Orinoco heavy oil deposits, upon which Venezuela expects to rely increasingly after the next decade, will require high prices since it may cost from $7 to $10 per barrel simply to produce this oil. This means that, in comparison to oil currently being produced, government income per barrel is likely to be very low. Assuming costs in the range indicated, Venezuela would have to produce enormous quantities to realize the same fiscal dividend: up to 16 million barrels per day.

Venezuela has pursued its objectives within OPEC in a number of ways. Wherever the opportunity has arisen, the Venezuelan government has tried to set an example by taking the first step, or initial risk, in the hope that this might convince the more reluctant members to follow along. In the early days this role was more pronounced, but Venezuela has resumed its efforts to become a kind of pacesetter. In 1970, for example, Venezuela moved ahead with a tax change timed precisely for its possible impact on the OPEC meeting of that year. And its success in extremely tough bargaining with the international oil companies over prices to a degree has served this function as well. More recently, while still aligned with those in OPEC asking for higher prices, Venezuela increasingly has assumed the role of mediator in the organization. As the world oil surplus has increased tensions within the price "camps" in OPEC, Venezuela often has been the initiator and promoter of compromise. In the critical Vienna meeting of September 1975, for example, the final decision to raise prices by 10 percent was the result of careful Venezuelan diplomacy. As one source reported it, Venezuela "emerged in a central role as a responsible conciliator, with President Carlos Andrés Pérez personally telephoning the Shah of Iran and Crown Prince Fahad of Saudi Arabia in pursuit of compromise."[2] To those familiar with the many compromises and reconciliations that have been required in the construction of Venezuelan democracy, the parallel is striking.

On the basis of current behavior, it seems reasonable to predict that Venezuela will continue to favor higher prices, will settle for prices that parallel world inflation rates, but will resist very strongly any reductions in price that are greater than about 5 percent. However, it also can be expected that Venezuela will continue to serve as a conciliator and mediator among the varied membership of OPEC, and will continue its deep commitment to the unity of the organization itself.

A natural extension of OPEC activities for Venezuela has been its promotion and support of other efforts at cartelization, including those in bauxite, copper, sugar, iron ore, bananas, and coffee. In the case of coffee, Venezuela has agreed to invest a minimum of $85 million to support an export control program proposed by Central American producers.

Venezuela also has been the initiator and chief promoter of formalized energy cooperation among the Latin American countries, helping establish first ARPEL (Association of Reciprocal Petroleum Assistance among Latin American States, created in 1961) to promote cooperation among state oil companies in Latin America, and then later OLADE (Latin American Energy Organization, inaugurated in 1973), as a forum in which the region's ministers of energy and petroleum could meet and discuss national energy policies.

Venezuela also has led the OPEC countries in committing its current and future reserves of oil earnings to recycling modes designed explicitly to aid developing countries and, more specifically, those suffering from the need to pay high prices for Venezuelan oil. Indeed, there is general recognition that Venezuelan response to the surplus generated by oil price increases has been the most sophisticated and carefully administered to date.

The loans, in almost all cases at an annual interest rate of 8 percent per year and for terms ranging from 15 to 25 years, have gone to the following: the World Bank, $500 million; the Inter-American Development Bank, to a special lending fund, $500 million; the Central American Bank for Economic Integration, $40 million; the International Monetary Fund, to help countries adjust to balance-of-payments problems caused by oil price hikes, $450 million; the Caribbean Development Bank, special development fund, $25 million; and the Andean Development Corporation, $60 million.

In addition, a special $500 million lending program was designed to help Central American governments finance oil imports from Venezuela. (Under these agreements, Venezuela will grant six-year credits equivalent to the first $6 of the price of each barrel of imported oil, also at 8 percent. Agreements have been signed with Costa Rica, El Salvador, Guatemala, Honduras, Nicaragua, and Panama. These subsidized volumes will decrease by one-sixth each year, but once the funds have been repaid, they will be available to the countries involved for long-term development loans.)

Finally, within the formal OPEC framework Venezuela led the way, with Iranian help, in establishing the special Third World Development Fund, which will receive 10 cents from the earnings of each barrel of oil produced by member countries and is expected to grow to some $5 billion by 1983.

It should be stressed that these aid activities, in addition to having a very real humanitarian component, have been selected carefully with an eye to their contribution to concrete Venezuelan interests. With the exception of the Central American arrangement and the OPEC tithing, these loans have not been on particularly concessionary terms; thus, they are also forms of income recycling. In addition, the Central American fund, if used, will have the result of tying Central American countries to Venezuela as a supplier, thus preventing or delaying a possible loss of this market to Mexico in the future.

Before turning to other dimensions of Venezuelan foreign relations, mention should be made of the possible impact that the nationalization of the oil industry may have on the conduct of petroleum policy at the international level. The nationalization itself has gone quite smoothly; the administrative reorganization is under way and production continues according to plans drawn up by the private companies (at the government's command) before the takeover.

At the outset, however, Venezuela was not able to place its oil at the levels desired—approximately 2 million barrels a day in exports—without some very tough bargaining with the former concessionaires. These companies sought to use their new position as "offshore buyers" to force the government to bring its prices below the levels the government negotiators had set as conforming to OPEC standards. Venezuelan negotiators held out and finally placed the amounts they intended, but only after some very frightening moments.

Since the original negotiations, just before New Year's Day 1976, the market has improved dramatically. But the lesson was not lost; Venezuelans were made to feel very insecure indeed. PETROVEN now will have to handle marketing, and this is the one area of the petroleum industry activity that Venezuelans have been least trained to handle. In several of the companies formerly controlling the industry, these decisions were taken for the most part by parent multinational headquarters. To make matters worse, Venezuela's marketing job is very difficult compared to that of the other OPEC countries. As one observer has noted, "there is not much doubt that the nationalization operation is a very much more ticklish one than any attempted in other areas such as the Middle East. Venezuela exports a much larger proportion of finished products than any Middle East Country."[3] Actually, just under half of Venezuela's exports are in the form of refined products.

All of this adds up to a new and very pronounced form of dependence on the international companies, and a new and direct vulnerability to the world oil market. It also means that the Venezuelan government has a strong incentive, already mentioned by top officials, to reorient the country's markets to circumvent the international companies wherever possible and to diversify markets.

SECURING THE BORDERS

Venezuela currently is involved in border controversies of varying intensities and future significance with (1) the Netherland Antilles (maritime delimitations); (2) Trinidad-Tobago (maritime delimitations and fishing rights); (3) Guyana (over Venezuela's continuing but currently dormant claim to more than one-third of that country's territory); (4) Brazil (involving a thinly disguised Venezuelan suspicion of the long-term implications of the very active Brazilian military and civilian presence across the line from Venezuelan territory that is nearly uninhabited); and (5) Colombia (over the delimitation of the waters of the Gulf of Venezuela).

Only the last of these is currently the subject of active controversy, since the deeper issue involves the possible oil reserves under the disputed land, and since the Venezuelan military has expressed considerable concern and involvement in the matter. Active military conflict with Colombia seems very unlikely in the immediate future but cannot be discounted. Colombia, despite its surface stability, may be subject to sudden and rapid sociopolitical change in the future, and Venezuela, like most democratic countries, is subject to considerable mood reactions with respect to issues touching on the sanctity of national territory.

LEADING A NEW HEMISPHERIC SYSTEM

In the last half-decade, hemispheric international politics have been changing rapidly, and Venezuela has worked diligently and in surprisingly diverse ways to build a strong reputation as a leader of this process. It has experienced some success, but it also has been forced to recognize the very real limits to collective action in the region.

Latin America has, so to speak, opened up as far as international relationships are concerned. There is a marked new heterogeneity, a new fluidity in bilateral and multilateral relationships, a kind of groping for a regional understanding about objectives and appropriate policy means.

This is to be explained in large part by the fact that a number of Latin American countries have grown more experienced, more self-confident, and more self-assertive, accepting the responsibility for shaping their own future. This is true especially of countries that have begun to consolidate strong central governments. Closely related to this trend is the inclination of a number of states to dismantle or at least modify the U.S.-designed hemispheric institutions originally created to handle cold war problems, and to replace them with institutions that (1) address the more immediate issues of development and facilitate the cooperative action needed to boost that development and (2) tolerate diversity and ideological experimentation.

For a number of countries this has led to a hesitant but growing advocacy of a more openly adversarial relationship with the United States, a relationship that would keep the United States at arm's length, available for bargaining on problems of clear concern to most or all Latin American countries but distant enough to open up the Latin American region to more active subregional international interaction—this to be increasingly shaped by the Latin American "middle powers" themselves. Economic arrangements and experiments designed to bring Latin American countries together and to control the intrusion of overseas economic influences form an important part of this new commitment to autonomy and self-control.

As indicated, Venezuela has been an active promoter of this image of a more "open" hemisphere in which the major countries engage in freer, more active subregional diplomacy and in which the emerging cleavage between rich and poor countries is allowed to enter the hemisphere and to texture relationships between the United States and Latin American countries. An exhaustive list of Venezuelan positions and activities that have contributed to this change is impossible, but a summary will outline the pattern.

President Pérez at the outset of his administration set as a primary goal the bringing together of Latin American heads of state in a series of consultative meetings, using as a pretext the anniversaries of key events in the struggle for Latin American independence 150 years earlier. After two such meetings—in Buenos Aires in September 1974 (Bolivarian and San Martinian countries) and in Lima in December 1974 (the anniversary of the Battle of Ayacucho)—the initiative petered out as the Venezuelan leader, while benefiting from some personal diplomatic successes, received an education in the limits of subregional cooperation. All of this was to lead to a final 1976 meeting in Panama to celebrate Bolívar's famous congress, but this plan eventually was abandoned.

Venezuela also was a prime mover, with Mexico, in the creation of the SELA (the Latin American Economic System) an institution that Venezuela hoped would facilitate communication among Latin Americans and provide a constructive framework for an adversarial dialogue with the United States on key development issues. Here also, the compromises necessary to launch the organization and the apparent lack of early dynamism have served to blunt the enthusiasm of Venezuelan diplomats.

Finally, in the Organization of American States (OAS), Venezuela strongly supported the effort to reassimilate Cuba as well as the reform of the Rio Treaty codifying the acceptance of "ideological pluralism" in the hemisphere. It joined Mexico and others in asking the abolition of the special Inter-American Defense Commission Against Communism.

These measures in support of ideological pluralism deserve special mention because they constitute the most important change in Venezuela's foreign policy in the years since the overthrow of Pérez Jiménez. In the early days, when Betancourt struggled to preserve his government from a military coup and nearly lost his life to an assassination squad sent by Dominican dictator Rafael Trujillo, Venezuela actively promoted what has since come to be known as the Betancourt Doctrine. It asserts the obligation of democratic governments to refuse recognition to military juntas that overthrow other freely elected governments. Beginning with the Rafael Caldera government, Venezuela gradually has muted its formal adherence to the Betancourt Doctrine because it has proved an obstacle to the accomplishment of other key foreign policy objectives. However, the importance of this change easily can be overstated. Venezuela always has been willing to deal with nondemocratic governments (as in the Middle East), and it has not become an eager supporter of military coups against democracies. Its attitude toward the new Chilean government—Venezuela is a home for many Chilean exiles—is perhaps the clearest manifestation of this.

ESTABLISHING VENEZUELA AS A SUBREGIONAL LEADER

Within the context of the new, more open hemisphere, Venezuela has recognized and begun to take account of several special relationships that in a sense arise out of its geographic setting and out of its need to establish bilateral ties with countries that, like itself, have begun to extend themselves into the international system. Two such relationships are especially interesting: one with Peru, within the framework of the Andean Pact and the belt of Spanish-speaking countries to the north of Chile, and the other with Mexico, within the context of the Central American countries and the Spanish-speaking Caribbean. (Relations with Brazil, with the English Caribbean, and with the Dutch Antilles have been conducted primarily on a bilateral basis and mainly have to do with oil, bauxite, or other economic matters, as well as borders. With Argentina, there is hardly any relationship at all.)

These subregional geopolitical relationships are interesting and worth mentioning for several reasons. The geographic areas are of primary economic concern and extension for Venezuela, and thus are places where patterns of rivalry might be expected to arise. And in fact there has been a good deal of speculation in the press about Venezuelan-Peruvian rivalry in the Andes and Venezuelan-Mexican conflicts over influence in the Caribbean and Central America. Venezuela has been very active diplomatically in these areas, extending special loans, promising to fund development projects, and even taking publicized positions on boundary issues it previously might have ignored (on Belize, the Panama Canal, and Bolivia's exit to the sea, for examples).

However, one of the most distinctive aspects of Venezuelan diplomacy in these areas is that Venezuela has gone out of its way to avoid conflict and rivalry and instead to work out direct, friendly relationships of mutual respect with the other active powers. This pattern first was established on a direct, personal level (Lima and Mexico City meetings between heads of state) and has extended to the point where the relationships between the countries have the distinct character of cooperation or "coleadership." This approach has been extended beyond the subregion to mutual sponsorship of important Latin American initiatives such as the Ayacucho Summit and the SELA system itself.

It is quite possible that much of this cooperation is superficial and may dissolve into direct conflict, but this does not seem likely at present. Perhaps the most serious dispute is the potential one with Mexico over its oil sales and its pricing policies in the U.S. market. Mexico, at Venezuela's urging, actually applied for membership in OPEC and the application was received in Kuwait, but Mexico felt obliged to withdraw its application, apparently because of the terms of the 1974 U.S. Trade Act. However, Mexico did say that it would follow OPEC price policies, clearly a gesture to calm Venezuelan fears.

FORGING A NEW GLOBAL ECONOMIC ORDER

In working with the OPEC and in oil matters generally, Venezuela has acquired considerable global experience in the conduct of international economic diplomacy. Actually, few Latin American countries have been involved so consistently at this level, although many have greater experience within the hemisphere.

Venezuela has a strong stake in reinforcing the legitimacy of nonmarket arrangements designed to improve the position of developing nations. In particular, it has promoted strongly the idea that prices for raw materials from developing countries and prices of manufactured goods from developed countries should be considered together by the international economic community. For these reasons, it is likely that Venezuela will continue to cultivate a global leadership role, especially in such forums as the United Nations, the Group of 77, U.N. Conference on

Trade and Development (UNCTAD), and The Conference on International Economic Cooperation (CIEC).

DEALING WITH THE U.S. OIL IMPORT SYSTEM

An important foreign policy objective remains to be mentioned. It is important because it relates to oil and because it is likely to take on greater importance in the future. Put in the simplest, most direct way, the Venezuelan government feels and has argued for years that it should be granted a special status in its trade relationship with the United States because of its role as a major supplier of oil and oil products. Venezuela contends: (1) it is currently and for years has been the single most important source of petroleum imports to the United States; (2) although a member and founder of OPEC, Venezuela never has embargoed the United States or used its oil as a means of political blackmail—indeed, its current trade pattern shows such great interdependence that such action would be virtually impossible; (3) during times of crisis—World War II, Korea, the various Mideast wars—Venezuela proved to be a reliable provider of petroleum; (4) although Venezuela has moved to nationalize its industry, it has paid adequate compensation that all the important companies have accepted (the companies have accepted, but many do not agree the amounts were adequate), and perhaps more important, it has established a good working relationship with the large U.S. multinationals, thus assuring the continuation of supply to its established U.S. markets; and (5) it is a fellow democracy.

Venezuela consistently has been denied special trade status for a number of reasons. These include the nearly Byzantine interest group struggle affecting U.S. decision on oil imports, the influence of the major oil companies that have a stake in Venezuela, the general lack of central coordination in energy matters in the United States, and the lack of congressional expertise in these matters. When mandatory oil import control was established in the United States in 1958-59, Venezuela suggested an intergovernmental agreement among the hemisphere countries supplying oil to the United States (Canada, Venezuela, and to a lesser degree Mexico) in order to prorate supply according to U.S. requirements. Such an agreement would grant hemispheric producers a preference, recognizing their status as more secure sources. But the U.S. decision was to exempt Canada and Mexico from the mandatory system while leaving Venezuela out entirely. This goal was accomplished by exempting overland imports.

The mandatory oil import program was a source of continuous strain and friction between the United States and Venezuela until its termination in 1973. Immobilized by an interest group conundrum, drifting along without a real energy policy, and desiring to protect the interests of U.S. corporations operating in Venezuela, the U.S. government repeatedly turned down Venezuela's petitions for preferential status in the U.S. market. This, despite the recommendation of a high-level U.S. task force that a hemisphere preference be adopted in order to avoid increasing reliance on less secure Arab oil. The only exception to this was with respect to imports of heavy fuel oil, and in this case the exception was made for the wrong reasons from Venezuela's standpoint. After about 1966 the quotas for residual fuel oil were set at such high levels as to be nonoperative since U.S. refineries preferred to produce as little as possible, instead turning their crude into more profitable commodities such as gasoline and using imported residual to supply the U.S. demand. With this exception, however, Venezuela could accomplish little; the large international companies had firmly decided upon a nonhemispheric preference with respect to imports since costs were lower in the Middle East and North Africa and since they strongly resented Venezuela's tougher controls and tax laws.

After the energy shortage and the OAPEC (Organization of Arab Petroleum Exporting Countries) embargo of 1973-74, a few Venezuelans hoped that they finally would receive special status. But this did not come about. In fact, when the old import control program finally was abandoned, subsequent regulatory changes tended to place Venezuelan imports, especially fuel oil, at a price disadvantage in their traditional East Coast U.S. market. The severity of this disadvantage was reduced by a spring 1976 administrative adjustment in what is known as the entitlements program (a program designed to equalize the benefits among refiners accruing from the price difference between domestic and imported oil), and Venezuela hopes that Congress will acquiesce to the administration request that fuel oil prices be decontrolled, so as to further improve its competitive standing in U.S. markets.

But meanwhile, literally adding insult to injury, the U.S. Congress included in the important Trade Act of 1974, signed by President Gerald Ford in January 1975, a provision excluding by definition all OPEC members from the benefits conferred by the new system of Generalized Tariff Preferences (GSP) authorized by the Act. This apparently was done as the result of the common misconception that it was OPEC, rather than OAPEC, that embargoed the United States. Both President Ford and Secretary of State Kissinger subsequently urged a reconsideration of this provision, introducing legislation into both houses of Congress to modify the "OPEC clause" so as to permit Venezuela (and Ecuador, also affected) to benefit from GSP adjustments. However, despite considerable urging, including a personal appeal by Secretary of State Kissinger, Congress did not act on the Ford administration's request.

Carlos Andrés Pérez reacted vigorously to the special discrimination in the trade act. He sent an urgent message to all OAS members requesting a special meeting of the OAS council to consider the action. A meeting of that group two weeks later produced a resolution (20 votes in favor) condemning the act and expressing "profound preoccupation with the deterioration of the inter-American solidarity provoked by certain clauses of the law." There was a great deal of sympathy among the other Latin American countries for the Venezuelan position on this issue. The precise effect of the exclusion is not yet known—in 1977 the general preference system had just been put into effect—although one estimate was that about $35 million in annual Venezuelan exports of manufactured goods to the United States would be affected. Oil is not affected.

The real damage of the act, of course, is symbolic. It confirms the worst fears and frustrations of Venezuelans who hoped for recognition of the special role Venezuelan oil has played in supplying U.S. needs. For practical purposes, there can be no doubt: Venezuelan oil is the same as Arab oil in U.S. eyes. With PETROVEN now taking over the job of marketing, and with the United States finally admitting to itself that energy independence is not to be forthcoming in the near future, this mistake may have unfortunate consequences.

CONCLUSION

Having reviewed the central concerns and objectives of Venezuelan foreign policy, what can we conclude about the view from Caracas on hemispheric and global international relationships in the future? How will Venezuelan elites define their interests, and what kind of role will they seek for their country?

First, it seems unlikely that the overall profile of foreign policy priorities described above will change significantly in the near future—say, the next five years. Domestic development goals—political and economic—and a binding pattern of economic ties with the outside world, mainly involving oil, are likely to continue to provide the constraints and incentives that have impelled Venezuelan elites along their current trajectory.

Thus, Venezuela will continue to place OPEC and bilateral trade ties with the United States at the top of the policy agenda. Given U.S. inattention, even rebuffs, this may be accompanied by an effort to diversify oil markets, but if PETROVEN does this it probably will amount to a gradual reallocation of small amounts for the first few years.

Venezuelan elites also will continue to seek a leadership role in global resource bargaining, while carefully cultivating other bilateral and multilateral ties that have a bearing on the success of Venezuela's developmental program and touch upon the Andean and Caribbean zones of interest. The election in December 1978 of a president less concerned with foreign leadership and the historical "mission" of Bolívar, may mute the emphasis placed upon such activities as the sesquicentennial summit meetings (if the mixed success of these has not already done so), and the promotion of developing nations' interests in such forums as the Group of 77.

Traditional regional collective institutions, most notably the OAS, probably will continue to be of secondary concern to Venezuela. However, it is unlikely that Caracas will seek to dismantle inherited institutions of this kind, if only because they again may serve as useful instruments of diplomatic self-protection and protest and because, perhaps in modified form, they may remain the best forums for the conduct of regional adversarial interaction.

In its diplomatic activities generally, it seems likely that Venezuela will continue to favor the establishment of international and transnational institutions to handle problems and pursue collective goals. This attribute of Venezuelan foreign policy, or "consociational" orientation to international relationships, is worth special mention since it suggests an important future role for Venezuela: that of bridge builder and intermediary.[4]

After stressing the likelihood of continuity in Venezuela's foreign policy, it also should be noted that it seems reasonable to expect a gradual decrease in the overall intensity and scale of Venezuelan involvement and initiative at the international level in the coming half-decade, as Venezuelan elites turn their attention inward to the enormous challenges posed by the nation's ambitious and demanding development program, and as the country experiences a sharp decrease in the resources available to support diplomatic initiatives—thut is, money that can be loaned or granted or invested abroad.

For within Venezuela it seems clear that the next few years will be extremely important, perhaps the most critical period in the country's modern history. Structural problems in the economy remain to be overcome before self-sustaining, oil-independent growth will be possible, and pressures are mounting for a significant redistribution of wealth and income. Further, although the state still is deeply addicted to a constant growth of income from oil, the country seems certain to enter a period of moderate fiscal leveling after 1979 and lasting into the 1980s as petroleum revenues cease to grow and the government must make major new investments in industry and mining. All these factors are sure to direct attention inward to domestic problems and away from international leadership activities, which promise to contribute less to the consolidation of the country's developmental strategy.[5]

NOTES

1. In the preparation of this study, I have drawn freely upon material in my earlier essays on "Venezuelan Foreign Policy" (prepared for the Office of External Research, U.S. Department of State, Spring 1976) and "The United States and Venezuela: Prospects for

Accommodation" (prepared for the author's workshop on Venezuela's role in international affairs, Council on Foreign Relations, Sept. 30-Oct. 1, 1976).

2. Latin America Economic Report (London, Oct. 3, 1975).

3. Hugh O'Shughnessy, *Survey of Venezuela,* Financial Times (Annual Report, London, 1975).

4. *See* Tugwell, *The United States and Venezuela, supra* note 1.

5. Should Venezuela experience a radical change in domestic politics—a circumstance I view as improbable in the next five years but conceivable as a consequence of domestic problems of the kind mentioned—foreign policy concerns might change somewhat. Should the military intervene, for example—a takeover from the left is hard to imagine—the government might place heavier emphasis on oil sales, less on independent control of the industry and its activities; and conciliation and institution building at the international level might be abandoned as a policy objective. Overall, however, the consequences of such a change are difficult to fathom, given the variety of authoritarianisms possible and the paucity of information on the military in Venezuela.

INDEX

ABOUT THE EDITOR AND CONTRIBUTORS

TOM J. FARER is Distinguished Professor of Law at Rutgers University and is Vice President of the Inter-American Commission on Human Rights. He also was Vice-Chairman of the Human Rights Working Group of the Council on Foreign Relations 1980s Project. Mr. Farer holds an A.B. from Princeton University and an LL.B. from Harvard Law School.

WERNER BAER and DONALD V. COES are Professors of Economics at the University of Illinois.

RICHARD J. BLOOMFIELD is U.S. Ambassador to Portugal, former Ambassador to Ecuador, and has been Director of Planning for the Latin American Bureau of the Department of State.

JOHN CHILD is a Lieutenant Colonel in the U.S. Army and a member of the Staff of the Inter-American Defense Board.

SYLVIA ANN HEWLETT is Professor of Economics at Barnard College and at the Graduate School of Arts and Science of Columbia University.

JO L. HUSBANDS is Senior Analyst at the Center for Defense Information.

RIORDAN ROETT is Director of Latin American Studies and Director of the Center for Brazilian Studies at the School of Advanced International Studies of Johns Hopkins University.

STEPHEN H. ROGERS is Director of the Economic Policy Section of the Latin American Bureau at the Department of State.

WILLIAM D. ROGERS, a former Assistant Secretary of State for Inter-American Affairs and Undersecretary for Economic Affairs, is now a partner in the law firm of Arnold and Porter.

FRANKLIN TUGWELL is Professor of Government at Pomona College.

BRYCE WOOD is Executive Associate Emeritus, Social Science Research Council, and former Deputy Director for Latin America of the Foreign Area Fellowship.